Jackie Ryan holds a PhD in history and political science from The University of Queensland, where she was an Honorary Research Fellow. She wrote the didactic text for the Museum of Brisbane's 'Light Fantastic' exhibition on Expo 88 in 2013, and has devised audiovisual material on Expo for the South Bank Corporation and the Queensland Museum. She produces the Aurealis Award-winning *Burger Force* comic series and founded comedy writing collective the Fanciful Fiction Auxiliary; the websites for both of these projects have been archived by the National Library of Australia as sites of cultural significance. Jackie is the programs manager at the Queensland Writers Centre. She still has her Expo season pass.

www.jackieryan.net
@JackieRyan_Inc

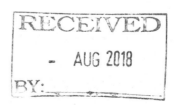

JACKIE RYAN

WE'LL SHOW THE WORLD

EXPO 88

UQP

First published 2018 by University of Queensland Press
PO Box 6042, St Lucia, Queensland 4067 Australia

uqp.com.au
uqp@uqp.uq.edu.au

Cover design by Christabella Designs
Author photograph by Carody Culver
Typeset in Adobe Garamond 11.75/15 pt by Post Pre-press Group, Brisbane
Printed in Australia by McPherson's Printing Group, Melbourne

 The University of Queensland Press is supported by the
Queensland Government through Arts Queensland.

 A catalogue record for this
book is available from the
National Library of Australia

ISBN 978 0 7022 5990 6 (pbk)
ISBN 978 0 7022 6088 9 (pdf)
ISBN 978 0 7022 6089 6 (epub)
ISBN 978 0 7022 6090 2 (kindle)

Contents

To the people who conceived, planned, and executed World Expo 88, the people who objected to it, and the people who loved it.

You were all right.

Abbreviations

ABA	Australian Bicentennial Authority
ABC	Australian Broadcasting Commission (Corporation after 1983)
AEO	Australian Exhibits Organisation
ALP	Australian Labor Party
ALS	Aboriginal Legal Service
ASIO	Australian Security Intelligence Organisation
BCC	Brisbane City Council
BESBRA	Brisbane Exposition and South Bank Redevelopment Authority
BIE	Bureau of International Expositions
BLF	Builders Labourers Federation
BP	British Petroleum
BTQ	Brisbane Television Queensland
CCC	Crime and Corruption Commission
CJC	Criminal Justice Commission
DAS	Department of Administrative Services
DLP	Democratic Labor Party
EARC	Electoral and Administrative Review Commission
FAIRA	Foundation for Aboriginal and Islander Research Action
GOMA	Gallery of Modern Art
JLW	Jones Lang Wotton
MACOS	Man: A Course of Study
MLA	Member of the Legislative Assembly
NSW	New South Wales
PED	Post Expo Development
QAG	Queensland Art Gallery
QCC	Queensland Cultural Centre
QCOSS	Queensland Council of Social Service
QPAC	Queensland Performing Arts Centre
QTC	Queensland Theatre Company
QTTC	Queensland Tourist and Travel Corporation
QUT	Queensland University of Technology
RNA	Royal National Association
RSL	Returned Services League
SEMP	Social Education Materials Project
SEQEB	South East Queensland Electricity Board
SP	Starting Price
SURG	Southside Urban Research Group
TAB	Totalisator Administration Board
THG	Trades Hall Group
UQ	University of Queensland
USSR	Union of Soviet Socialist Republics
WA	Western Australia

Introduction

What If You Threw an Expo and Nobody Came?

The extraordinary part of the exposition being put together on the banks of the Brisbane River, for me, is this: that of all the places on earth where the 21st century could have been unveiled, mankind chose Queensland.

Robert Haupt[1]

IT WAS BIG. IT WAS BRIGHT. It was the pre-crash 1980s: a period of bacchanal consumption in which media-feted financial cowboys were flanked by celebrities, politicians, and socialites as they championed extraordinary ventures, staged extravagant parties, and raised their glasses to risk.

But even in this climate of gilded confidence, it was difficult to persuade anyone to take a chance on World Expo 88 (Expo).

It seemed that *everyone* knew the exposition was going to be a disaster – and the only people insisting otherwise were being paid to. There were so many unknowables that potential investors were reduced to performing the business equivalent of studying tea-leaves.

One such pursuer of portents, American businessman Chuck Sanders, scoured Brisbane in 1987 for 'some sort of omen' that could induce him to set aside common sense and take part in Expo.[2]

As an eleven-time world exposition veteran, Sanders knew such events entailed financial risk; but investing in this instance was more akin to a leap of faith. Those who had even heard of the host city were most likely aware that Brisbane, capital of the state of Queensland, Australia, was an international minnow. With a population barely touching a million (and just over 2.5 million in the entire state), organisers could not expect to fund this extravaganza through local and intrastate ticket sales alone – yet the prospect of securing high-profile exhibitors capable of luring interstate and international tourists was bleak.[3] World expositions were in decline: many contemporary host cities had failed to break even with their events.[4] A relic of a bygone era, expositions seemed to have been superseded by newer and shinier toys. If the vast cities of Europe and America were encountering difficulties sustaining such festivities, what chance had Brisbane – for six months? An increasingly unpopular event in a largely unheard-of city sounded decidedly resistible.

One night during his Brisbane sojourn, Sanders observed a couple and their teenage children as they joined him in the elevator of the recently completed Hilton hotel, situated in the city's central mall. Sanders intuited they were not guests of the establishment, and was puzzled when they pressed the button for the highest floor, as he knew there was little of interest there. When the elevator began its ascent, the family peered excitedly through the glass-sided vessel as the ground receded beneath them – at which point it dawned on Sanders that such an experience was still a novel form of entertainment in this city. When a member of the family was inspired to cry out 'Wooooo!!!', Sanders had his omen: if Brisbane locals were this enchanted by elevators, surely they'd embrace a world exposition in 1988.[5]

Expo defied problems, precedents, and pundits to become the largest, longest, and loudest of Australia's bicentennial events. A colourful 1980s amalgam of cultural precinct, theme park, travelogue, shopping mall, and rock concert, the Expo behemoth had the formerly sleepy city of Brisbane bedazzled. During its six-month run, over eighteen million visits were recorded (including staff, VIPs, and repeat visits from season-pass holders) – a figure that exceeded Australia's population at the time.[6] From 10 am to 10 pm, seven days a week, for six months, attendees wandered slack-jawed around the otherworldly environment that its chairman, Sir Llew Edwards, referred to as 'the happiest place on earth'.[7]

Expo is popularly perceived as the catalyst for Brisbane's 'coming of age'. And, like most coming-of-age experiences, some of it was awkward. Expo was a product of its 1980s environment: a time of big hair and big objects, when having an event meant having a *spectacular*. It was also a product of its place – arguably the wrong place: Brisbane, Queensland. Under the premiership of the National Party's Sir Joh Bjelke-Petersen, the state was frequently the subject of derision. Mad cousin Queensland was different. Parochial. Corrupt. A relentlessly backward source of embarrassment that was best kept locked in the national cupboard. Such criticisms played to a cornucopia of patronising generalisations ... many of which were not unjust.

In the years prior to Expo, Queensland exhibited some of the hallmarks of a police state: public gatherings were discouraged, protesting was virtually illegal, and small groups of people could be subject to police questioning for being outdoors. Rumours of corruption within the police force were frequent – and frequently ignored. The dark absurdities of the period include confiscation of the *Hair* soundtrack on the basis of obscenity by police later linked to a prostitution protection racket, and the premier's invocation of 'State of Emergency' powers to facilitate a rugby match.[8] Bjelke-Petersen's role in the Whitlam government's dismissal and the sacking of striking South East Queensland Electricity Board (SEQEB) workers confirmed his reputation for authoritarian politics. His publicly expressed desire for Queensland to secede from Australia was, for many, the icing on the Queensland nut cake.

The state government appeared to prioritise development and control over culture. What passed for popular culture in Queensland tended to manifest itself in a tourist-oriented predilection for big things: the Big Pineapple, the Big Cow, the Big Dinosaur. The Bjelke-Petersen years were also about big development – if development can be taken to mean the destruction of landmarks such as Cloudland and the Bellevue Hotel, a high-rise construction free-for-all on the Gold Coast, schemes for the sale and redevelopment of the Botanic Gardens, and the premier's unrealised dream of drilling for oil on the Great Barrier Reef.[9] It has been suggested that some of Bjelke-Petersen's wealthy business associates (colloquially known as the 'white shoe brigade', owing to their predilection for such footwear and their showy business style) also looked with the lust of Gollum upon a certain piece of South Brisbane real estate.[10] A run-down industrial slum to many, a place of character to some, and home to a few, the bank of the Brisbane River opposite the CBD was ripe for redevelopment. What was needed, claimed the cynics, was an event to justify the resumption of such prized land. Something for the people. A *spectacular*, if you will.

As unofficial underdog, Queensland was not expected to host Expo 88. The more populous – and polished – cities of Sydney or Melbourne were deemed a better fit, especially by the powerbrokers who lived in them. Expo was secured for Queensland through an unprepossessing combination of skulduggery and bull-headedness, against the wishes of Prime Minister Malcolm Fraser, and to the dismay of other states. The announcement was greeted with blank confusion within Queensland itself. For a long time, other (predominantly Labor-run) states refused to participate in what was expected to be a 'Joh Show'. Commitments from international participants were also torturously slow to eventuate. Public opinion about Expo in Queensland ranged from protest to ambivalence. In the years leading up to the event, there was a genuine possibility it would be an expensive and humiliating flop.

Expo organisers encountered an extraordinary array of challenges, including public ignorance of world expositions, the perilous state of such events, media criticism, controversial land resumptions, anti-Queensland bias, strained intergovernmental relations, the conflicting

requirements of multiple organisational bodies, bicentennial controversies, and protests.

The exposition's theme song, 'Together We'll Show the World',
became a rallying cry for Queenslanders to support the event in the
face of local, national, and international doubts. The herculean efforts
of Expo's organisers against such odds returned great dividends. The
year after Bjelke-Petersen's premiership came to an ignominious
end with the thwarted 'Joh for PM' campaign and revelations of
police and political corruption, Expo presented Brisbane with an
all-singing, all-dancing, government-sanctioned gathering place.

Through night parades, the Aquacade, smoke machines, and
laser beams, Expo held the people of Brisbane enthralled. With the
aid of thirty-eight international, fourteen government, and twenty-
four corporate display pavilions, attendees could 'travel the world'
in a day.[11] They could ski at the Swiss Pavilion, view artefacts from
the Vatican, inspect a terracotta warrior from the Qin Dynasty, and
learn about leisure in the USSR; they could witness the wonders
of high-definition television, dancing robots, and 'text internet',
ride the monorail, sight the Magna Carta, star-spot dignitaries
and celebrities, and watch tap dancers on a pink submarine in the
Brisbane River; they could 'go for a bit of a rave' at the Heat Shield
disco, view a rock concert performed on a river stage, and partake
in the notorious 'Chicken Dance' at the Munich Festhaus. The
breadth of experiences on offer meant season passes were deemed of
such value they were still being bought just weeks before the event's
conclusion. The city went Expo crazy.

But the exposition wasn't the only transformative event in town.

Two of the most significant events in Brisbane's recent
history – Expo 88 and the Commission of Inquiry into Possible
Illegal Activities and Associated Police Misconduct (hereafter
referred to as the Fitzgerald Inquiry) – took place side by side. The
then premier of Queensland, Mike Ahern, had the delicate task
of inviting the world's gaze to the state while some of his former
ministers were testifying at the inquiry – several en route to jail.

Somewhere between the fluorescent festivities at Expo and the muted tones of the courtroom across the river, the Bjelke-Petersen government lost much of the credit for its extraordinarily popular endeavour. Expo began as one of Joh's 'big things', but it grew into something bigger. Its organisers and participants helped steer the event from the 'old ways' into the new, producing a comparatively apolitical event. In the process, mainstream Brisbane assumed a sense of ownership over Expo – most evident during the redevelopment controversies that arose in relation to the site. The land belonged to the people now. At least ... the most recent people. And they would exert their democratic right to enjoy the fake beach subsequently built upon it. Thirty years later, Expo continues to be venerated at key anniversaries long after events such as Brisbane's 1982 Commonwealth Games have faded from memory.

Given the impact Expo is credited with having had upon its host city, there has been surprisingly little analysis of it, which may be partly attributable to a 'sense that Expo was a parochial Queensland event, primarily focused on entertainment and consumption, and therefore not of national significance'.[12] It is also possible that those familiar with the less palatable aspects of its originating government may have struggled to appreciate the event's virtues. World exposition research is itself a relatively new field: Robert Rydell's 1984 book, *All the World's a Fair*, is credited with being the first 'to argue that world's fairs merited serious attention due to their complex nature and overlapping discourses that illustrated the zeitgeist of an era'.[13] There has been excellent consideration of select aspects of Expo,[14] but little engagement with its broader journey from political tool to cultural phenomenon. *We'll Show the World* considers the shifting social and political environment in which Expo was conceived, planned, and executed, and the manner in which such factors shaped – and were in turn shaped by – this event.

The first chapter, 'On the Origin of the Expo Species', locates Expo in world exposition history by outlining the development and meaning of expositions, the motivations for hosting one, and the risks associated with doing so. Chapter Two, 'We Need to Talk about Queensland', contextualises the local and national opposition to Brisbane as Expo host, the challenges negotiated by organisers, and the effect the event was to have upon its host city. Chapter Three, 'The Getting of Expo', considers the state government's circuitous world exposition manoeuvrings, and the manner in which some of its controversial traits helped secure the event for Brisbane. Chapter Four, '"Brending" the Rules', details the array of impediments to producing Expo and the managerial decisions that helped avert a 'Joh Show'. Chapter Five, 'We'll Show the World', considers the steps taken to persuade ambivalent government and public particpants to embrace the event amid the death throes of the Bjelke-Petersen premiership. Chapter Six, 'Brisbane Comes of Age – Again', examines the euphoric public response to Expo alongside criticisms of the event and challenges arising from the contemporaneous Fitzgerald Inquiry. Chapter 7, 'After Party', explores the bitter battles for the meaning, legacy, and ownership of Expo. The conclusion, 'Shine on Brisbane', draws together the previous chapters to illustrate the zeitgeist of this era, and illuminate Expo's significance to Brisbane.

Sources consulted for this book include newspapers, magazines, parliamentary records, official documents and reports, private collections, promotional materials, television segments, speeches, biographies, oral histories, academic works, alternative press publications, protest materials, and interviews conducted by the author. Interviewees include Expo Chairman Sir Llew Edwards, General Manager Bob Minnikin, Queensland Premier Mike Ahern, Brisbane Lord Mayor Sallyanne Atkinson, Queensland Under Treasurer Sir Leo Hielscher, a number of Expo division directors and producers, early exposition proponents James Maccormick and Sir Frank Moore, 'Together We'll Show the World' campaign and theme devisor Carol Lloyd, Queensland Events Corporation Chairman Des Power, *Expo Schmexpo* protest film director Debra Beattie, 'Cyclone Hits Expo' protest song co-writer Adam Nash, Executive Officer of the Foundation for Aboriginal and Islander Research Action (FAIRA)

Bob Weatherall, Queensland Council of Social Service (QCOSS) director Tony Kelly, and *Cane Toad Times* editor Anne Jones. The interviewees were uniformly generous with their time and remarkably candid in their recollections. Given the disparate views canvassed herein, a reasonable indication of whether balance has been achieved may be (alas) that no one is entirely satisfied with the result.

Expo's highlights, pavilions, and guests are touched upon in this work, but it is not a catalogue of things to see and do at Expo. Many such guides were produced at the time and are readily available from online auction sites. This is an examination of what took place around, behind, and between the Expo cracks. It explains how the 'Joh Show' became the people's party, and how an event initially greeted with outrage, scepticism, or indifference came to mean so much to so many. It is the story of how, to Brisbane, Expo was personal.

1

On the Origin of the Expo Species

Imagine an area the size of a small city centre, bristling with
dozens of vast buildings set in beautiful gardens; fill the buildings
with every conceivable type of commodity and activity known,
in the largest possible quantities; surround them with miraculous
pieces of engineering technology, with tribes of primitive peoples,
reconstructions of ancient and exotic streets, restaurants, theatres,
sports stadiums and band-stands. Spare no expense. Invite all
nations on earth to take part by sending objects for display and
by erecting buildings of their own. After six months, raze this
city to the ground and leave nothing behind, save one or two
permanent land-marks.

Paul Greenhalgh[1]

THEY GO BY MANY NAMES: great exhibitions, international
expositions, world fairs, and world expos. The titles are inter-
changeable, but the meanings attributed to them vary widely.
Exposition enthusiasts might consider them peaceful, educational
affirmations of the onward march of civilisation, the flow-on effects
of which include economic stimulus, revitalisation of degraded or
under-populated areas, and cultural and technological exchange.
World exposition sceptics might view them as tools of governments

and corporations for manufacturing consent through the demonstration, celebration, and legitimisation of their worldview; outcomes are of the 'bread and circuses' variety.

The purity of organisational motive may vary, but there are some constants in the results: a successful exposition can debut an aspirational host city as a new world force on the modernising stage; confirm the social, political, and technical superiority of an established power; and secure a place for the event and its location in the nostalgia-tinged memories of attendees. An unsuccessful exposition can bankrupt the host, destabilise its government, and become a source of domestic and international ridicule.

Put simply, a world exposition can be a dangerous thing. At their best – and, indeed, their worst – they affect the course of history. This chapter outlines the extraordinary highs, lows, risks, and benefits of the world exposition form with a view to contextualising the temerity required to host one in Brisbane.

Antecedents

World expositions have their origins in the medieval fairs and trade shows of the nineteenth century; they were part of a curatorial culture that, at a time of limited literacy, taught people to comprehend the world through display.[2] In his book *The Birth of the Museum*, Tony Bennett argues that museums and world expositions of this era were part of an 'exhibitionary complex', functioning (in tandem with emerging modes of display such as arcades, department stores, and dioramas) as tools for social instruction and crowd discipline while simultaneously modernising cultural infrastructure.[3]

Victorian-era politicians were familiar with the civilising properties of culture, having established public parks, theatres, libraries, and art galleries – ventures that exposed the lower classes to bourgeois social protocols and opportunities for self-improvement through imitation, and that offered avenues of cultural engagement such as commentary, literary journals, and debating societies.[4] Fears the lower classes would bring an ale-house atmosphere to such forays were mitigated through 'soft approach' techniques involving entertainment and example, and architectural designs conducive to 'panoptic surveillance' in which attendees were semi-directed through displays while being displayed to each other via viewing galleries, observation towers, and promenades.[5]

In the wake of social upheavals wrought by the industrial and French revolutions, display practices shifted from elite private collections of irregularly arranged treasures and cabinets of curiosity to public showings of pedagogically ordered objects that also demonstrated a government's power 'to organise and co-ordinate an order of things and to produce a place for the people in relation to that order'.[6]

Displays were influenced by the emerging disciplines of history, geology, archaeology, biology, and anthropology, and by scientific principles of specialisation and classification.[7] Significantly for world expositions influenced by this thinking, museums positioned the present as the cumulation of progress, placed 'man' at its evolutionary peak, and devised natural history exhibitions denoting imperial superiority over 'primitive peoples'.[8]

French philosopher Michel Foucault considered the curatorial concept of 'indefinitely accumulating time' a peculiarly Western one, and contrasted it with the ephemeral nature of festivals and fairs where time was 'fleeting, transitory, precarious'.[9] Bennett believed that organising powers used such nuances to great effect: where museums provided 'a deep and continuous ideological backdrop', the focus of a world exposition could pivot to meet shorter term ambitions.[10]

Early World Expositions

The first event for which invitations to exhibit were issued and accepted internationally, the Great Exhibition of the Works of Industry of All Nations, was held in London in 1851. It was conceived as an educational celebration of the industrial age, and combined techniques developed in museums, art galleries, arcades, and Mechanics' Institute exhibitions (though the focus shifted from individual achievement to equipment, products, and 'collective national achievement with capital as the great co-ordinator').[11] At a time when the concept of progress was linked with the exploitation of natural assets, international participants were invited to prove their advanced status through displays of industrial technology and mineral or agricultural wealth. Queensland, appearing as a district of New South Wales (NSW), centred its display around wood.[12] Contributions from other participants included microscopes, sewing machines, locomotives, needlework, an electric telegraph, hydraulic presses, architectural models, and the Colt revolver.[13]

The exhibition took place at Hyde Park in a purpose-built single building, the Joseph Paxton-designed Crystal Palace. Though enthusiastically promoted by influential figures such as Queen Victoria's consort, Prince Albert (a key organiser of the event), the lead-up was characterised by negativity and dissent, echoes of which were encountered by many subsequent expositions.[14] Obstacles included press scepticism, complaints about site suitability, doubts about attendance figures, and accusations of monetary waste. When questioned about such criticisms by the King of Prussia, the beleaguered Prince Albert replied:

> Mathematicians have calculated that the Crystal Palace will
> blow down in the first strong gale; Engineers that the galleries
> would crash in and destroy the visitors; Political Economists
> have prophesied a scarcity of food in London owing to the
> vast concourse of people; Doctors that owing to so many races
> coming into contact with each other the Black Death of the
> Middle Ages would make its appearance as it did after the
> Crusades; Moralists that England would be infected by all the
> scourges of the civilised and uncivilised world; Theologians that
> this second Tower of Babel would draw upon it the vengeance
> of an offended God.[15]

The exposition proved an extraordinary success, recording over six million visits (equivalent to a third of the British population at the time) across its five-month run. Charlotte Brontë considered it 'a wonderful place, vast, strange, new, and impossible to describe' and felt that 'its grandeur does not consist in one thing, but in the unique assemblage of all things'.[16] It also celebrated and affirmed the sources of colonial power – trade and industrialisation – while unleashing an exhibitionary phenomenon that helped birth the consumer society by teaching the middle class to want newer and better things – and a lot more of them.[17]

A plethora of world expositions ensued as other countries were inspired to demonstrate their magnificence. The concept eventually attracted host cities as diverse as Dublin, Calcutta, Vienna, Madrid, Johannesburg, St Petersburg, Nanking, Guatemala, New York, Hanoi, Constantinople, Rio de Janeiro, Turin, Lima, Kyoto, Prague, Dijon, and Christchurch.

This growth in world exposition stature prompted a commensurate escalation in extravagance. The 1867 Exposition Universelle in Paris (held during the reign of Emperor Napoleon III) boasted no less an ambition than cataloguing every aspect of human endeavour and investing it with moral purpose. The result – spreading from the central building to surrounding parklands (providing a carnival-like atmosphere emulated in subsequent expositions) – was of such impregnable mass that the visiting Mark Twain observed, 'We saw at a glance that one would have to spend weeks – yea, even months – in that monstrous establishment to get an intelligible idea of it.'[18]

Queensland exhibited at world expositions in its own right following its separation from NSW in 1859, and as an Australian state after Federation in 1901. Numerous expositions were held in Australia during the nineteenth century, the host cities being Sydney (1870, 1879–80), Adelaide (1881, 1887–8), Melbourne (1854, 1861, 1866–7, 1875, 1880–1, 1884, 1888–9), Launceston (1891–2), Hobart (1894–5), and Brisbane (1897).[19] These cities typically aspired to demonstrate their sophistication, and were backed by agricultural societies and manufacturing associations desiring commerce and industry opportunities.[20] Their events inspired grand architecture such as the Garden Palace (constructed for the 1879 Sydney exposition and destroyed by fire in 1882), and the Melbourne Royal Exhibition Building (constructed for the 1880–1 Melbourne exposition and host venue for the opening of the first parliament of Australia in 1901) – one of the last surviving nineteenth-century exposition buildings in the world.

Many expositions also had applications for urban renewal, a revitalisation concept that typically involved demolishing slums or dilapidated structures and relocating residents and ageing businesses – processes often facilitated by government land resumptions. The 1879 Sydney exposition prompted the development of a tramway system, new cultural institutions, and the improvement of city services, lighting, and pavements – actions spurred by local fears that visitors would judge Sydney 'out of harmony with our pretensions'.[21]

Local coverage of the 1897 Brisbane exposition claimed it 'has transformed Brisbane from dullness and emptiness into a scene of bustle and energy never before witnessed here'.[22] Burgeoning local pride prompted the NSW commissioner of exhibitions to remark, 'hardly one person enters the grounds but asks me, "Well, what do you think of our exhibition?"'[23]

As expositions grew in popularity, they also grew beyond the capacity of a single building. Vast themed sites came to be constructed for these ephemeral events, with some hosts introducing additional competition by inviting exhibitors to design their own pavilions. Afterwards, cities sometimes gained new buildings and facilities along with large tracts of 'revitalised' land.

Historian Paul Greenhalgh posits that by the 1880s, 'an atmosphere of megalomania came to surround the exhibitions, as nations struggled to distinguish themselves from preceding events'.[24] Some merely crafted great platforms from which to fall. The organisers of the World's Industrial and Cotton Centennial

Exposition in New Orleans (1884–5) were so far behind schedule that the event commenced without flooring in some buildings, with a number of displays still in shipping cases, and with empty spaces where even shipping cases had failed to arrive.[25] The 1897 Central American Exposition led to insolvency for the Guatemalan Government and a failed unification attempt with Costa Rica and the Greater Republic.[26] Rain for 107 of the 184 days of Philadelphia's 1926 Sequi-Centennial International Exposition sealed that event's fate, prompting critics to predict the end of world expositions.[27]

The exposure and vulnerability of hosting governments could be used to great advantage by opponents: the Dreyfus Affair (a scandal in which French artillery officer Captain Dreyfus was wrongfully convicted of committing treason) divided Paris until a presidential pardon was extracted – reportedly to quell threats that his supporters would boycott the 1900 Exposition Universelle.[28] Exponential pressures could also tempt organisers to countenance the unconscionable: the stakes were evidently so high for Chicago's 1893 exposition that the city's health department covered up proof that a smallpox epidemic had originated on the site, resulting in thousands of deaths.[29]

Some exposition costs could be rationalised through indirect benefits in the form of economic stimulus, exposure, and increased public standing. The world exposition in Adelaide (1887–8) provided work for thousands and helped extract the South Australian capital from economic depression.[30] With over thirty-two million recorded visits, the popular Paris 1889 Exposition Universelle is credited with keeping its government in power.[31] San Diego's Panama California Exposition (1915–16) transformed the city's architecture, led to the foundation of the San Diego Zoo (with leftover animal exhibits), and contributed towards doubling the city's population within a decade.[32] Chicago's 1893 event, with its 600-acre site, architecturally designed White City, engineering marvels, attendant conferences, and 21.5 million visits, is considered one of the greatest world expositions of all time.[33] It began as a battle for civic supremacy between New York and upstart Chicago, but came to be viewed as a 'coming of age' for the United States. It also provided anonymity for one of that country's first documented serial killers, Dr H.H. Holmes, who lured victims to his 'World's Fair Hotel'.[34]

Anthropologist Burton Benedict observed that world expositions came to function as cultural shrines, drawing visitors from around the globe to engage in rituals based on material exchange – while explicit and implicit negotiations about social and political hierarchies were taking place.[35] Scholar Lisa Munro suggests the conscious and unconscious themes on display had a substantial life beyond these events:

> Millions of people constructed, found employment within, or attended world's fairs. Millions more heard stories about the fairs from friends and relatives who visited and saw advertising for the fairs that had spread far and wide … More importantly ephemeral ideas and discourses from expositions moved to museums, where they became institutionalised as a permanent part of national consciousness.[36]

Governments were swift to realise the potential of world expositions to educate, socialise, and inculcate. The 1876 Philadelphia Centennial International Exhibition was held to demonstrate that city's recovery from the American Civil War (the hand and torch of the Statue of Liberty were also on display in order to convert patriotism into funds for its completion).[37] The Guatemalan national anthem debuted at its 1897 world exposition, and the Pledge of Allegiance (recited in American schools to this day) was devised for Chicago's 1893 event.[38]

World expositions also provided platforms for social movements and scholarly endeavours. Booker T. Washington delivered his historic speech on race relations at the Atlanta Cotton States and International Exposition of 1895.[39] Chicago's World's Columbian Exposition (1893) included a women's pavilion and associated convention highlighting female accomplishments; 'More important than the discovery of Columbus', pronounced the exposition's honorary president of the Board of Lady Managers, Bertha Palmer, at the dedication ceremony, 'is the fact that the General Government has just discovered woman.'[40] At the Congress of Historians led by Henry Adams at the same exposition, Frederick Jackson Turner presented his paper 'The Significance of the Frontier in American History', which is credited with changing the course of American historiography.[41]

Late nineteenth- and early twentieth-century expositions often included displays propagating Social Darwinism. In the ethnological court of the Sydney International Exhibition of 1879–80, Aborigines were declared the world's most primitive people, and the Queensland court displayed mummified Aboriginal and Torres Strait Islander remains that the Sydney press dubbed 'distinguished Queenslanders'.[42] The Louisiana Purchase International Exposition (1904) contained a living anthropological display of American Indians, African Pygmies, giants from Argentina, and a Filipino village of 1200; it also featured a laboratory designed to demonstrate Anglo-Saxon superiority.[43] The 1915 Panama–Pacific International Exposition included eugenics conventions on the 'race betterment' ideas of cereal magnate John H. Kellogg, and the Ku Klux Klan controversially booked auditorium space at Philadelphia's Sequi-Centennial International Exposition of 1926.[44] There was considerable division within the black communities of America about the value of participating in these events – and whether some recognition was better than none.[45]

Ruling elites retained a determinedly utopian approach to world expositions, as exemplified by American president William McKinley in the 6 September 1901 edition of *The New York Times*:

Expositions are the time-keepers of progress. The records of the world's advancement. They stimulate the energy, enterprise and intellect of the people, and quicken human genius. They go into the home. They broaden and brighten the lives of the people.

They open mighty storehouses of information to the student.
Every exposition, great or small, has helped this onward step.[46]

The day of publication, McKinley was assassinated at the
Pan-American Exposition in Buffalo. He was seriously wounded
when shot twice by an anarchist. The attending physician
(a gynaecologist) failed to detect the second bullet. It has been
suggested that if the X-ray machine being featured at the exposition
had been used, McKinley might have lived.[47] Theodore Roosevelt
ascended to the presidency in his place.

The Pan-American Exposition fared little better than McKinley;
it closed with a loss of three million dollars, multiple lawsuits,
and newspapers declaring 'the whole exposition business has been
heavily overdone'.[48] The prediction was again premature. The 1904
exposition in St Louis was among the largest and most elaborate ever
held. To provide the 1272 acres required for the event, organisers
drained a lake, removed a hill, rerouted a river, built or rebuilt over
a hundred miles of streets, added extra rail lines, cleaned up yards,
added new parks, and arranged for smoke polluters to be fined.[49]
The exposition attracted twenty million visits, made a substantial
profit, and inspired the popular song 'Meet Me in St Louis'.[50]

Prior to the disruption of World War I, numerous expositions
were staged around the globe each year. With twenty to thirty
exhibiting nations expected at each event, rival hosts strove to
differentiate their festivities to lure exhibitors and participants, some
linking with a prominent anniversary or occasion. One such novelty
involved holding the second, third, and fourth modern Olympiads
in conjunction with world expositions (in 1900, 1904, and 1908).
Ensuing Olympic events included cannon firing, pigeon flying,
tobacco spitting, and the 'Anthropology Games', in which members
of ethnological exhibits were coerced into activities such as the
Pygmy mud fight.[51] The founder of the modern Olympics, Pierre de
Coubertin, was nonplussed; the games were subsequently severed
from world expositions.[52]

To attract an exposition-sized crowd, organisers initially distinguished their events from museum exhibits with live specimens, working displays, novel sculptures carved from chocolate or butter, and various food and mineral samples stacked into imposing 'trophies'. As expositions increased in popularity and sophistication, they begat great crowd-pleasing monuments to ingenuity, such as France's Eiffel Tower (1889) and the American Ferris Wheel (1893). Such initiatives were not always welcome. The director of the Paris exposition received a manifesto objecting to the winning design (over submissions that included a giant guillotine) that stated, 'we, the writers, painters, sculptors, and architects come in the name of French good taste and of this menace to French history to express our deep indignation that there should stand in the heart of our Capital this unnecessary and monstrous Tour Eiffel'.[53]

Exposition organisers also sought to broaden their events' appeal by engaging influential representatives from the arts. Contributing world exposition artists, architects, and entertainers include Victor Hugo, Buffalo Bill, Annie Oakley, Giuseppe Verdi, Paul Gauguin, Henri Matisse, Auguste Renoir, Auguste Rodin, Claude Monet, Edvard Munch, Richard Wagner, Rudyard Kipling, Johnny Weissmuller, Howard Hughes, Esther Williams, Frank Lloyd Wright, Le Corbusier, Saul Bass, Charles and Ray Eames, Buckminster Fuller, Jerry Lee Lewis, Bob Hope, Bill Cosby, and Johnny Cash.

Art and entertainment devised for these events often transcended the world exposition sphere. The 1925 Exposition des Arts Decoratifs Modernes in Paris gave its name to the style it helped popularise: art deco.[54] Chicago's 1893 neoclassical White City influenced American architecture into the 1930s and inspired a City Beautiful movement.[55] James Earle Fraser's statue of a weary American Indian rider, , was designed for the 1915 San Francisco exposition.[56] The film *To Be Alive*, produced for the 1964–5 New York World's Fair, won an Oscar for Best Documentary, and the song 'It's a Small World' was a Disney contribution to this same exposition.[57] Amusement zones developed for world expositions, including Chicago's 1893 Midway Plaisance (which introduced the term 'midway' to describe carnival zones), inspired Coney Island and entities such as Disneyland.[58] Expositions also provided fanciful settings for alternative entertainment mediums, such as when the Elvis Presley film *It Happened at the World's Fair* incorporated scenes shot at the 1962 exposition in Seattle.

Entertainment zones – the meeting point between expositions and their fairground predecessors – initially operated as unapproved adjuncts to world expositions. When formally included (and brought under a measure of control), they remained segregated from educational aspects of expositions such as display pavilions, but were no less susceptible to prevailing social views. 'African Dips', an amusement attraction at the 1933–4 Chicago A Century of Progress Fair, offered visitors the chance to 'throw a ball through a hole; if they were successful, an African American was dropped into a tank of water'.[59] This exposition and the 1935–6 California Pacific International Exposition both featured midget villages, and the 1939–40 New York World's Fair boasted the freak show 'We Humans'.[60]

Some entertainment operators veered in a salacious direction to lure exposition crowds. Visitors might have been shocked to observe belly dancers at the 1893 Chicago exposition, but by the time of the 1933–4 event in that same city they could watch naked ladies cavorting with robots.[61] Lurid displays along the entertainment precinct known as 'the Pike' at the 1904 St Louis event inspired one critic to write, 'If the Pike had been a mile longer it would have led to hell.'[62]

World expositions prior to World War I continued to affirm the prevailing powers' progress and status, but signifiers of these qualities gradually shifted from raw materials and industrial technology to scientific achievement and consumer comforts – bringing greater prominence to inventors and brands. Products unveiled at world expositions during this period include Alexander Graham Bell's telephone; Thomas Edison's telegraph, megaphone, and phonograph;

Hershey's chocolate; and Juicy Fruit gum.[63] The 1915 San Francisco exposition featured General Electric's consumer-friendly 'The Home Electrical' display, Eastman Kodak's two-tone Kodachrome photographs, and a Ford assembly line that constructed eighteen Model-T vehicles a day.[64] Inventor and brand rivalries also came into play in the planning and execution phases of expositions – such as when Nikola Tesla and Westinghouse were selected over Thomas Edison and General Electric to provide electricity for the 1893 Chicago event.

Interwar Expositions

World War I temporarily diminished the capacity of aspiring host cities to undertake the risk that expositions had come to represent, but the events returned with such vigour in the 1920s that the Bureau of International Expositions (BIE) was formed at a convention in 1928 to control their frequency and duration, and to exert some measure of control on quality.[65] It was determined there would be two types of exposition: a universal exposition and a smaller, specialised version aligned with a particular theme.[66] Only the government of a country could apply to host one. The BIE met twice a year to consider world exposition bids. Regulations relating to frequency, duration, and forms of exposition fluctuated over the years, but many governments refrained from nominating a rival exposition date close to a bid already under consideration.

Australia became a signatory to the International Convention Relating to Exhibitions in 1935, but withdrew ten years later in the belief that there were better ways to promote exports (then its primary motivator for participation).[67]

World expositions' return to favour after World War I has been attributed to the ideological opportunities they continued to represent. In *Fair America*, Robert W. Rydell, John Findling, and Kimberly D. Pelle argue that the colonial and American world expositions of the 1920s and '30s were strategic responses to worldwide crises threatening the capitalist system: those held in Europe garnered support for imperialism, while those held in America built a case for intervention in countries deemed essential to its growth, and helped extract America from the Great Depression by focusing attention on past glories and future hopes.[68]

As exposition organisers increasingly linked better living with entertainment and leisure, the concept of progress became wedded to technological advancement and material growth. Amusement zones and technological corporations slowly advanced from expositions' periphery to centre stage, lending legitimacy to the idea that corporations could be trusted with society's future.[69] The New York World's Fair of 1939–40 promoted such views via the large utopian 'Democracity' model within the Perisphere and General Motors' highway-positive Futurama ride (an updated version of which also appeared at the New York 1964–5 exposition).[70] Thirty-four major corporation buildings were prominently featured, including RCA, Heinz, Eastman Kodak, General Electric, and Westinghouse.[71] This forward-looking event nevertheless failed to foresee the future of its own site. An ash dump in Queens (*The Great Gatsby*'s 'valley of ashes') had been heroically reclaimed to stage the event at the instigation of New York park commissioner and urban renewal exponent Robert Moses, but the site lay dormant for years afterwards when a planned parkland conversion proved financially unviable.[72]

The thriving world exposition circuit – and the premise of progress – was again curtailed in the shadow of World War II. The decision to situate German and USSR pavilions opposite each other at the 1937 exposition in Paris proved ill-advised (especially as Hitler's architect Albert Speer obtained a sketch of the USSR Pavilion in time to dwarf it with his own creation); ideals of education and exchange were hijacked by suspicion, with pavilion guards preventing photographs and sketches of the technology on show. Peace medals were distributed at the exposition three years before the Nazis overran France.[73] During the 1939–40 New York World's Fair, the flags of the French and Polish exhibits were draped in black, the Soviet Pavilion was razed (at its request), and a notice outside the incomplete Czech Pavilion explained work had ceased due to Nazi invasion (Germany had not participated in the exposition, but Japan's pavilion included a model of the Liberty Bell).[74] At the exposition's conclusion, the iconic Trylon and Perisphere constructions were scrapped for steel as part of the war effort.[75] The 1939–40 San Francisco exposition was closed in its second year so the US Navy could turn Treasure Island into a naval station.[76]

Few countries possessed the resources or wherewithal to mount a world exposition in the aftermath of World War II; Tokyo's anticipated 1940 exposition debut was jettisoned, as was the grand exposition Mussolini had planned for Rome in 1942.[77] World exposition veteran Sol Bloom (who had made his reputation managing the Midway entertainment at Chicago's 1893 exposition before becoming a Broadway producer and a member of Congress) entered a different realm of world representation as part of the US delegation at a conference that birthed the United Nations at the conclusion of the war.[78]

The Ascendance of the Olympic Games

The Olympic Games were also cancelled in 1940 and 1944 owing to war, but they resumed in 1948 – ten years before the next world exposition – after which they came to succeed expositions as the primary proving ground for national strength.[79] The Games' ascendance as a 'mega event' increased exponentially after the 1956 Winter Olympics, the first to be broadcast live internationally via satellite. The degree to which the Games embodied motivations and fears once associated with world expositions was evident at the 1956 Melbourne Summer Olympics (the event's Australian debut). Historian Graeme Davison observes that the Melbourne Games were born of a desire for international recognition for the city and social recognition for its 'business elite', and that the event inspired City Beautiful initiatives, a drive for more sophisticated architecture such as the Olympic Pool, and a campaign for the liberalisation of liquor licensing laws – lest the city be deemed a 'hick town'.[80] The anticipated international visiting audience largely failed to eventuate, but euphoria was extracted from a simple absence of overt disasters, with the local press declaring 'we've grown up overnight'.[81]

The Cold War Period

The next world exposition was held in Brussels in 1958 (the Japanese, German, and Italian pavilions were modest), attracting forty-two million people at the onset of the Cold War.[82] The event's ideological subtext was the struggle between communism and the globalisation of corporate capitalism. The escalating arms race between America and the USSR brought additional tensions; the Soviets had achieved a public relations coup with the launch of *Sputnik* the previous year, prompting the US commissioner-general to request funding to 'do a Sputnik culturally, intellectually, and spiritually' in Brussels.[83] Years later, it was revealed that the American pavilion operated as a front for highly sensitive US intelligence-gathering activities in Europe.[84]

The ideological stand-off also influenced Seattle's space-themed Century 21 Exposition (1962), which was supported by the American Department of Defense and the National Science Foundation; both organisations sought to rally the public's faith in American innovation in the aftermath of *Sputnik*.[85]

Western expositions continued to legitimise – and reflect – the growing influence of transnational corporate capitalism.[86] Exhibitors at the 1964–5 New York World's Fair included IBM, Kodak, General Motors, Westinghouse, Ford, DuPont, Pepsi, and Coca-Cola.[87] Corporate pavilions included General Electric's Disney-designed theatrical monument to technology, Progressland.[88] The event suffered a financial loss of $21 million – despite attendance figures in excess of fifty-one million.[89] The loss is generally attributed to its president, Robert Moses, who alienated the press, made economically crippling arrangements with exposition executives and contractors, and excluded potential participating nations by holding the event without sanction from the BIE, which he denigrated as 'three little men in a cheap hotel room in Paris'.[90] The perceived failure prompted *Harper's Magazine* to declare that world expositions would be superseded by stores, televisions, museums, and travel.[91]

World expositions staged in the 1970s and early 1980s reflected the questioning of modernity that took place in the second stage of the twentieth century, as evinced by the exposition themes 'Man and His World' (Montreal, 1967), 'Celebrating Tomorrow's Fresh New Environment' (Spokane, 1974), 'Energy Turns the World' (Knoxville, 1982), and 'Progress and Harmony for Mankind' (Osaka, 1970). The Montreal and Osaka expositions also signalled a change in the image that Australia (exhibiting for the first time since World War II) sought to project, shifting emphasis from primary production to science, technology, and modernist design, with sophisticated contributions from Australian Pavilion architect James Maccormick, exhibit designer Robin Boyd, and furniture designers Grant and Mary Featherston.[92]

The Osaka world exposition was the first to be held in Asia (tickets purchased for the unrealised 1940 Tokyo exposition were honoured at this event thirty years later).[93] Companies promoted included Fuji, Hitachi, and Mitsubishi.[94] The exposition was an enormous success, with over sixty-four million visits and profits in excess of $146 million.[95] At the event's commencement, Premier Satō said he was pleased Japan had finally 'acquired sufficient national strength to sponsor a world exposition and to discharge important responsibilities in the international community'.[96]

The Divisive Pervasiveness of Urban Renewal

In the latter half of the twentieth century, smaller, 'specialised' world expositions were held in developing towns such as Spokane (1974) and Knoxville (1982) in America. They functioned as catalysts for urban renewal while supplying an altruistic explanation for government land resumption and property redevelopment.[97] The urban renewal approach is exemplified by Seattle's Century 21 Exposition (1962), which was instigated by developers and designed with its physical legacy in mind – seventy-five per cent of its constructions were permanent.[98] At the exposition's conclusion, the site became the Seattle Center, incorporating shops, restaurants, museums, arena facilities, theatres, amusement attractions, an opera house, the exposition's monorail, and its iconic Space Needle.[99]

A growing disenchantment with unfettered urban renewal was articulated by civic observer Jane Jacobs, whose 1961 book, *The Death and Life of Great American Cities*, challenged modernist excesses responsible for a great loss of historic housing, urban sprawl, social dislocation, and the isolation and destruction of (typically lower socioeconomic) communities by freeways. Jacobs believed the City Beautiful movement bequeathed by the 1893 Chicago exposition could more accurately be called the 'City Monumental' movement (after its White City architectural component), and that its true legacy was lifeless, underutilised civic centres in 'city after city' embodying 'dispirited decay'.[100] She noted that 'when the fair became part of the city, it did not work like the city'.[101] Jacobs advocated for mixed-use space, preservation of historic housing and communities, economic diversity, and public participation in planning.

One of her main opponents was the polarising New York bureaucrat Robert Moses, who figured prominently in the 1939–40 and 1964–5 New York world expositions (both of which failed to achieve their urban renewal ambitions). Moses was an advocate of French architect and urbanist Le Corbusier, who had controversially proposed demolishing entire blocks of historic Paris at that city's 1925 world exposition and replacing them with high-rise apartments. Moses embraced renewal dogma with such effectiveness that he cleared hundreds of acres of character houses and land (displacing tens of thousands of people) while modernising New York City.[102] Jacobs was instrumental in thwarting his scheme to level Greenwich Village (and what is now SoHo) for an expressway. She argued that city planning and transportation had stagnated: 'nothing is offered which was not already offered and popularised in 1938 [*sic*] in the General Motors diorama at the New York World's Fair, and before that by Le Corbusier'.[103]

American enthusiasm for freeways and urban development influenced Australian planners after World War II, when ageing city developments were considered slums in need of demolition.[104] Victorian-era homes and Carlton terrace houses faced destruction in the state of Victoria, and much of historic inner-city Sydney was replaced with high-rises in the 1960s.[105] Resident action groups (many influenced by Jacobs) formed to preserve historic buildings, multicultural inner-city life, and cheaper living expenses (at the eventual cost to migrants and lower socioeconomic groups via gentrification), while 'green bans' enacted by sympathetic unions were instrumental in saving Sydney's Rocks district and Collins Street in Melbourne.[106]

Second-tier cities eager to exploit the redevelopment potential of a world exposition in the latter half of the twentieth century thus faced increasing opposition to urban renewal – in addition to the basic illogicality of attempting to position a city that was demonstrably in need of redevelopment as the embodiment of 'progress'. There was also – yet again – the matter of the decline of the exposition form.

The Rise of Alternative Events

With the notable exceptions of Expo 67 in Montreal (fifty million visits) and Expo 70 in Osaka (over sixty-four million visits), public interest in the ageing concept dwindled in the late stages of the twentieth century.[107] Prior to Expo 88, a number of hosts proved unable to break even with their events; the 1984 New Orleans exposition was 'a financial disaster unmatched in the annals of world expositions', and so unpopular (with less than half the projected attendance figure of fifteen million) it was forced into bankruptcy during the event, with debts in excess of $120 million.[108] The world exposition planned for Chicago in 1992 was cancelled, prompting a new round of media speculation that expositions were no longer a source of wonder.[109]

The 'wonder' mantle was arguably assumed by the popular and financially successful 1984 Los Angeles Summer Olympics, in which the games re-emerged from a fraught decade of cost overruns, drug cheat scandals, boycotts, and terrorism – just as world expositions looked doomed to disinterest.[110]

Emerging festivals and events were also syphoning public attention – and changing leisure patterns. In the late twentieth century, Graeme Davison noted that 'in the global economy of tourism and high finance, cities have been turned from workshops into playgrounds', producing a commensurate shift in rituals and celebrations:

> Theatres, sporting arenas, casinos, convention centres,
> museums and art galleries, river walks and festival markets
> are the focal points of the post-modern city. Its calendar is no
> longer that of the agricultural seasons or the business year but
> the round of conventions, sporting contests, arts festivals and
> street processions that draw tourists and locals to its cafes and
> hotels.[111]

Atop 'this cycle of celebration', said Davison, 'are the mega-events in which the city performs on an international stage'.[112] These events 'define the post-industrial, post-modern city just as international exhibitions once symbolised the modern industrial city'.[113]

While many traditional world exposition hosts had lost enthusiasm for the concept, some champions remained. Future Australian prime minister Gough Whitlam retained an interest even after a 1960s Victorian proposal failed to proceed, and he was instrumental (while in Opposition) in persuading the federal government to again become a signatory to the International Convention Relating to Exhibitions.[114] In 1974, with encouragement from Canadian

BIE delegate (and future BIE president) Patrick Reid, Australian delegate Bill Worth, and Special Minister of State Lionel Bowen, the Whitlam government informed the BIE of Australia's interest in staging a world exposition in 1987/88; this intention was formalised at a BIE meeting in 1975.[115] There was an underlying assumption on the part of both the Whitlam and succeeding Fraser governments that the only cities capable of sustaining such an event were Sydney and Melbourne.[116] Nevertheless, the Queensland Government made several unsuccessful early attempts to secure the event for Brisbane – an inelegant but not unsurprising situation for a city unheard of by most, and mocked by many of those who had.

The Inglorious Emergence of the City of Brisbane

Founded without treaty upon the homelands of the indigenous Turrbal and Jagera peoples early in the nineteenth century, and named after the river that divides it (itself named for Sir Thomas Brisbane, governor of NSW and instigator of the penal settlement established in the area to receive secondary offenders from the Sydney colony), the town of Brisbane was created when local government commenced after separation from NSW in 1859.[117]

The Brisbane River also divided the city metaphorically, with an informal class system emerging as government administration and commercial headquarters were established on the north side, and factories and warehouses arose near the south-side port and the coal rail terminal at Kangaroo Point.[118] The divide was mirrored in living conditions, with grand estates appearing in north Brisbane, and multicultural working-class suburbs in the south attracting immigrants from Europe and Asia.[119]

In 1925, the Theodore Labor government amalgamated approximately twenty municipalities and shires into the City of Greater Brisbane – the largest municipal government in Australia, and the only local government authority with an Act of Parliament.[120] The Brisbane City Council (BCC) initially maintained complex utilities such as water, sewage, public transport, and electricity (infrastructure that, in other states, was typically the responsibility of central authorities) while hamstrung with a limited revenue base composed of rates, charges, and loans.[121] State and federal neglect added challenges in the form of unequal grant distribution, and restrictions on loan amounts and sources. Brisbane was further buffeted by the Great Depression, World Wars I and II (the second placing enormous strain on fragile infrastructure when the state became the centre of Allied efforts in the Pacific War), postwar scarcity, a skilled labour drain, paternalistic state interventions by rural-focused governments, and onerous town-planning legislation.[122]

As late as the 1950s, the city boasted few grand structures beyond Brisbane City Hall, Cloudland, and the Story Bridge. In the early 1960s, eighty per cent of its suburbs were unsewered, and a statutory town plan only transpired in 1965.[123] Most roads weren't sealed between kerbs until 1972.[124] Prior to completion of the Merivale Bridge in 1978, it was not possible to take a train from South Brisbane into the city.[125] The Brisbane River was variously viewed as an obstacle to be crossed, a force to be wary of (as per the 1893 and 1974 floods), and a resource for the drawing of water and the disposal of waste. There was little impetus to construct parks or allow public access to the dilapidated wooden wharf-lined river, and buildings typically faced the city rather than Brisbane's natural asset.[126]

It could be argued that Brisbane was not in need of renewal, since the city had not really begun. It was an unlikely world exposition contender even by the fluctuating standards of second-tier cities entranced by the urban development potential of such events. But there was also the matter of the volatile state of which Brisbane was both capital and casualty.

2

We Need to Talk about Queensland

Once upon a time an academic said to me: 'In thirty years people will wonder what happened in Queensland in the seventies. It will all sound like a fairy tale – a man ruling with 19 percent of the vote, a state politician whose manoeuvres removed a federal government.'

Hugh Lunn[1]

THE NATURE OF MUCH OF the criticism directed at Queensland during Sir Joh Bjelke-Petersen's premiership can be gleaned from the titles of contemporary publications: *The Deep North*; *The Hillbilly Dictator*; *Behind the Banana Curtain*; *Queensland Leaves the Planet*; *Back to Queensland (You Can't Go Forward)*; *State of Mind: Why Queensland is Different*. The notion of Queensland's 'difference' preceded Bjelke-Petersen, but reached almost mythological proportions during his premiership, spurring debate as to why Queensland was – or was not – different, the extent to which such difference could be measured, and what difference any differences might make. The term was rarely used in a positive sense. To comprehend the local and national antipathy to the prospect of Queensland's capital city hosting Expo 88, the challenges faced by organisers, and the seismic impact the event was to have, it is essential to understand the state Brisbane was in.

The Difference Debates

Claims of Queensland's 'difference' were often rooted in tangible facts: harsh climate, dependence upon primary industry, lack of established secondary industries (and associated migratory inducements), sustained underinvestment in education, great distances and rivalries between the capital and satellite cities at ports and mining locations, and the tendency of some politicians to eschew democratic conventions. An egregious example of Queensland's democratic 'difference' as a self-governed colony in the nineteenth century was its endorsement of practices tantamount to slavery in the treatment of South Sea Islanders in the sugar industry.[2] After Federation, Queensland Labor governments proved adept at eroding democratic safeguards and conventions, controversially abolishing the (admittedly problematic) Legislative Council in 1922, proclaiming a State of Emergency to deal with strike actions (1946–8), and introducing the zonal electoral system commonly referred to as the malamander or gerrymander in 1949, which gave greater weighting to votes in regional areas (then Labor heartland) than in populous metropolitan zones.

By 1957, Labor had been in power for thirty-nine of the previous forty-two years, and only returned to Opposition as a consequence of internal strife. The Country Party won power in coalition with the Liberal Party after Labor separated into the Catholic-dominated Australian Labor Party (ALP) and Queensland Labor Party (later the Democratic Party) during the 'Gair split' (after former premier Vince Gair). Under the Coalition agreement, the position of premier and various influential ministries went to the partner with the greatest number of seats; the junior partner filled the positions of deputy premier, treasurer, and lesser ministries unpopular with the electorate or with few 'pork-barrelling' opportunities – though the potential for largesse was limited.

Sir Leo Hielscher (under treasurer from 1974 until the commencement of Expo) recalls Queensland's fraught economic situation prior to the minerals boom: 'We had a very, very poor economy up until say '64 or so when I came into the Treasury. The state finances were broke and the economy was third world, really. We had no big companies except Mount Isa Mines – and it was handicapped by a clapped-out railway line; but all of our infrastructure was damaged – rode into the ground – mainly from the war effort. We were front-line during the war. Before the war, we had ten years of depression, and then another ten years of war, and then another ten years of austerity – and by the time the mid-'60s came we were really down and out: we had more or less a subsistence economy; everyone worked for themselves ... you painted your own house; you dug your own garden; you had your own chooks in the backyard – that sort of thing.'[3]

Hielscher is widely credited (along with Liberal parliamentary leader Sir Tom Hiley, his successor Sir Gordon Chalk, and Coordinator-General Sir Sydney Schubert) with modernising the Queensland economy – though their unorthodox approach raised the ire of federal counterparts.[4] 'We invented a new term,' says Hielscher. 'We didn't break the rules, we didn't bend them, we would "brend" the rules'.[5]

Coalition relations were congenial under the premiership of Country Party leader Frank Nicklin, whose rural focus allowed the Liberal Party a measure of independence with its city base. This changed when Country Party strategists realised that, with Labor in disarray (with its ageing blue-collar organisational wing dominated by the Trades Hall Group [THG], and its members dubbed the 'Breakfast Creek Gang' in reference to the hours logged at a pub near their headquarters), the greatest threat to their political ascendancy was the Liberal Party. Country Party State President Sir Robert Sparkes and State Secretary Mike Evans orchestrated a rebranding as the National Party in 1974 to broaden their appeal in metropolitan areas and in the Gold Coast (a move followed in other states). Successive Country/National Party-led governments adroitly manipulated the zonal system to both disadvantage Labor and ensure their own seniority; National Party Member of the Legislative Assembly (MLA) Russ Hinze boasted of advising the premier, 'If you want the boundaries rigged, let me do it and we'll stay in power forever. If you don't do it people will say you are stupid.'[6]

Many Liberals expected to displace their Coalition rivals in the 1970s and failed to appreciate the seriousness of their situation until the party had been substantially weakened – an oversight that, coupled with Labor lethargy, contributed to the thirty-two-year governance of Queensland by conservative country interests prone to directing funds away from the capital towards regional industries and their own electorates.[7] The most significant factor in the longevity and character of that governance – and the inspiration for much of the antipathy towards Brisbane as host city for Expo – was Queensland's entrenched premier, Sir Joh Bjelke-Petersen.

Difference Personified

Bjelke-Petersen's remarkable political career could not have been predicted from an early age – or, indeed, from middle age. Born in New Zealand in 1911 to Lutheran parents of Danish descent, he moved with his family to Kingaroy, Queensland, in 1913. An indifferent student, he worked full time on the family farm from age fourteen. His extraordinary work ethic – in combination with canny farming innovations, business enterprise, disregard for environmental conservation, and the capacity to live alone in a cowbail on remote land for fifteen years – resulted in successful land-clearing, crop-dusting, and peanut-farming businesses, and the right to the descriptor 'self-made man'. His first biographer, Hugh Lunn, notes that this path to financial success eschewed socialising activities such as negotiating the workplace environment, sharing knock-off drinks, playing sports, and joining special-interest groups.[8] Having suffered polio at age nine, Bjelke-Petersen was also excluded from the then common socialising aspects of military service, and participation in World War II.

As a successful rural entrepreneur, Bjelke-Petersen was courted by conservatives to enter politics. He was elected to the Kingaroy Shire Council in 1946, and won the vacant state seat of Nanango in 1947 at age thirty-six. As a non-drinking, non-smoking, committed church-goer, he was mocked by the Opposition and eschewed by many in the Coalition as a country redneck fundamentalist of little consequence. Communist Party member Fred Patterson once nominated him as the only person less likely than himself to become premier of Queensland.

At age forty, Bjelke-Petersen married Florence Gilmour, with whom he had four children. 'Flo' was a political asset, winning hearts with her country charm and homemade pumpkin scones, while serving as a backup 'personality' when her husband was unavailable. Bjelke-Petersen was finally offered his first ministry in 1963, when he was fifty-two. He used his position as minister for Works and Housing to accrue favours by fast-tracking projects and services in the electorates of fellow parliamentarians. Such favours were called in when Nicklin retired and Bjelke-Petersen sought the position of deputy party leader – a role not considered important, as Jack Pizzey was expected to lead the party for at least ten years. Bjelke-Petersen became deputy party leader and minister for Police in 1968. Six months later, Pizzey died of a heart attack and Bjelke-Petersen thwarted Liberal parliamentary leader Gordon Chalk's ambition to extend his eight-day term as the premier of Queensland.

Bjelke-Petersen's lack of formal education was no impediment to his holding this position; the senior Coalition party typically comprised poorly educated white agrarian businessmen in their sixties who had raised their children in simpler times, and whose uniformly blinkered social and political outlook was credited with creating an 'official Queensland view of the world [which] has often been archaic, expressing conservative and simplistic views of complex issues'.[9] Rosemary Kyburz, a former schoolteacher and

Liberal MLA for Salisbury (1974–83), has little time for the 'self-made man' conceit:

> Unfortunately, when people are, for want of a better term, self-taught, they become quite righteous about the fact that they've made it. And 'made it' in their terms is having money. They haven't made it in the broad learning spectrum of having read Dante and Homer and understanding poetry and that sort of thing ... Shakespeare could well be the next cab driver for all they cared.[10]

A Cultural Desert?

It was easy to position Queensland as antithetical to the arts. Its capital was the city in which The Beatles had been egged (by a group that included future National Party MLA Bob Katter), of which Bob Dylan had said, 'progress doesn't seem to have touched down here' (after being jeered in the streets), and in which the premier sought to intervene in the shared living arrangements of visiting pop group ABBA.[11] The government was slow to establish arts bodies or support artistic endeavour, yet swift to empower censorship bodies for film and literature. It also figured prominently in the destruction of culturally significant heritage sites.

Some have argued that the popular view of Brisbane as a 'cultural desert' at this time was more of a reaction to conservatism and 'Queensland difference' rhetoric than a genuine assessment of artistic merit. In his book *The Third Metropolis*, William Hatherell chronicles the transformative influence of the American 'cultural invasion' (when thousands of American troops based in Brisbane during World War II exposed locals to new entertainment and social attitudes), and the emergence of an arts scene that birthed the *Meanjin* and *Barjai* journals, Miya Studio, the Johnston Gallery, Jacaranda Press, and University of Queensland Press – entities that supported Brisbane artists such as David Malouf, Judith Wright,

Janette Turner Hospital, Thea Astley, Oodgeroo Noonuccal, Thomas Shapcott, and Margaret Olley.[12] Artistic outlets in the late 1970s and early 1980s included the Institute of Modern Art, the Milburn and Bellas commercial galleries, and numerous artist-run spaces and projects. As chronicled in Andrew Stafford's book *Pig City*, Brisbane's music scene was similarly fertile, producing groups such as The Saints, The Go-Betweens, The Riptides, The Apartments, and The Screaming Tribesmen.[13]

Areas of artistic endeavour favoured by conservatives (such as opera, fine art, traditional theatre, and ballet) enjoyed state patronage at the behest of Gordon Chalk, who also drove development of the Queensland Cultural Centre (QCC) – despite Bjelke-Petersen's objection that there was nothing in it for country voters.[14] The Coalition's rural bias was evident in the naming conventions of institutions such as the Queensland Ballet, the Queensland Symphony Orchestra, and the Queensland Theatre Company, all of which acknowledged the state, rather than the city in which they were based.[15]

Bjelke-Petersen's extreme conservatism prompted many artists and alternative thinkers to leave the state in an informal movement known as the 'Brisbane exodus'.[16] Other incentives included superior interstate and international career opportunities, and the simple if ineluctable fact that Brisbane could be dull. Anne Jones (an editor of satirical magazine *The Cane Toad Times*, which targeted Bjelke-Petersen and Expo) paints a bleak picture of entertainment options at this time: 'All the licensing laws were so restrictive, the only things going on were the casinos and strip clubs down the Valley – which were illegal – so you've got a few alternative types making their own fun, a few inveterate gamblers down the Valley, and the vast mainstream going to the movies.'[17]

Jones was drawn to the magazine as an outlet for creative work: 'We would be cartooning or writing funny stuff, and there weren't places for it to be published. It's hard for people to imagine these days ... but there was nothing for young people to do.'[18]

The city's sparse leisure options were further curtailed by weekend trading regulations and restrictions on Sunday activities. Tony Kelly (director of QCOSS and senior lecturer at the Department of Social Work at The University of Queensland [UQ], where he backed a study into the social impact of Expo) recalls that, beyond meeting for dances and concerts at venues such as Cloudland and Festival Hall, people of mainstream Brisbane were more inclined to entertain family and friends in their backyards than congregate in the few existing coffee shops or public spaces.[19]

The deputy director of entertainment and walkways producer for Expo, Barbara Absolon, says restrictive health regulations limited outdoor dining opportunities, and that when they were 'loosened up a bit' a few years prior to Expo 'it was so innovative we were all rushing to Giardinetto's [Italian restaurant in Fortitude Valley] to sit on the street and watch the buses go by'. She recalls there were few large-scale gathering activities in Brisbane prior to the exposition: 'the Ekka [Royal Queensland Show] and Warana [Arts Festival] were the two highlights of the year – and the Christmas characters in the old Allan & Stark building ... work Christmas picnics ... those were the big things for people to do.'[20]

Those with the means to do so could embark on a weekend getaway to the Gold Coast – lured by the prospect of surf carnivals, family fun, or shadier diversions in the form of drugs, sex, and vice on the pleasure strip. Other options included zoos and attractions such as Magic Mountain and the Big Pineapple, Grundy's Entertainment Centre, Conrad Jupiters casino (Queensland's first legal gambling establishment), and ticketed utopias such as Dreamworld and Sea World; many of these escape outlets were envisioned by white shoe developers.[21]

Developers in Paradise

Support for Brisbane development was not the sole province of the Coalition government. Labor's Vince Gair had opened the

Chermside shopping centre (the first large suburban shopping development in Australia) in 1957 – the year planning began on Queensland's first residential high-rise, Torbreck.[22] Labor lord mayor Clem Jones (1961–75) increased Brisbane height restrictions to allow inner-city skyscrapers in 1964.[23] Having caught up on the city's utilities and infrastructure backlog (aided by heavy borrowing during the boom and a convivial relationship with city-focused Treasurer Chalk), Jones was able to turn his attention to other areas, including BCC's bid to secure the 1978 or 1982 Commonwealth Games, and the beautification of public areas with libraries, picnic spots, walking tracks, sports fields, swimming pools, and – importantly for Expo – the purchase of large tracts of land along Brisbane's South Bank for conversion into parkland.[24]

Brisbane's ageing infrastructure finally received state government attention in the 1960s, when the minerals boom necessitated good roads and sophisticated locales for Queensland businesses. At the height of the urban-renewal-led fervour for freeways and integrated transport, American consulting engineers Wilbur Smith and Associates were commissioned to assess Brisbane's travel and traffic requirements, resulting in a modernised railway, the much-contested (council-assisted) abolition of trams, and a system of freeways and expressways along the northern riverbank, disparaged by some as an aesthetic blight.[25] Such actions entailed resuming the homes of thousands of Brisbane residents (far more than were displaced by Expo) amid claims of undervaluations, Special Branch police intimidation of protesters, and expedited demolition of vocal objectors' homes.[26]

The intensity of development thrust upon Brisbane at this time engulfed all previous efforts, and took place within a conservative, anti-urban, anti-intellectual environment that alienated and politicised large sections of the community; it was all the more inflammatory for taking place in the midst of conflict-of-interest scandals and curtailed civil rights.[27]

Trouble in Paradise

As Bjelke-Petersen was an unexpected premier, media and opposition attention only belatedly turned to his business interests. He continued many of his former operations during his parliamentary career, while adding some ethically ambiguous new ones. In 1969, it was revealed that he had prevailed upon Minister for Mines (and his former oil search partner) Ernie Evans to grant him authority to prospect for petroleum, which he parlayed into Exoil shares worth $720,000.[28] His government also awarded leases to prospect for oil on the Great Barrier Reef to companies in which he owned shares.[29] Bjelke-Petersen denied using his position for financial gain and refused to divest himself of shares that implied a conflict of interest, insisting, 'selling your shares will not make you an honest man'.[30]

Other scandals included revelations that the state government granted Bjelke-Petersen Enterprises permission to expand its kaolin (white clay) mining operation, the premier's insistence that a power station be built in his electorate near his investment property (an action that cost the state an additional 300 million dollars over the site recommended by the State Electricity Commission), and revelations that his wife accepted preferential shares in the mining company Comalco (along with several MLAs dealing with the company in a ministerial capacity).[31]

Such scandals were closer to tradition than exception. Ned Hanlon's Labor government had been rife with corruption, and Nicklin Coalition MLAs were known to attach themselves to businesses specifically to profit from insider information.[32] Successive scandals and poor media performances nevertheless prompted a challenge to Bjelke-Petersen's leadership in 1970. He was informed that he lacked the numbers and was advised to step down, but he spent the night calling in favours; the next day, he used the proxy of an absent member (whose preference was never confirmed) to bring voting to a tie, then voted for himself. A subsequent attempt to install Chalk as premier was thwarted when Bjelke-Petersen convinced Sparkes it would result in a split.[33]

Former Australian Broadcasting Commission (ABC) journalist Allen Callaghan is often credited with helping Bjelke-Petersen restore his political fortunes. When appointed as the premier's media adviser in 1971, Callaghan introduced public relations techniques that were ahead of their time. Favourable footage shot by government cinematographers in distant locations was often the only material available to the media. Well-written press releases were telexed to news outlets shortly before deadline – increasing the chances that they would be published unedited.[34] The premier was a regular guest on call-back radio before it was the norm, and had government-funded prime-time slots such as *Queensland Unlimited* and *The Joh Show* on commercial television.[35] He was coached to be civil to the media, answer the question he wanted asked (rather than what was actually asked), and talk unusable nonsense to avoid difficult questions while on location, as portable cameras contained only four minutes of film.[36]

Bjelke-Petersen's infamous verbal stumbles are believed to have endeared him to 'ordinary people' over his more polished critics. Brisbane correspondent for *The Sydney Morning Herald*, David Monaghan (who later joined with Expo protesters), was less impressed:

> Joh used to call his press conferences with us journalists 'feeding the chooks' and you'd always get a funny Johism that could make a line. What the funny line hid was the truth of how Joh with his crooked Cabinet and police chief ran the regime through crime, corruption and fear.[37]

Callaghan's job was made easy by a poorly resourced, unquestioning, uninspired, and generally conservative press.[38] A 1980 survey of state and suburban newspapers found the majority were firmly anti-Labor.[39] The state's largest newspaper, *The Courier-Mail*, endorsed the Bjelke-Petersen government at every election the premier contested.[40] Journalists critical of the government risked being denied access to it (and to the second-largest employer of journalists: the government), while media organisations risked defamation actions and loss of government advertising.[41]

Contemporary journalist Steve Bishop believes some of his peers failed to report on government and police scandals, as they were 'in thrall' to characters later found to be corrupt, and were stymied by the belief that 'this was the way it had always been'.[42] In 1989, the Fitzgerald Inquiry found that systemic corruption within the Queensland Police Force took root during Nicklin's premiership and was overseen by Police Commissioner Frank Bischof; corrupt networks also formed between NSW and Queensland police at this time.[43] Their perfidious activities are chronicled in Matthew Condon's true-crime trilogy *Three Crooked Kings*, and include protection rackets for illegal casinos, brothels, and unlicensed bookmakers.[44] Bischof was exposed in 1964 when Starting Price (SP) bookmakers approached Treasurer Hiley with objections to an increased police 'levy'. Subsequent investigations revealed a betting scam through which Bischof laundered his corrupt earnings. Astonishingly, Nicklin and Hiley merely requested that he refrain from doing it again.[45]

Bischof's bagmen were identified by witnesses on various occasions as police officers Terry Lewis, Glen Hallahan, and Tony Murphy – referred to in some circles since the 1960s as the 'Rat Pack'.[46] Other police suspected of corruption included Jack Herbert (linked with gambling, kickbacks, and consorting with prostitutes) and Don 'Shady' Lane, who had markedly little success when tasked with investigating corrupt police or reducing gambling and prostitution in Fortitude Valley. Lane became a Liberal MLA in 1971. He used his position to deter inquiries into police corruption and hamper the careers of police critics such as Labor's Col Bennett (who lost his seat after Lane orchestrated a redesign of electoral boundaries) – all while reportedly receiving half the money collected by corrupt police in his electorate.[47]

Several inquiries into police corruption at this time failed to produce results, including a Royal Inquiry into allegations that Bischof and his police colleagues ignored prostitution at the National Hotel (which they frequented). Conservative Royal Commissioner Harry Gibbs (later knighted and appointed chief justice of the High Court) ruled vast amounts of evidence inadmissible, accepted perjured testimony, did not seek to expand the limited terms of the Inquiry, and then found no evidence of police corruption.[48] Lewis, Murphy, and Hallahan were cleared on other occasions through restrictive terms of reference, police coaching or verballing of witnesses, inadequately skilled lawyers, campaigns to discredit accusers, and threats to the wellbeing of potential witnesses.[49] Notorious prostitute, brothel madam, and whistleblower of corrupt police Shirley Brifman died in suspicious circumstances days before she was due to give evidence that Murphy had perjured himself during the National Hotel Inquiry; she had been promised police protection. There was no inquest.

Des Power, the executive producer of the National Nine Network's *Today Tonight* and the ABC's *This Day Tonight* (both of which broke important stories on Queensland corruption in the 1970s and 1980s), believes Bjelke-Petersen's protection of the police stemmed from wilful naivety: 'Joh was fed the line that if you want a stable society, you've got to have a relationship with the police; they're the key to everything … he idolised them because they all spun him this yarn: "Joh, we're here to help you, we're your eyes and ears, we can give you information, we can ensure stability, we can control and stop crime" – and he swallowed all that … Bischof was the master of saying things like, "Joh, if only you knew what was going on – but I don't want to worry you – we'll look after it."'[50]

It has been suggested that Bjelke-Petersen's 'lack of formal education and curious trusting simplicity has rendered him vulnerable to the most appalling quacks and frauds'.[51] Supporting examples include his advocacy of Milan Brych (a cancer-cure charlatan), and Steven Horvath (who convinced the premier he'd invented a water-powered car). National Party management committee member and businessman Sir Frank Moore recalls that opportunists 'hung around the edges' of Bjelke-Petersen 'like bloody flies around a dead beast'.[52] Sir Leo Hielscher defended the Queensland Treasury from a number of grafters, and noted, 'We didn't need economics degrees ... we needed psychology degrees.'[53] His diversionary tactics when the plane-loving premier 'got a bee in his bonnet about something' included shiny brochures and the phrase 'I just want to show you this new jet, premier'.[54]

Bjelke-Petersen was also unduly influenced by Christian fundamentalists such as Rhonda Joyner (a National Party member and friend of Flo's), who petitioned him to ban the teaching programs 'Social Education Materials Project' (SEMP), which considered the forces shaping society, and 'Man: A Course of Study' (MACOS), which contained footage of gulls mating.[55] Bjelke-Petersen obliged, noting, 'the notion that children should be allowed to do their own thing and be turned out as little liberal arts graduates must go'.[56] Other unelected individuals with significant government sway included Sparkes, Callaghan, and Bjelke-Petersen's pilot Beryl Young (with whom he formed a close friendship).[57]

Bjelke-Petersen relinquished the Police portfolio to Max Hodges in 1969 when the latter suggested a police scandal could threaten Bjelke-Petersen's premiership if he were still Police minister.[58] Hodges coaxed Bischof into retirement and replaced him with the respected Ray Whitrod, who held a degree in economics from the Australian National University and a diploma in criminology from the University of Cambridge, had helped establish the Australian Security Intelligence Organisation (ASIO), and had been the first commissioner of the Commonwealth Police Force (later the Australian Federal Police).[59] Whitrod was shocked by the scale of corruption within the Queensland Police Force, and by the unwillingness of government, police, religious organisations, and those in professions such as law and academia to address it.[60] He alienated 'three power bases on the sociopolitical scene: the Irish, the anti-Irish and the squattocracy', by refusing to side with any of them.[61] Fatally for his Queensland career, he also alienated Bjelke-Petersen – by insisting that the Westminster separation of powers principle be upheld:

> He treated me as though I were another of his clerks, there
> to carry out his instructions while not impeding his plans. I
> kept trying to get through to him that I had a responsibility to
> maintain the law ... I would implement any legal instructions
> given to me by him or by my minister, but how I did this was
> my decision. Joh sensed, I think, that I would do no more,
> and perhaps that wasn't sufficient. Certainly his subsequent
> relationship with Terry Lewis was quite different.[62]

The state's first director of public prosecutions, Des Sturgess, believes Whitrod's focus on corruption, ceremony, and clearance statistics neglected procedural problems such as verballing witnesses and fabricating evidence – practices that indoctrinated police in a culture of deceit, and compromised those seeking to expose other corrupt activities.[63] He also believes that Whitrod paid insufficient attention to police incompetence of the kind that allowed clear warnings prior to the 1973 bombing of the Whiskey Au-Go-Go nightclub (which resulted in fifteen deaths) to pass unheeded.[64]

Whitrod's initiatives prompted reprisals in the form of anonymous telephone calls, unscheduled home visits by taxi drivers and medical personnel under the impression they had been sent for, and a truckload of gravel being dumped in his driveway, testing him to the point where 'I had taken to locking my bedroom door at night and keeping a firearm with me'.[65]

Des Power was familiar with such reprisals, having broken several current affairs stories critical of the government or police, including one on a paedophilia ring involving the legal fraternity, a story alleging Senior Constable David Moore (who was also a children's television star in a police public relations capacity) was involved in a child pornography ring linked to radio star Bill

Hurrey (both Hurrey and Moore were separately convicted of sex offences relating to young boys), and a story exposing the cover-up of a drink-driving incident involving police and the death of a young woman.[66] Retaliatory actions involved interference with the television station's automobiles and police speed traps set between that station and Power's home, after which an anonymous caller asked, 'Did we get you?' Reprisals from government or police supporters included threats of cancellation, defamation, jail, and death. Power recalls Whitrod offering him some unsettling advice: 'Don't worry about the threats. It's the ones you *don't* get that you've got to worry about.'[67]

The climate of fear extended well beyond police activities. In his capacity as director of QCOSS from 1973 to 1976, Tony Kelly held regular meetings with government ministers: 'You've got no idea how emotionally violent it was to go and visit: if you didn't come out with the right line, the abuse was incredible ... we were dealing with ministers who were covering child abuse and ignoring psychiatric issues – who instead accused *us* of being perverted and mischievous.'[68]

When Kelly went public with concerns about an unprecedented number of suicides at the psychiatric facility known as Wolston Park (later revealed as the site of some of the worst child abuse cases in the state's history), he got 'one of the most awful phone calls I've received across my entire career' from someone in a position of considerable power, in which he was warned to drop the matter or 'never work again in Queensland'.[69]

Public retaliation on the part of the state government became increasingly normalised. Bjelke-Petersen threatened teachers of SEMP and MACOS with dismissal and prevented teachers who had unsuccessfully contested an election for Labor from returning to work 'for opposing the coalition'.[70] Conservationist John Sinclair was bankrupted in court actions after his central role in preventing mining on Fraser Island.[71] The Labor Party was refused facilities in government buildings and space in government aeroplanes used by the Coalition for vote-enhancing visits to electorates or disaster areas; it was also denied essential information about the contents of bills.[72] Entire electorates could be subject to intimidation, as when Bjelke-Petersen warned that 'Mackay is lucky to get what it does after all the attacks on me … if Mackay reciprocates and gives the government a go, it will get what it is entitled to'.[73]

Some communities endured government intimidation in the form of controls on the right to protest. The South African Springbok rugby tour of 1971 provoked anti-apartheid protests around Australia, and managers of the Brisbane match venue, the Royal National Association (RNA) showgrounds, feared similar actions (and union reprisals).[74] Bjelke-Petersen prompted outrage in sections of the community by declaring a State of Emergency based on the unlikely premise that Brisbane protesters would use homemade bombs and glass-filled tennis balls at the match.[75] When 2000 protesters (including future Queensland premiers Wayne Goss and Peter Beattie) marched on the Tower Mill Motel, where the Springboks were staying, a rock was allegedly thrown through a window, prompting a police charge with 'fists, batons and boots'.[76] Whitrod ordered his officers to desist, but few did. Unbeknown to him, Bjelke-Petersen had offered police immunity and financial incentives for assistance with the protests, saying, 'You stay with me and I'll stay with you.'[77] The National Party won two by-elections that day, which was attributed to Bjelke-Petersen's hardline display. The Police Union launched a motion of no confidence in Whitrod.[78]

The politicisation of the police force continued apace after the Springbok tour. During a 1976 protest against small living allowances for students (held without a permit), an officer was filmed striking a female student on the head with his baton; Bjelke-Petersen said there would be no repercussions. When UQ vice-chancellor Sir Zelman Cowen (later Australia's governor-general) objected, Whitrod announced an inquiry with the support of Minister for Police Hodges. Bjelke-Petersen relieved Hodges of the Police portfolio and terminated the investigation.

47

The battle for control of enforcement was further exacerbated when Bjelke-Petersen sought to prevent an inquiry into the use of excessive force during a police raid, also in 1976, on a hippie commune at Cedar Bay.[79] For Whitrod, the situation became untenable when the premier transferred Rat Pack member Terry Lewis back to Brisbane (from the outpost where Whitrod had sent him to restrict his capacity for corruption) and promoted him – over 106 police of equal rank and sixteen senior officers – to the role of assistant commissioner.[80] Kelly recalls unexpectedly encountering Whitrod (whom he knew from his QCOSS role) at a urinal as these dramas unfolded, and the police commissioner's frustration with Bjelke-Petersen's latest power play: 'We were both pissing in the toilet at the time and he basically said, "I'm fucked. They've got me. Joh's got me."'[81]

Whitrod disobeyed Bjelke-Petersen and ordered an investigation into Cedar Bay. At its conclusion, he had summonses issued against four officers on charges including arson, and then he tendered his resignation.[82] His departure prompted a front-page story in *The Australian* headed 'The Last of the Honest Cops'.[83] When asked at a press conference if Queensland was becoming a police state, he said, 'There are signs of that development.'[84] Whitrod accepted a position in Canberra and organised for his files and possessions to be relocated, but the delivery van and its contents were later found burnt and abandoned. As any investigation would involve newly appointed police commissioner Terry Lewis, Whitrod didn't bother.[85] The Criminal Intelligence Unit he had established to identify corrupt police was soon under the control of an officer widely suspected of corruption, Rat Pack member Tony Murphy.

The following year, Bjelke-Petersen refused to make public or table in parliament a report on corruption in the Queensland Police Force prepared by Scotland Yard detectives.[86] Des Sturgess recalls that the government had such a reputation for ignoring damning reports by this stage that, at the conclusion of the 1976–7 Lucas Inquiry into police enforcement of criminal law (which Sturgess worked on, and which found that a large amount of police evidence was fabricated), Justice George Lucas held the completed report aloft and joked, 'Let's take this across to the shredder.'[87] The state government set up a private committee (overseen by Terry Lewis) to examine the Lucas recommendations – none of which were implemented or made public.[88]

Sturgess endured further frustrations when Minister for Police Russ Hinze acceded to a Police Union request (against the Lucas Inquiry's recommendations) to establish a Police Complaints Tribunal to vet allegations against officers. It was headed by Eric Pratt, a barrister, former policeman, and long-term friend of Terry Lewis (who advocated for his appointment as a judge). It was a notoriously ineffective tribunal, regularly discounting evidence that could lead to charges or censure against police.[89]

During the halcyon days of near continual vindication of police later found to be corrupt, dangerous criminals operated with so little interference as to suggest cooperation at an institutional level. There was a proliferation of illegal gambling machines in the state, provided by a company with links to the American mafia. Significant drug-smuggling operations were established in Far North Queensland, and the head of the 'Mr Asia' heroin syndicate, Terry Clark, gained access to police recordings proving drug couriers Douglas and Isabel Wilson had informed on him. (They were murdered the following year.)[90]

The premier and Rat Pack members thwarted several attempts to establish the National Crime Authority in Queensland. Bjelke-Petersen's friend Supreme Court Justice Edward Williams (later appointed commissioner-general of Expo) recommended disbanding the Federal Narcotics Bureau in 1979 as part of his findings for the Australian Royal Commission of Inquiry into Drugs – just as the bureau was poised to begin a major investigation into corruption allegations encompassing Terry Lewis, the Queensland Police Force, and parliament.[91] At Bjelke-Petersen's invitation, he then headed the Williams Royal Commission Special Investigation into Allegations against Senior Police Officers and Parliamentarians, which first sat in 1980. Counsel Assisting the Commissioner Cedric Hampson reportedly spent more time character-assassinating whistleblowers than pursuing cross-examination opportunities against the accused, and ignored relevant written and recorded evidence.[92] Steve Bishop analysed both inquiries and concluded that the decision to clear Lewis and other police of corruption was 'a travesty of evidence, logic and justice' so 'demonstrably a fix' as to be 'aiding and abetting organised crime'.[93]

Bjelke-Petersen's resistance to negative findings and inconvenient recommendations extended into the parliamentary arena, with his dismissal of a 1978 auditor-general report that revealed twenty-three current and former MLAs had misused public funds.[94] Sir Llew Edwards (Liberal MLA from 1972 to 1983 and chairman of Expo) is candid in his recollections of this time: 'I think that probably all of us were guilty of not making certain that expenses were watched so carefully – but because you were a minister in the Bjelke-Petersen early days … you suddenly became almost God – I hate to say that – and therefore you just put the claim in – nobody would check it, they'd automatically be paid.'[95]

Attempts by Labor, Liberal, and National parliamentarians to convince Bjelke-Petersen of the need for a Public Accounts Committee to scrutinise government activities went unheeded – even though Queensland was the only Western parliamentary democracy without one (which was especially problematic in the absence of an upper house).[96] The premier also overrode recommendations from statutory bodies, such as when he ignored warnings of both the Port of Brisbane Authority and an independent assessor that giving control of a new terminal to the company operating the existing one (a suspected political donor) would create a monopoly.[97]

Other procedural subversions included a refusal to answer questions without notice in parliament, placing difficult questions on notice ad infinitum, ordering a new mace engraved 'Government of Queensland' rather than the democratically apt 'Parliament of Queensland', and allowing ministers to remain in position after making serious mistakes.[98] The premier's limited grasp of parliamentary procedure produced some awkward scenes, such as when he mistakenly voted with the wrong side in divisions. 'He was a very interesting man,' says Edwards. 'He appeared never to have read a Cabinet paper, for example'.[99]

Sir Leo Hielscher recalls a plethora of parliamentary irregularities at this time – including the extent to which decisions were made outside of it: 'You'd come to him [Bjelke-Petersen] with an issue – or if it's a problem, you knew what the answer was before you gave him the problem – then steer him around ... he decides the answer – which is the one you want – then it's law ... whereas these days they'd have to go to committee. We'd make sure that the principal decisions were taken like that in the kitchen cabinet – had all the approvals in place before long. It might have been following the facts, but we'd go away and get it going and write a Cabinet submission and Cabinet would okay it. We always made sure we had our backs covered. That's not the way it works now.'[100]

Rosemary Kyburz was part of a 'small l' Liberal or 'ginger group' frustrated with parliamentary irregularities and backbenchers' inability to be heard: 'In the privacy of the party room we were supposed to do our whinging [the consequences for crossing the floor in protest were severe] ... and it would be just overruled because people didn't want to hear it ... Joh ruled the land – put it that way – in the Liberal Party room ... it was like being a foot person to Cinderella.'[101]

Bjelke-Petersen may have kept his front bench relatively free from talent to minimise the risk of a leadership challenge – an approach most evident in the notoriously slow political ascension of the promising young Mike Ahern, elected in 1968. Bjelke-Petersen disliked Ahern's father (a former Country Party president), and resented the younger Ahern's ambition, education (he was one of only a few Queensland politicians with a university degree), and closeness to former premier Nicklin. In an era of bitter religious divisions, Bjelke-Petersen and much of his Cabinet were also averse to Ahern's

Roman Catholicism – though it was the premier who was more likely to evoke biblical cliché. 'He'd only ever read one book,' says Ahern, in reference to Bjelke-Petersen's fundamentalist tendencies, 'and he only read half of it. He didn't read the *new* part.'[102]

The speed with which Bjelke-Petersen's gentlemanly demeanour contorted to ferocity when challenged (a trait Sparkes dubbed 'schizophrenic') may have had a bearing on lopsided Cabinet deliberations observed by Hielscher, who recalls seeing Bjelke-Petersen 'win a cabinet decision one to seventeen – he's the one'.[103] Ahern's assessment of Bjelke-Petersen's parliamentary conduct is withering: 'He viewed everything as a fencing contractor would do. Get the boys in the morning and tell them what they're going to do – then go and do it … Those were the rules as far as he was concerned. Didn't understand parliament, didn't want to understand it. He knew how to get a job done. He knew Les Thiess could do it – he gave it to him.'[104]

Friends with Benefits

Sir Leslie Thiess (whose company, Thiess Watkins, was awarded the construction manager tender for Expo in controversial circumstances) was one of a cavalcade of businessmen and entrepreneurs who profited from close relations with Bjelke-Petersen. Thiess's government-sanctioned good fortune included selection as operator of the Townsville casino (on a lower tax rate than its Broadbeach competitor), interference on his behalf to void a cultural centre tender the Gold Coast Council had awarded to a competitor (it was given to Thiess instead), and local government minister Russ Hinze's decision – over the objections of locals – to zone an area for high-rise development to facilitate a Thiess construction (on land later revealed to be held by Hinze's future wife and his accountant), which Labor's Ken Hooper labelled 'thinly disguised corruption'.[105]

Hinze was himself something of a controversy magnet; his improprieties included maintaining commercial interests in horse racing while serving as the minister for that industry, relocating a road to the benefit of one of his companies, interfering with a rival group's Totalisator Administration Board (TAB) application to his advantage, and being wrongfully involved in milk quota distribution.[106] Hinze's association with Theiss yielded the thrifty politician benefits such as a $500,000 'loan' that was never called in. Other 'Theiss-friendly' parliamentarians availed themselves of perks such as 'good deals' on new cars, while Bjelke-Petersen's 'gifts' from this seemingly benevolent connection included a built-in swimming pool.[107]

Such largesse may have been rationalised by recipients as a form of 'mateship', but Ahern has little time for such leaps in ethical logic: 'That's the sort of stuff that eventually got him [Bjelke-Petersen] into really big trouble. You can't do it today – you'd go to jail. But in those days he had a friendship with Thiess; he had a property next to him. There's a history there of quite corrupt endeavour: he had two bulldozers on site there and Channel Nine ran a story on who maintained these – Joh's bulldozers – and they discovered that Thiess maintained them. *What a scandal*. What they didn't ask was who gave Joh the bulldozers. And it wasn't Thiess, of course, it was the company – which was the shareholders. That's what was done in those days.'[108]

Many of the premier's friends and associates were well compensated for their allegiance. Allen Callaghan was appointed chairman of the Queensland Film Corporation; under secretary of the Department of the Arts, National Parks and Sport; and deputy chairman of the Queensland Day Committee (of which his wife was appointed executive officer). Retired or defeated government ministers could also expect lucrative positions on boards and in the public service.[109] The politicisation of the public service became entrenched at this time; nominees for senior positions were scrutinised for loyalty to the Coalition and its development agenda, and expected to act as party advisers.[110]

Bjelke-Petersen's support for business and development can arguably be viewed through the lens of his enthusiasm for 'progress', which he famously linked with the sight of cranes on the skyline. His government's pursuit of overseas investment – and its willingness to build infrastructure at public expense for industries such as mining (which had overtaken the pastoral industry in export earning, and was eighty-five per cent foreign owned) – can be viewed through a lens of similar focal length.[111] Levels of foreign investment were an Australia-wide concern at this time, with Japanese land acquisitions infuriating vocal members of the Returned Services League (RSL). Tensions reached a flash point in Queensland in 1974 when the government prioritised business and development over protesters – and its own interdepartmental committee of inquiry – to pass special legislation allowing Japanese developer Yohachiro Iwasaki to purchase and lease a large, environmentally sensitive area of Crown land off coastal Central Queensland at Yeppoon, and then develop a $20 million resort. Construction was delayed when a bomb blast caused $1 million of damage to the site, attracting national criticism of the decision to grant Iwasaki freehold land, and of the racist response this provoked.[112]

Political scientist Rae Wear observes a pronounced disconnect between the government's largesse with entrepreneurs and trans-national corporations and its expenditure on welfare (less than any other state), and suggests that Bjelke-Petersen subscribed to an American style of fundamentalist Christian moralism in which economic success was considered a reward for virtue and industry, and the poor were simply victims of their own indolence.[113]

The relationship between the National Party and vested business interests came to national attention in 1982 when ABC's *Four Corners* program investigated the Bjelke-Petersen Foundation (established in 1979), revealing that donors viewed it as the cost of doing business in Queensland.[114] Businessmen were pressured to donate upwards of $10,000 to the foundation; rewards included a private dinner with Bjelke-Petersen. There was a suspicious link between large donors and their success with government contracts, rezoning applications, and knighthoods.[115] The names of those who declined to donate were kept on file.[116]

Knighthoods were dispensed to Coalition allies with dizzying regularity – a practice that reached its bizarre crescendo when Bjelke-Petersen nominated himself for one. 'We'd all worked out that if you'd been there long enough it was your turn for a knighthood,' recalls Edwards.[117] Businessman Justin Hickey trod an alternative path to this accolade: he was knighted a year after offering $100,000 towards a senior citizen centre near the premier's home at Kingaroy.[118] Other avenues to the honorific were decidedly unvaliant. 'The word was that if you wanted a knighthood you paid $50,000 for it to Joh,' remembers Ahern.[119] When asked if Terry Lewis paid for his knighthood, Ahern says, 'He did other things which were worse.'[120]

Pig City

In a 1977 manoeuvre designed to thwart protests that were expected to disrupt uranium shipments pertinent to Coalition business interests, Bjelke-Petersen made police directly responsible for implementing government policy by ordering the police commissioner to refuse protest march permits, and then transferring the right to appeal away from the courts to that same police commissioner. 'The day of the political street march is over,' crowed Bjelke-Petersen; 'don't bother applying for a march permit. You won't get one.'[121]

While not without precedent (Queensland refused permits for marches against conscription and Vietnam in the 1960s), such hardline actions politicised large segments of Brisbane, resulting in thousands of arrests, a Right to March campaign, and protest songs such as 'Pig City'.[122] Bjelke-Petersen also provoked censure from religious bodies: Anglicans, Catholics, Lutherans, and the Council of Churches issued a joint political statement against the bans, and an Anglican assistant bishop cancelled the Palm Sunday procession in solidarity.[123] The premier dismissed them as having been 'manipulated into supporting communists' (for whom he had an abiding and vote-yielding hatred).[124]

Rallying points for youthful protesters and those of an alternative mindset included UQ and independent radio station 4ZZZ. Station volunteer Adam Nash (also co-writer and vocalist of the protest song 'Cyclone Hits Expo') recalls the spirit of the time: 'If you were in any way alternative – or even just to be young – I think was accompanied by a great kind of outraged sense of injustice and unfairness ... you have to remember that the mainstream at the time was completely psychotic. The alternative was to try and behave like a sane person.'[125]

Sallyanne Atkinson (Liberal lord mayor of Brisbane during Expo) cautions that the protest movement does not uniformly reflect the experiences of mainstream Brisbane: 'Somebody said to me recently, "Oh, it must have been terrible growing up here – being young under Bjelke-Petersen." I said no – we did everything we wanted to do – didn't particularly want to march in the streets – they were isolated incidents; it wasn't as though there was stuff happening all the time – that every morning you got up and said "God, I've just got to get out there and protest today."'[126]

Some of the consequences for those who did protest, or who found themselves in opposition to the government, included police surveillance and harassment, raids by the notorious Task Force, and Special Branch files compiled on citizens that could be used to limit their employment opportunities.[127] Adam Nash says harassment was omnipresent: 'We were always hassled by the cops. Always. It didn't matter what you were doing. It used to remind us of idiot bullies at school – they could really fuck you up if they wanted to.'[128]

Of particular annoyance to Nash was the likelihood that their harassers were corrupt: 'They used to make jokes about it to us; we were in the Valley – usual thing – cops came up and were hassling us for no reason ... and I remember them joking and saying, "You haven't seen any illegal casinos around here, have you, fellas? You'd let us know if you did, wouldn't ya?" Everybody knew about it [illegal casinos and police corruption]. Everybody. Even my parents knew about it. It was so absurd the only sane response was humour.'[129]

'The Joke' was a term used by corrupt police in reference to their complicity in illegal activities. So many were familiar with this joke by the late 1970s and early 1980s that it was difficult to believe the state government didn't get it. When Des Power informed Russ Hinze that he and reporter Kerry Lonergan had won $1400 at one of the illegal casinos the government claimed did not exist, Hinze's response was, 'You're dreaming.'

Power says this was typical: 'They bluffed their way through this sort of stuff; they pooh-poohed it. They tried to make out that journalism was inexact at best. They were basically accusing us of telling lies. What do you do, though? You can't go and complain to the police, because they're in the swim. You can't go and complain to the politicians, because they're also in the swim. The simple backbencher is going to go and talk to the Police minister and he's going to tell them they've got it all wrong, buster, back off, go away. That's how corruption survives. The worst form of corruption is silence: it's the public servant who's too frightened to speak – who retires harbouring all those secrets, knowing what went wrong but never having the courage to tell. There weren't too many whistleblowers around then.'[130]

In his 1979 book, *The Deep North*, author Deane Wells (then a lecturer in philosophy at UQ, later the Labor MLA better known as Dean Wells) identified several totalitarian traits in Bjelke-Petersen: an inability to conceive of criticism as a legitimate public function, the characterisation of people with opposing views as criminal or deviant, the use of power to harm such people, treatment of public institutions as if they were his property, and seeing himself as being in personal command of the police force.[131] Some of these traits were apparent in the premier's interactions with the first federal Labor government since 1949, his continual clashes with which ensured him – and Queensland – national notoriety.

Despite the economic assistance that the Whitlam government offered Queensland from 1972 to 1975, its centralist nature – coupled with Bjelke-Petersen's inability or unwillingness to differentiate between Labor and communism – ensured clashes over issues such as commodity prices, mining royalties, offshore resources, conservation, national borders, and control over Aboriginal reserves.[132]

From the early 1900s, Queensland Labor and Coalition governments had engaged in a litany of discriminatory activities against Australia's original inhabitants, including enforced Aboriginal residence in reserves, unequal pay and stolen wages perpetually held in 'trust', disproportionate arrest rates, minimal educational opportunities, forced assimilation, and land rights concerns.[133] Prior to the 1950s, human rights issues relating to Aboriginal and Torres Strait Islander people (who were effectively wards of the state) received scant political attention in Queensland.[134] This changed – for the worse – when it transpired that some Aboriginal reserves and settlements were on promising mining sites. In 1957, the state government made an agreement with Comalco that would disrupt traditional ways of life in Weipa, and in 1975 mining was permitted in the Aurukun reserve. Bjelke-Petersen resisted the efforts of the Gorton, McMahon, Whitlam, and Fraser federal governments to address Aboriginal human and land rights issues. His actions again aroused the concern of religious organisations (some of which had pre-existing arrangements with the reserves). A legal adviser to the Queensland Catholic Bishops found that Queensland's indigenous peoples had fewer legal protections than flora and fauna.[135]

Bjelke-Petersen accused Aboriginal land rights activists of being communist puppets, academic sympathisers of being blind to a plot to annex parts of the north for 'guerrilla training centres for coloureds', and religious organisations of associating 'with communists who denounce God and religion'.[136]

By 1975, the Whitlam government had assumed control of Aboriginal affairs in every state except Queensland.[137] Bjelke-Petersen's antipathy towards Whitlam was so pronounced that his 1974 state election campaign was run against what he positioned as the 'alien and stagnating, centralist, socialist, communist-inspired' Canberra, and he appeared to take pride in the appearance of outwitting his ostensibly more powerful foe (however ethically elastic the victory).[138]

The premier's machinations against Whitlam included the infamous 'Night of the Long Prawns', in which Democratic Labor Party senator Vince Gair (who, a press leak revealed, had been appointed ambassador to Ireland by the Whitlam government in the expectation that the ALP could win his vacated Senate seat) was entertained by National Party allies and delayed from resigning while Bjelke-Petersen issued writs for the election – making it a casual vacancy that could be filled by the Queensland Government.

Bjelke-Petersen's later refusal to follow democratic convention and accept a nomination from the same party of a deceased Labor senator (instead appointing Whitlam-hating maverick Albert Field) created a situation in which federal Opposition leader Malcolm Fraser could block supply – resulting in the Whitlam government's dismissal by Sir John Kerr, and gifting Fraser the benefits of campaigning from office. Bjelke-Petersen was an unconventional presence in the federal campaign, travelling the country to insist that Whitlam threatened the Australian way of life, financing newspaper and television advertisements depicting 'a country in chaos', engaging a detective in Switzerland to search for damaging information about the so-called 'loans affair', and promising – under the protection of parliamentary privilege – to make dramatic revelations about kickbacks received by Whitlam government ministers (no such evidence was ever produced).[139] When Whitlam lost the election (which he did emphatically in Queensland, where only former police officer Bill Hayden kept his seat), Bjelke-Petersen announced, 'what Queensland started Australia finished'.[140]

Queensland political experts Margaret Bridson Cribb and Dennis Murphy believed the 'Queensland is different' view came to national prominence through Bjelke-Petersen's activities during the Whitlam period.[141] Supporting evidence was abundant: Bjelke-Petersen endorsed apartheid in South Africa, congratulated President Suharto on Indonesia's invasion of East Timor, refused to conform to daylight saving time, and threatened that Queensland would secede from Australia and develop its own currency.[142] The level of national condescension directed at Queensland's capital at this time is evident in the Barry Humphries quip 'Australia is the Brisbane of the world', and in the work of journalists such as Mungo MacCallum:

> There is a certain symbolic irony in the fact that, with the advent of daylight saving in the most civilised parts of the country, it takes just a quarter of an hour on the clock to get from Sydney to Brisbane, but two and a quarter hours to get back ... Queensland must be the only place in the Western world where candidates still think it's good campaigning to nail pictures of themselves to trees, with slogans like 'Don't fuss, vote Russ', on the bottom of them.[143]

To the extent that Brisbane was known internationally, it seemed to be for similarly uninspiring traits, as with the 1982 *Doctor Who* episode in which the Doctor's Australian companion, Tegan, joins with another character (Nyssa) to find a 'zero room':

> **Tegan:** I know the Tardis is huge, but it can't be taking them this long, surely. What's a zero room anyway? The Doctor said something about null interfaces.
> **Nyssa:** I suppose some sort of neutral environment. An isolated space cut off from the rest of the universe.
> **Tegan:** He should have told me that's what he wanted. I could have shown him Brisbane.[144]

Bjelke-Petersen appeared comfortable with his growing notoriety, even nominating a favourite among the rising tide of 'Joh jokes':

> When Gough died and went to Heaven, St Peter told him to sit on his right side. When Big Mal died and went to Heaven,

St Peter told him to sit on his left side. When Joh died and went to Heaven, he said to St Peter: Get out of my chair.[145]

The 'Queensland is different' mindset often conflates Bjelke-Petersen with the state – something he himself was inclined to do. It neglects to account for the zonal manipulation that allowed his party to govern with as little as nineteen per cent of the vote, or for dissension from organisations, the public, and within Coalition ranks. It also positions these differences within a conservative reactionary sphere – ignoring the historic radical aspect to Queensland's 'difference' that made it the first state to introduce compulsory voting and to abolish hanging, the only Australian state to elect a member of the Communist Party or to oppose conscription during World War I, and the site of the first elected Labor government in the world.[146]

Many critics also failed to make a distinction between Brisbanites and other Queenslanders. The director of the protest film *Expo Schmexpo*, Debra Beattie, says Brisbane artists experienced considerable prejudice from their contemporaries in the southern states: 'They thought, "Oh, you've come from Queensland – you must have voted for Joh." There was a real disconnect between the world that I lived in and the way that we were perceived in Sydney and Melbourne.'[147]

Tony Kelly says the levels of interstate ridicule necessitated organisational coaching on how to 'be' at national meetings: 'I was told, you've got to play the Queensland game ... there's two options: "Duh, I'm from Queensland and I dunno nothing about nothing", or you can say, "Oh, I'm from Queensland, but I'm not really, you know, I'm a different type".' He found the situation untenable: 'The behaviour of the southern states was appalling. Appalling. Very similar to the way we behaved to the Vietnam vets when they came back. We were so busy campaigning, we forgot about the people in front of us. And the way the rest of Australia treated Queensland at that time of its democratic fragility was appalling. The ignorance of the southern states about the realities in Queensland was terrible. Terrible.'[148]

In *State of Mind*, Peter Charlton argues that Bjelke-Petersen exploited the 'Queensland is different' concept for electoral gain, but that he was only a 'typical Queenslander' in so far as he reflected – and appealed to – the suspicions, prejudices, inferiority complexes, and resentments of his rural voting base.[149] His inflammatory actions rarely inconvenienced regional voters, as they were confined to an area unlikely to yield his party many seats: Brisbane. Some of those who conflated Bjelke-Petersen with Queensland – and Queensland with Brisbane – saw a city in which staunch conservatism was incxplicably wedded to police corruption, where cronyism and development went unchecked while critics were reined in, where essential services were underfunded and government spending was unexamined, where legal entertainment venues were raided more than casinos or brothels, and where stubbornness and prejudice trumped intellect. Bjelke-Petersen was a divisive premier, but he succeeded in uniting large parts of Australia – in horror – at the prospect of Brisbane, Queensland, as host city for World Expo 88.

3

The Getting of Expo

It was so much a different time. I mean … when Joh decided
that we were going to have Expo there was no public consultation
or anything about it. He just went off one day and we got Expo.
I don't even know where he got it from.

Sallyanne Atkinson[1]

BRISBANE'S SUCCESSFUL WORLD EXPOSITION BID was many
years and myriad twists in the making. Over the course of this
circuitous journey, the Bjelke-Petersen government exhibited a
number of the traits for which it had become infamous, including
stubbornness, parochialism, disdain for due process, and a proclivity
for Machiavellian intrigue. These characteristics combined to
improbable effect in pursuit of Expo 88, helping the Queensland
Government thwart a prime minister, vex rival states, and confound
its own constituents.

Early Architects

It began in a civilised fashion. Early Expo instigator UQ architect
James Maccormick (later joint chief architect of Expo with
architectural firm Bligh Maccormick 88) had a substantial world

exposition background: while serving as principal architect at the Commonwealth Department of Works, he designed the Australian pavilions for Expo 67 (Montreal), Expo 70 (Osaka), and Expo 74 (Spokane). Upon learning that the impetus for the Spokane event was to revitalise the derelict riverside area, it occurred to him that 'nobody had discovered the Brisbane River except for when it flooded', and that the old Evans Deakin shipyards at Kangaroo Point would make an ideal site for a world exposition of the urban renewal variety.[2]

In 1976, Maccormick broached the idea with his colleague Bill Worth, who was the Australian representative to the BIE and commissioner-general of the Australian Exhibits Organisation (AEO). Worth advised him that a 1987/88 Australian world exposition had been slated with the BIE at the Whitlam government's request, but that the succeeding Fraser government was ambivalent about the prospect (possibly because such a commitment might be electorally unpalatable when coupled with building an expensive new Parliament House); should it proceed, the preferred host city was reportedly Sydney – though Worth conceded that the NSW capital 'has not shown a great deal of interest because they seem mesmerised with trying to get the 1988 Olympic Games'.[3]

Worth reminded Maccormick that there were two types of world exposition: the large and costly 'universal' kind with sweeping themes, in which pavilions were designed and built by international participants, and a smaller, 'specialised' model with a more narrow theme, in which the host built and rented pavilion space to exhibitors. As it was assumed that only Sydney or Melbourne had the capacity for a universal exposition, Worth suggested a specialised event for Brisbane.[4]

Maccormick gained the support of Royal Australian Institute of Architects president Graham Bligh (later joint chief architect of Expo with him), who in turn enlisted Australian Chamber of Commerce president Tom Burrell to sway the Brisbane Chamber of Commerce to support the cause.[5] Multitudinous meetings with government and industry figures ensued.

Brisbane's special-events CV gained heft in 1976 when the city 'won' the right to host the 1982 Commonwealth Games (a BCC initiative supported by the state government) after all other competitors withdrew their bids.[6] In a 1977 newspaper article, industry advocates mobilised by Maccormick proposed a Brisbane world exposition funded by private enterprise.[7] An attendance estimate prepared by Wilbur Smith and Associates anticipated that between 1,982,000 and 2,478,000 visitors would generate between 10,671,000 and 13,341,000 exposition visits, and that fifty-five per cent of total visits (and nearly eighty-eight per cent of total visitor days) would stem from the local population.[8]

In May 1978, the Brisbane Chamber of Commerce announced it had become the prime mover in the exposition bid, with support from the deputy premier and treasurer of Queensland, Sir Bill Knox (Chalk's successor).[9] This support proved as rickety as the South Brisbane wharves; instead of pressing Queensland's case at a premiers' conference in which potential bicentennial activities and host cities were discussed, Knox merely speculated (arguably correctly) that Australia's centenary of Federation might make a better celebration date.[10] In any case, Brisbane's chances were slim; Fraser had upheld many of Whitlam's policies relating to Queensland on issues such as land rights and environmental protections, and intergovernmental relations were ornery as a result.

After the premiers' conference, the Australian Bicentennial Authority (ABA) was formed to consider a range of celebratory options, including an Olympic event for Melbourne or Sydney. The ABA was answerable to the AEO, a division of the Department of Administrative Services (DAS). The combined power of these initialisms resulted in feasibility studies into a universal exposition at Sydney's Darling Harbour or Melbourne's Fishermans Bend.[11] The suggestion that Brisbane could be added to the candidate mix was dispatched with southern certitude. 'It's too big for Brisbane,' claimed ABA and James Hardie Industries chairman John Reid, 'and it's got to be held where our history started, in Sydney.'[12] BIE president Patrick Reid nevertheless confided to Maccormick that Brisbane might be 'the joker in the pack'.[13]

A Changing of the Political Guard

Sir Bill Knox was deposed in December 1978; his detractors felt he had offered insufficient resistance to Bjelke-Petersen, and that the Liberals had lost power and credibility as a result. His successor, Sir Llew Edwards, had some form resisting the premier, having opposed Albert Field, Milan Brych, and the street march ban. Edwards attributes his ascension to his performance as minister for Health, where (with support from Chalk) he persuaded Bjelke-Petersen to accept the Whitlam government's Medibank funding, which Edwards channelled into a construction program – a move that saw him dubbed 'Llew the builder'.[14] He credits his good working relationship with the premier with creating a space in which ministers such as himself, Ron Camm, Fred Campbell, and Neville Hewitt could become 'the whole strength of the government; let Joh play it all out and run around and become a pilot and this and that, and we'll do the work'.[15]

Bjelke-Petersen's ongoing ambivalence towards the minutiae of governance was witnessed by Terry White, a Liberal elected to parliament in 1979: 'The premier would come in and if he had particular issues ... he did have them dealt with. And then he'd order a cup of tea and a biscuit and read *The Courier-Mail* whilst Llew Edwards [ran] the government.'[16]

Against this background, the lacklustre Labor Opposition was considering its position. A rebel group that included Peter Beattie and UQ academic Dennis Murphy agitated first for reform, and then for the national intervention that took place under Federal Labor leader Bill Hayden in 1980 (after which Beattie became state secretary and Murphy state branch president). The intervention ushered in generational change and diluted the entrenched power of the THG, which was poorly equipped to respond to the social changes of the 1970s and 1980s, and had failed to capitalise on public anger over issues such as civil rights, the environment, and cultural heritage.[17]

Bjelke-Petersen did little to help his reputation – or Coalition relations – when he orchestrated the midnight demolition of the heritage landmark Bellevue Hotel (by the National Party's favoured heritage destruction workhorses, the Deen Brothers) in 1979. Anger within the Liberal Party was such that Edwards allowed a censure motion, which was supported by thirteen Liberal backbenchers and the Opposition. Kyburz gave an extraordinary speech to parliament in which she condemned the 'stealthy, sly, snide manner' in which the 'iniquitous' destruction of the Bellevue occurred, implied the Police Commissioner's complicity, and condemned parliament's inability to extract answers from Bjelke-Petersen as 'he unmitigatedly bends the truth', while noting the 'fear in this city' such activities engendered. She also denounced 'the manner in which the Premier has tried to divide this State', the autocratic methods that belied his statement that 'we are here to govern', and asserted that 'some of the criticisms that have been levelled at this Government now stick – and they stick like dung on rotten walls'. Kyburz predicted her own government would respond to such criticisms with misdirection:

> Probably it will call out its wild dogs in their hunting packs, who will yap around our heels and start barking about what they see us doing or not doing ... I know the way that the Premier's mind works. He will muck-rake, he will do everything he can to discredit not only the Liberal Party but all other people who criticise him ... the word 'democracy' in this State is dying a slow, painful, lingering death from a malignant cancer.[18]

The censure motion was defeated. Coalition relations soured further with proposed revisions to the state's anti-abortion laws in 1980 that Kyburz considers 'the most frightening piece of fascist legislation I have ever seen in my life' (the original bill refused abortion for rape or incest victims, and sought jail terms for anyone advising a woman to have an abortion – including fourteen years' hard labour for doctors who performed one).[19]

Kyburz had other reasons for concern. She had been approached by a delegation of senior police officers who 'told me some scandalous things ... the sort of corruption that came out in the Fitzgerald Inquiry', and warned her of possible reprisals should she continue to speak out:

> I said, 'You know, what are you talking about?' And they said, 'Anything could happen. When there's people who are vocal opponents of this government anything can happen, and has happened.' And I, I was just aghast ... you could have a car accident, or you could be poisoned or something ... you couldn't go to a minister 'cause you didn't know who to trust. You certainly couldn't go to Joh. He'd just laugh at you and say, 'You're making the whole thing up' ... So we didn't know what to do.[20]

Two other events occurred around this time that affected the Coalition – and the eventual shape of Expo 88. Terry White was promoted from the Liberal backbench to the ministry, and Russ Hinze persuaded the premier to give serially overlooked back-bencher Mike Ahern a ministry (by warning him that Ahern might challenge for the leadership if slighted again). Bjelke-Petersen also provoked local and national scorn when he contrived to have Flo enter the Senate, prompting Bill Hayden to remark, 'He gave us the hillbilly approach to politics in Queensland. And now it is the Ma and Pa Kettle Show for Australian politics.'[21]

Queenslander!

The NSW and Victorian studies determined it was not financially viable to host a world exposition in either city, but that a smaller (still 'universal') variant could be managed at Darling Harbour more economically than at Fishermans Bend – although this still entailed capital outlay of a billion dollars.[22] Fraser offered to share costs with NSW premier Neville Wran, but the state Treasury concluded that the resources required would adversely affect areas such as education and health; early in 1981, the Wran and Fraser governments publicly conceded there would not be an Australian world exposition in 1988.[23]

James Maccormick took the news better than most; the door closing on a universal exposition in Sydney might open a specialised window in Brisbane. In a well-tailored pitch to National Party management committee member Sir Frank Moore, Maccormick positioned a potential Brisbane exposition as a political triumph for the Nationals.[24] Moore was a business and development dynamo; he was chairman of the Australian Tourist Industry and the Queensland Tourist and Travel Corporation (QTTC) and a member of the Lands Court and of the Queensland Liquor Licensing Board, and his financial interests included tourism, television, and radio. His exuberant entrepreneurial ethos encapsulates the mentality of the day: 'When you're in this position, you sometimes have to cut corners – if you're going to lead, you've got to make decisions. You can't have committees and meetings – you've got to actually do things and get on and drive the damn thing – and if you come to a problem, you blow it up and move on to the next one.'[25]

A spectacular of the world exposition variety broadly appealed to Moore – especially given the rise of hallmark events, 1980s Australian incarnations of which include Adelaide's Formula One Grand Prix and the America's Cup off the coast of Fremantle. Moore was intrigued by the marketing and tourism potential of such festivities, and was convinced of the need, 'every three or so years, to have a major or world-class thing in Queensland.'[26]

Australia had become a viable international travel destination in the 1960s and 1970s, when improvements to flight capacity and technology enabled reduced fares and travel times just as the country blipped onto the international radar with various sporting and cinematic achievements. Moore believed a marquee event could direct this nascent interest towards Queensland. He had little time for those who conceived of such manoeuvrings as parochial: 'So much of the talk about us being parochial in Queensland emanates of course from Sydney and Melbourne, who would like to think they're not ... if we had sat here without having a go, Queensland would still be an agricultural mining state.'[27]

Many Queenslanders enjoyed a surge of patriotism in 1980 when their rugby team won the first State of Origin match against NSW. In the lead-in to the 1982 Commonwealth Games, BCC's 'Image 82' campaign and 'Shine on Brisbane' civic relations promotions invited locals to celebrate their city and themselves, with the associated jingle urging people to tidy up, cheer up, and 'face each day with a smile', so that 'everyone will enjoy us and love our friendly style'.[28] Brisbane Television Queensland (BTQ) Channel Seven launched a similarly parochial call to arms in the wake of this successful campaign: its station identification, 'risbane', featured the new Queen Street Mall (the lower half of which had been completed for the Commonwealth Games), and Kim Durant singing 'She's the city we love, she's the best in the world and there's no place I'd rather be'.[29] The originator of this campaign, John Garnsey of Garnsey Clemenger advertising, says such adverts were designed to tap in to the 'more positive, more aggressive, even, at times, arrogant' shift in perceptions of Queensland that accompanied Bjelke-Petersen's skirmishes with Whitlam and Fraser.[30] He identified similar adverts in the 'tapping the wells of parochialism' vein, including the Castlemaine Perkins Fourex jingle 'That's what I like about Queensland' and the Bank of Queensland's 'You can count on a Queenslander'.[31] The dominant rural and blue-collar images fostered by these campaigns were unlikely to have been embraced as emblematic of Australia by the more patrician members of the Fraser government.

Despite the terminal state of Australia's world exposition prospects, various entities retained an interest in administering CPR – especially as the country's Olympic Games hosting options had dissipated and bicentennial organisers were without a marquee event. Exposition enthusiast Bill Worth had retired from the AEO and the BIE, and had become a consultant to the ABA; his replacement, Eric Wigley, looked favourably upon a renewed exposition push.[32] BIE president Patrick Reid secured the support of Prime Minister Fraser and Home Affairs and Environment Minister Bob Ellicott to investigate the possibility of a specialised exposition – although it later transpired that there was only one suspect. Despite urgings from ABA General Manager David Armstrong and the Department of Prime Minister and Cabinet that the prospect of a specialised exposition be canvassed among all states, John Reid pragmatically reversed his anti-Queensland position to court the only state expressing a lingering interest in the prospect – he urged the chairman of the Queensland Council of the ABA, the prominent businessman Ian Russell, to support a specialised exposition in Brisbane.[33]

Russell brought powerful connections to the exposition cause: the president of the Queensland National Party Sir Robert Sparkes, the treasurer of the Queensland Liberal Party Sir Robert Mathers, and QTTC co-founder and multi-island resort owner (South Mole, Tangalooma, and Daydream) Jim Kennedy.[34] As treasurer of Queensland, Sir Llew Edwards was wary of reviving the exposition bid, but he was eventually persuaded of its potential benefits. 'I think Queensland was at a time where it needed to change from wheat farmers and coal miners,' he says. 'We've got to look at the development of technology and see if we can make this a better, broader-minded state.'[35] This opinion was not uniform across the rural-focused state government. Russ Hinze (whose business interests were centred on the Gold Coast) reportedly asked, 'Why would we do this for Brisbane when we've got to look after the rest of Queensland?'[36]

Coordinator-General Sir Sydney Schubert was receptive to the bid by virtue of the urban development opportunities it represented.[37] Under Treasurer Sir Leo Hielscher had reservations about the extent to which Treasury was (and would continue to be) bypassed during various feasibility studies, but was optimistic that such an event – in tandem with the Commonwealth Games – could show 'that Queensland was not what it used to be': 'By the early '80s, we were running along nicely – the budgets were balanced, the coal industry was going well, the bauxite industry was coming along ... we were trying to get the tourist industry going, but our record was not known. And we were desperately needing the world to know about us – because to fund some of the infrastructure we needed, we had to approach the world as well as the domestic financial markets ... Expo would tell the world that we were not a bad sort of a place to do business with.'[38]

Edwards wrote to the Fraser government requesting a jointly funded feasibility study along the lines of the Commonwealth's earlier arrangements with NSW and Victoria. Fraser neglected to reply. A reminder letter from Bjelke-Petersen requesting that the Commonwealth also match exposition capital costs in line with its NSW discussions was not responded to in any haste, either.[39] Edwards recalls that 'there was great conflict ... He [Fraser] was very much against Queensland getting it. I think in hindsight he didn't think Joh or Queensland could do it – that they were all "Joh-types" in Queensland.'[40]

News of the Queensland proposal was leaked to the press, angering Fraser and prompting Premier Wran to deride it as a 'watered-down version of Expo' and proclaim, 'we have watered-down expos in Sydney every week. Sydney is the capital of Australia. This is where Australia was born and this is where the greatest celebrations will take place.'[41]

Much of the intrigue around the Queensland proposal excluded the increasingly isolated Liberal backbench. Kyburz gave voice to this frustration in an April 1981 address to parliament:

I rise this evening ... concerning the staging of an Expo in 1988. As every member knows, it is most unlikely that that motion will ever be debated in the House because of the anachronistic way in which the House is run, but I choose to raise the matter now and will do so at every other opportunity. The thing that concerns me about the staging of an Expo in 1988 is that the public will probably be bled, bled and then bled again just as they have been bled for the staging of the Commonwealth Games ... The only people I can see who would gain from the staging of an Expo are big business, the hotel trade and some sections of the restaurant industry. But who will pay for the staging of the Expo? ... Why can it not be that those who gain have some share in the paying, and the larger share at that? ... The money should be spent where it is needed, not on some hot-air balloon to push big business.[42]

But the balloon had been freed from its tethers and begun its expensive ascent. A Queensland-funded feasibility study by consultants Cameron McNamara recommended the eventual South Brisbane site and anticipated capital and operating costs in the vicinity of $266 million.[43] James Maccormick and Bill Worth also surveyed potential locations, including land near the Gold Coast recommended by Russ Hinze (which, it transpired, he owned).[44] Maccormick was partial to the South Brisbane site, as he considered it 'close to the city, on the railway line' and 'a slum waiting for clearance and updating'.[45] The dilapidated and ineffectual old port occupying the space had been superseded by a newer incarnation at the mouth of the river and by advancements in containerised shipping. The site was ripe for razing.

Kyburz challenged the projected exposition costs in parliament, prompting a wry exchange with Liberal MLA Robert Moore:

Mrs Kyburz: I issue a very strong warning that the staging of an Expo in Queensland at a cost of $200m plus could break the State. Quite frankly, it would not cost $200m plus; it would cost $200m plus, plus, plus ... how dare anybody

discuss sinking the State into a financial morass just to pay
for something as 'frippy-frappy' as an Expo ... In my opinion
the Commonwealth Government ... should say 'No' to
Queensland, because Australia has far more urgent priorities.
Mr Moore: If it does that, we will secede.
Mrs Kyburz: The honourable member for Windsor will be
doing it on his own.[46]

Malcolm Fraser ordered a separate analysis of the Queensland/
ABA initiative, which determined that the exposition would
cost significantly more than previously estimated – an ill-timed
development at the onset of the early 1980s recession. He rejected
the proposal in December 1981, reasoning (oddly, given his support
for a Sydney or Melbourne exposition) that 'such an expenditure for
a single, fixed event would be both inappropriate and inconsistent
with the need for the Government to support national and
international events which would reach people across the nation'.[47]
In a letter of commiseration to Maccormick, Ian Russell wrote, 'As
a seasoned Expo veteran, you must have been bitterly disappointed
that the Expo was lost to Australia, not because we were defeated
at the BIE, but by Australia's most powerful club!'[48]

The BIE required a formal application from an aspiring host
nation's representative government – without it, Queensland's exposition hopes were lost. A new proposal was nevertheless underway
within the month. The instigator, Sir Frank Moore, was incensed by
the antipathy of 'southern interests and Canberra bureaucrats' to the
prospect of a national event staged in Queensland.[49] Moore favoured
a 'free enterprise' funding model in which the state government and
private enterprise would become shareholders in an Expo Company
(though a high-risk special event underwritten by a government
entering a conflict-of-interest quagmire is not commensurate with
most understandings of 'free enterprise').[50] In acknowledgement of
the differing private and governmental motivations underlying an
exposition, Edwards and Bjelke-Petersen opted for a model funded

and controlled by the public sector with assistance from private enterprise.[51] Merchant banker David Graham (who had organised finance for the Gateway Bridge) estimated that a Brisbane exposition could be financed with $100 million from the government, recoverable through the sale of the site at the event's conclusion.[52] Suggested post-exposition land uses included a luxury hotel, a casino, a convention centre, a theme park, and a zoo.[53]

Fraser was persuaded to keep the 1988 exposition slot open with the BIE on the condition that Queensland would not seek Commonwealth financial support for the venture. Edwards recalls, 'Malcolm Fraser – I think probably on the advice of his treasurer at the time [John Howard], they were very rigid in the negotiations … very opposed to any funding for Queensland.'[54]

The expected private enterprise enthusiasm for a Brisbane exposition failed to materialise. Faced with Commonwealth resistance, an encroaching recession, and tumbleweeds in lieu of the state's fabled frontier entrepreneurial mentality, Schubert and Hielscher deemed the event too risky to pursue; in April 1982, Chicago and France became the host city frontrunners for the next world exposition when Queensland scuppered its bid.[55]

Not to be deterred by Queensland's abandonment of its own proposal, Moore and Edwards revived their exposition ambitions in the inspirational wake of the 1982 Commonwealth Games. The event boosted business and government confidence in Brisbane's major-event-hosting capacity and lifted the morale of locals, some of whom donned T-shirts proclaiming 'It's hard to be humble. I'm a Queenslander'.[56]

The Brisbane Games inspired other changes that were to affect Expo and its legacy, including Liberal city councillor Sallyanne Atkinson's gambit to surrender her safe Indooroopilly seat and run for lord mayor. She had first run for council in 1978 with the slogan 'Let's show the world a better Brisbane', which was designed to address negativity stemming from Queensland's status as a 'Cinderella State'.[57] Her 1978 dining and entertainment guide, *Around Brisbane*, was re-released in the afterglow of the Commonwealth Games with a new introduction assuring readers that 'our citizens have acquired the confidence of coming of age'.[58]

Tourism entrepreneur Jim Kennedy suggested the exposition theme 'Man, Technology and Leisure', which gradually morphed into 'Leisure in the Age of Technology'.[59] The commercial applications of such a theme are readily apparent, but Barbara Absolon offers some contextual – though improvident – rationale: 'That was back in the era when the universities were introducing courses on recreational studies and things like that – because we were all going to be bored out of our minds within twenty years, as technology would have taken over; so each of us would only have to work twenty hours a week – and that's what it was about: "What will leisure be?"'[60]

The preliminary report for the exposition forecast twenty to thirty international participants and $105 million in acquisition and development costs, with $90 million recoverable from sale of the site at the event's conclusion.[61] The document was drafted by vested business and development interests with limited answerability or exposition experience, but it was nevertheless skimmed through Cabinet with unusual speed on account of the prime minister's bad back.[62] Fraser was on leave with this ailment in November 1982 when Moore persuaded Bjelke-Petersen to send an 'urgent' telex to the acting prime minister, National Party leader Doug Anthony, revealing that Brisbane's Expo bid had been revived and implying that this necessitated lodgement of a federal application at a BIE meeting the following week.[63]

Anthony resisted public service objections to the move and dispatched officials from the Department of Prime Minister and Cabinet and Home Affairs to Brisbane. They found that the study made insufficient allowances for inflation, interest charges, and infrastructure inputs, and that it entailed potential costs to the Commonwealth of up to $100 million … but that it was otherwise attractive.[64] Anthony authorised an application to the BIE with the proviso that a thorough feasibility study be undertaken, and that the event be held at no cost to the Commonwealth.[65] When Fraser discovered what had transpired, he was reportedly furious; he later confirmed that he would not have allowed Queensland's bid to progress to the next stage of the application process.[66]

Brisbane Commonwealth Games Manager Dan Whitehead and Deputy General Manager Bob Minnikin (later general manager of Expo) were engaged to coordinate the next stage of the exposition bid, which entailed a BIE assessment visit to Brisbane in March 1983, and production of a feasibility study capable of eliciting final exposition approval from the state Treasury and Cabinet, and the BIE. An Expo secretariat headed by Whitehead coordinated a number of consultants to this end, including David Graham, who collated and assessed operating costs provided by the secretariat and land costs evaluated by A.D. Taylor and P.G. Byrne and Company (in which Moore had a business interest).[67] The secretariat was overseen by Hielscher, Schubert, and Moore, who provided the group with QTTC office space, staff, and facilities.[68] Minnikin credits Moore with being 'the one ... more than any, that really lobbied the government – or in particular Joh – in terms of "Queensland needs to do this" for Expo 88.'[69]

A preliminary report in March predicting a net profit of $15 million was deemed gravely insufficient (and optimistic) by Treasury, which nevertheless proceeded with the BIE visit that month. The final report, in May 1983, envisioned a modest profit of $2 million, but was still light on economic data.[70] Despite the team's experience with the Commonwealth Games, Minnikin says exposition assessments were elusive: 'there were so many variables getting put into the feaso [feasibility study] we came up with attendance numbers of between five and ten million; the Treasury were not happy with such a wide range and they brought in an external expert from America [Nick Winslow]. He came up with 7.4 million and Treasury were then happy.'[71]

The secretariat recommended that the Coalition create two statutory authorities for Expo: one to acquire and manage the site (overseen by the Liberal minister for the Treasury), and one to run the event (overseen by the premier).[72] In a May 1983 submission to Cabinet, Edwards and Bjelke-Petersen backed this recommendation, summarised the recent feasibility study, proposed investigating the creation of special legislation to facilitate the event, and noted that the Commonwealth should be asked for a financial commitment 'at an appropriate time'.[73] The submission was approved. The generally positive local media response included the newspaper article 'Taking a Vital Step for City's Future', in which Moore predicted that the exposition would attract millions in tourist revenue.[74]

Edwards, Bjelke-Petersen, Schubert, and Whitehead obtained provisional approval to stage Expo at a BIE meeting in June 1983. Brisbane Labor lord mayor Roy Harvey declared the outcome 'damn great', and noted that 'in the past, other countries had heard of Sydney but very few knew of Brisbane. This signifies Brisbane is catching up the backlag and we are on the map.'[75] Possibly in a special-event-induced fervour (having already announced that the city would be bidding for the 1992 Olympic Games), Harvey claimed that Expo would also enhance Brisbane's chances of staging the Student Games in 1987.[76] Whitehead overlooked the 'coming of age' mantle so recently bestowed upon the Brisbane Commonwealth Games to ensure readers that the exposition 'will be a huge step in this city growing up'.[77]

Political Machinations

The malamandered public presumably received some Expo announcements more warmly than others. A *Daily Sun* article revealed, 'the Premier, who will be 77 in 1988, said "I intend to be around and still Premier to see this Expo", indicating his intention to contest at least two elections'.[78] One of his key Expo allies would not be contesting with him. Sir Llew Edwards had been elevated to the Liberal leadership with the expectation that he would temper the premier's less palatable inclinations. His successes in this area included rescinding a $6 million government loan to controversial businessman Shrian Oskar (later jailed for fraud in England) for establishing an oil seed crushing plant of dubious merit in Queensland. Failures included the Winchester South coal-mining rights being awarded against Edwards's wishes to a consortium including Bjelke-Petersen ally Sir Leslie Thiess (over a Queensland company with just three per cent overseas equity), and the National Party blocking Edwards's attempt to introduce a ministerial code of conduct.

Coalition antipathy manifested itself in increasing incidences of three-cornered electoral contests – despite an agreement that neither party would stand a candidate against each other's existing members. Liberal Party president Yvonne McComb supported these activities to prevent the election of 'unthinking acolytes' to Bjelke-Petersen, whom she considered 'an affront to democracy'.[79] One such affront had occurred in 1982, when the premier attempted to interfere with the judiciary to insert Terry Lewis's preference for a new chief justice – against the wishes of the Liberal Party (resulting in the elevation of a compromise candidate).[80] Liberals entertained the idea of severing the Coalition and courting the Labor Party at this point, but Edwards disallowed it.[81] Kyburz says many of her peers were uncomfortable with the close working relationship between Edwards and Bjelke-Petersen:

> Llew had a very good ability of ingratiating himself with everybody. He was able to do it well. He was … the sort of man who'd had 'McDonald's training', I always call it … If a marshmallow ever wore a suit it was Llew … We couldn't understand why he didn't see things the way we did. But then, young Turks are like that, aren't they?[82]

Terry White says he and 'ginger group' colleagues such as Terry Gygar and Ian Prentice 'were totally frustrated' and wanted the Liberal Party 'to take some action to let people know that we stood for something'.[83] Matters came to a head over a Liberal initiative to create a Public Accounts Committee to oversee government spending. With the exception of Mike Ahern, the Nationals opposed the idea. Edwards urged his party to avoid skirmishes on 'trendy policies ... with little or no electoral appeal to the average Australian', but in August 1983 Prentice moved that the Legislative Assembly discuss the proposal.[84] The ALP, seven Liberal back-benchers, and Liberal minister Terry White supported the motion, which was nevertheless defeated. Bjelke-Petersen pressured Edwards to remove White from the ministry for breaking Cabinet solidarity, after which White challenged for the Liberal leadership; the numbers were against Edwards, so he stepped down. When Bjelke-Petersen improperly refused to accept the new leader, White and seven Liberals resigned from Cabinet in protest. Bjelke-Petersen somehow overruled even this by convincing Governor Sir James Ramsay to refuse the resignations.

As the Coalition imploded, Bjelke-Petersen posed for a photo with recently elected Labor prime minister Bob Hawke (who had defeated Fraser in a landslide win) at the proposed Expo site in South Brisbane.[85] Given the premier's historic antipathy towards Labor, federal support for the exposition was far from certain, but Hawke consented for it to proceed.

The premier deftly avoided an early state election (as required by the tattered state of the Coalition) by calling for an early end to parliament; Liberal and Labor members assented, as they assumed that this would be followed by a call for an early poll. The National Party instead led Queensland as a minority government until the October 1983 election, which Edwards, then reportedly considering a return to medicine, did not contest.[86]

The election was an unusual affair even by Queensland standards, with Police Commissioner Terry Lewis improperly endorsing the Bjelke-Petersen government, and the premier expending more campaign energy on his former Coalition allies than on Labor – contributing to election losses for 'ginger group' members

Ian Prentice, Guelfi Scassola, Terry Gygar, Bill Hewitt, Rob Akers, and Rosemary Kyburz (who lost her seat to Wayne Goss).[87] He then offered Liberal ministers Brian Austin and Don Lane Cabinet promotions to defect to the Nationals, which gave the party the numbers to govern Queensland in its own right for the first time. It also gave corrupt police access to Cabinet deliberations via Lane.

After separate discussions with the premier and the prime minister, Edwards joined the lengthy list of ex-parliamentarians with prestigious chairmanships when he agreed to spearhead the exposition.[88] Dan Whitehead did not remain with the management team for the development phase, though he stated that the parting was amicable: 'I've done my job and that was to secure the Expo for Brisbane in 1988.'[89]

Parliamentary opposition to Expo grew fainter with the defeat of the 'small l' Liberals and the event's growing momentum, but resistance remained as to the location. Any negative electoral consequences from the event were likely to be felt in surrounding areas – most of which were held by Labor. The party's representative for South Brisbane, Jim Fouras, was in a difficult position: it was electorally unwise to support an exposition in his electorate, but it was also unwise to oppose a potentially popular event. In an address to parliament in November 1983, he supported Expo while condemning its location – anticipating many future criticisms in the process:

Expo will have an effect on the little people in my electorate.
As a result of Expo, rates and rents will rise. More than
50 percent of the people in South Brisbane and West End
live in rented accommodation. They will be pushed out.
What will be left there? There will be very expensive, high-rise
development ... It will be a concrete jungle with barricaded
doors. People will have to speak into a microphone before they
will be able to enter the high-rise apartments ... The whole
character of my electorate has been threatened by the decision
to hold Expo there.[90]

Fouras said the site was not as run-down as Expo proponents claimed, and criticised the vague redevelopment plans and formidable veto powers of Coordinator-General Schubert, noting, 'surely, in any democracy, the elected local authority members, and not a public servant, should make such decisions'.[91] His remarks went unheeded.

Thus, in the absence of interest or informed competition from any other state; without public consultation, a robust feasibility study, or meaningful parliamentary debate; with scant regard to the ideals of world expositions; against the wishes of a prime minister; and amid murmurings of cronyism, cultural backwardness, and corruption, a small coterie of politicians and business leaders ushered Queensland into the development phase of a stratospherically risky event that most of the population had never heard of.

4

'Brending' the Rules

Expo 88 needed a paternalistic dictator and obviously Bjelke-Petersen was perfect for that particular function. People did not question too much what was going on because they knew what the standard answer was going to be: 'don't you worry about that' and to a large extent that was exactly what was necessary to avoid the normal sort of criticism that would have occurred because all the procedures were not being followed to the letter of the law.

Bob Minnikin[1]

'YOU COULD NOT DO AN Expo today on a site like that,' muses Expo Chairman Sir Llew Edwards, in an interview some twenty years after the fact. 'I would never be able to get the Federal or State Parliament to give us laws they gave me as the chairman: the power to be able to walk in [at] nine o'clock one morning, three weeks after I was appointed ... to the governor with a piece of paper that said "the Cabinet has approved for the Brisbane Exposition South Bank Redevelopment Authority to resume the whole of South Bank".'[2]

The power made available to Expo's organisers by the Bjelke-Petersen government became a matter of contention, but the event was largely made possible through that power, and organisers' willingness to mimic the government's 'flexible' approach to rules and regulations. They also benefited from the state's preparedness to act as sponsor, guarantor, and legislative enforcer of an entrepreneurial event. But the levels of antipathy roused by Bjelke-Petersen's association with Expo almost condemned it to mediocrity. To extract Expo from its political mire, organisers strove to insulate it from the very government it was dependent upon while forging alliances so alien to Bjelke-Petersen as to prompt exclamations of incredulity.

Organisational Structure

In accordance with BIE regulations, Expo was established under the authority of the relevant minister of the Government of Australia, Barry Cohen (the minister for Home Affairs and the Environment, which encompassed the AEO). Oversight shifted to John Brown with the formation of the Department of Sport, Recreation and Tourism after the 1984 election, and to Graham Richardson in December 1987, when Brown was found to have misled parliament in relation to the tendering process for the Australian Pavilion at Expo.[3]

Despite the insistence of both the Fraser and Hawke governments that their support for Expo was contingent upon its costs (variously estimated at between $200 million and $625 million) being quarantined from the Commonwealth, it belatedly transpired that such 'conditions' were unenforceable. BIE regulations stipulated that the host nation act as guarantor of the event, and that it bear (at minimum) the cost of a national pavilion, a commissioner-general, and the hosting and security requirements of international VIPs – the combined cost of which was estimated at $40 million.[4] The Commonwealth reluctantly met these obligations but routinely rebuffed other requests for financial assistance. This earned the (admittedly already existent) antipathy of Bjelke-Petersen, who declared it 'typical of their lousy attitude' and who – seemingly without irony – accused it of political bias: 'We know what they're like. We're not a Labor State. If you're from Perth or Sydney or Melbourne you'd only have to ask and you'd have it the next morning.'[5]

Managing this anticipated half-billion dollar, six-month extravaganza necessitated more substantial arrangements than the comparatively brief (ten days), small (481,000 tickets sold), and inexpensive ($30 million) 1982 Commonwealth Games – a BCC initiative managed by a $2 company, the Commonwealth Games Foundation, with expenses split relatively evenly by each level of government.[6] Queensland briefly indulged the illusion of intergovernmental cooperation through its participation in the five-person Ministerial Council (with representatives from each level of government) established to oversee the planning of Expo, but only four meetings were held – the first in January 1984 and the final in December 1985.[7]

The true power behind Expo was the Brisbane Exposition and South Bank Redevelopment Authority (variously referred to in related literature as BESBRA, the Expo Authority, or the Authority), a statutory authority established by an Act of the Queensland Government – the *Expo '88 Act 1984* – in February 1984, to manage resumption of the land required for Expo; the exposition's construction, development, and operation phases; and the eventual redevelopment of the site. The executive comprised Sir Llew Edwards, who was appointed chairman in February 1984, Bob Minnikin, appointed general manager and executive officer in March 1984, and support staff.[8]

That same month, the federal government appointed Sir Edward Williams (chair of the 1982 Brisbane Commonwealth Games Foundation and the Supreme Court judge whose actions are believed to have delayed the exposure of corrupt Queensland police) as the commissioner-general of Expo, to represent the Commonwealth in dealings with the BIE and BESBRA.[9]

In September 1984, the government issued those countries with which it had diplomatic relations invitations to participate in Expo (except where the Department of Foreign Affairs deemed it contrary to Australian interests).[10] International participants liaised with the Australian commissioner-general and BESBRA via a fourteen-member Steering Committee of international participants' commissioners-general (elected on a world regional basis). Dr Damaso de Lario of Spain was elected committee president in 1987.[11]

The BESBRA board contained more state government representatives and associates than the ill-fated (more balanced) Ministerial Council, which would have seemed entirely reasonable to the Bjelke-Petersen government, given it was bearing the bulk of the exposition's cost and risk – a burden the Commonwealth, BCC, and assorted entrepreneurial interests proved continually reluctant to alleviate.

BESBRA BOARD MEMBERS
Sir Llew Edwards (Chairman)
Sir Sydney Schubert (Deputy Chairman and Queensland Coordinator-General), until 30 June 1988; replaced by Mr J. Moleton from July 1988
Sir Leo Hielscher (Queensland Under Treasurer) until June 1988; replaced by Mr E.J. Hall from May 1988
Sir Frank Moore (National Party figure) until 1986
Mr W.J. Baker (Chief Commissioner and Chairman of the Land Administration Commission)
Mr K.J. Driscoll (Chairman of Directors of National Homes Pty Ltd)
Mr F.G. Maybury (National Party figure and Commissioner of the Queensland Pavilion)
Mr J.B. Reid (Chairman of James Hardie Industries Ltd and ABA representative)
Mr H.B. MacDonald (Secretary to the Commonwealth Department of the Arts, Sports, the Environment, Tourism and Territories), until August 1987; replaced by Mr A. Blunn from August 1987

Source: BESBRA, *World Expo 88: Media Guide* (Brisbane: BESBRA, 1988), 23; Sir Edward Williams, *Report of the Commissioner-General of Expo 88 on the Australian Government's Involvement in Expo 88* (Canberra: Department of Sport, Recreation and Tourism, 1989), 17.

An ABA representative was only admitted to the board after considerable lobbying. Minnikin says the omission was intentional, as despite the ABA's role in the attainment of Expo, the relationship had devolved into a rivalry: 'They were very Sydney-centric. They'd put out publications and stuff and Expo would be almost a footnote to it. We saw it as being one of the most important events in the bicentennial; they saw it as being a Queensland event. That was not just with the ABA; that went right through – it was not easy to get a national perspective on Expo.'[12]

The national perspective was not easy to get at Expo, either. The Australian Pavilion commissioner-general, former test cricketer and Queensland Labor parliamentarian Tom Veivers, reported that the Commonwealth was 'grossly under-represented' on the BESBRA board, and blamed the Hawke government's early ambivalence towards Expo with fostering a deleterious power imbalance between Williams and Edwards, which was especially problematic given the 'differences and difficulties' between the two men.[13]

Lady Jane Edwards (née Brumfield, who married Edwards shortly after Expo concluded) confirms that BESBRA was frequently at odds with Williams: 'He was a cranky old thing – he's gone to the great racetrack in the sky, so I can say these things now – he was very stuffy and from a very different generation.'[14]

Williams's legendary candour was in evidence when a trainee director at the Queensland Theatre Company, John Watson (later appointed an Expo River Stage producer), was sent to his office in 1984 to investigate 'all this talk about World Expo 88 coming to Brisbane', and to see if the company could assist: 'Sir Edward said: well, I'll be fucked if I fuckin' know. The only fuckin' reason we got the fuckin' Expo was because fuckin' Hawkie said to fuckin' Joh if we tried to do the fuckin' Expo in fuckin' Melbourne or fuckin' Sydney those fuckin' BLF [Builders Labourers Federation] cunts will fuckin' fuck us over and we'll never get the fuckin' thing open on time.'[15]

Watson shakes his head at this recollection, and then laughs, 'You grow up quickly, you know?'[16] A clue to Williams's frustrations appears in his Commissioner-General's report, which noted (with a written eloquence Williams was also known for) that relations with BESBRA were 'at times fraught with considerable difficulty'.[17] He cited a 1986 report by French BIE delegate Marcel Galopin, which censured the Commonwealth's disengagement with Expo and its relegation of Williams's role to 'simple representational functions' rather than 'the necessary counterweight to the organising authority'.[18] Steering Committee President Dr Damaso de Lario echoed these sentiments in his report, noting that the committee had inadequate support when 'directly confronted with the Expo Authority'.[19] Sir Llew Edwards concedes he viewed the exposition 'differently' to Williams, and freely admits to seeking superior powers to his organisational rival while capitalising on his congenial relationships with Bjelke-Petersen and Hawke in order to get Expo 'done – built, open on time, and a success'.[20]

BESBRA also sought to limit BCC input. After the collegiality of the Jones–Chalk period, council–state relations soured during Knox's tenure as treasurer, when Commonwealth grants for BCC were diverted to state projects, and council was stripped of its few profitable responsibilities (notably electricity) without compensation.[21] A modicum of civility was maintained out of mutual interest: Brisbane Lord Mayor Roy Harvey and his successor, Sallyanne Atkinson, needed state government support for the 1987 World Student Games and the 1992 Olympic Games bid, and the government required essential BCC services and public works to facilitate Expo.[22] Harvey's early support for the exposition may have helped facilitate the appointment of a BCC representative to the BESBRA board, but this voice was silenced in 1986 when that figure left to pursue a career with the National Party; in a suspected retaliation against Atkinson's budget-driven refusal to provide BESBRA with a direct council grant, the BCC representative was not replaced.[23]

Edwards might have had such intergovernmental animosities in mind – along with the circumvention of red tape – when harnessing his political expertise to help craft the *Expo '88 Act*, which encroached significantly on BCC responsibilities while granting extraordinary powers to the unelected BESBRA: the exposition site was exempted from the *City of Brisbane Town Planning Act*, the *Building Act*, the *City of Brisbane Act*, and the *Local Government Act* – prompting academic Peter Carroll to assert that 'in effect, a large, inner-city site had been removed from the control of BCC, and the citizens which it represented'.[24]

Atkinson says her relationship with Bjelke-Petersen was 'prickly', and that heated discussions over expensive Expo infrastructure and works were exacerbated by 'a lot of carrying on with Llew Edwards'.[25] Lady Edwards believes the source of this intergovernmental consternation was council's unwillingness to accept the powers vested in BESBRA by the state: 'The organisation which most profoundly opposed things like eating and drinking outdoors and serving food and alcohol outside regulation hours was in fact the Brisbane City Council ... she [Atkinson] kept saying, "The council bylaws are this and we won't allow that," and Llew and the team kept saying, "Well, on the Expo site you've got no jurisdiction," so there was a lot of squabbling with government authorities who hadn't realised that they'd kind of created this little area in the city which had no rules and regulations except the Expo Act. That made a lot of things possible but it also attracted a lot of hostility from people who were used to running things.'[26]

Atkinson takes a dim view of Expo-induced incursions into BCC responsibilities, noting, 'I think the state government regarded itself as the owner of Brisbane.'[27] She was astonished at the transformation the event had wrought in formerly regionally focused parliamentarians: 'All of a sudden with Expo, they started to get much more interested in the city. I can remember Russ Hinze once saying to me, "The city of Brisbane is like a beautiful woman; you want to spend money on it."'[28]

Smooth Operators

Minnikin and Edwards reported weekly to the BESBRA board, and oversaw eight divisions between them (which were assembled and shaped over several years). 'We had very good team leaders internally,' says Edwards, 'an excellent accountant [Tony Philips], "Scrooge", we called him; Peter Goldston, who was in charge of construction; Ross Given [Operations] was a lawyer – and he'd never done anything like this before – but I just liked his style. Bob Minnikin, to his credit, was also a very good general manager; that team met weekly [joined by other directors as their respective divisions formed] and literally put the Expo together.'[29]

EXPO DIVISIONS AND DIRECTORS (AS AT 30 APRIL 1988)		
DIVISION	DIRECTOR	OVERSIGHT
Communications	Jane Brumfield	Sir Llew Edwards
Entertainment	Ric Birch	Bob Minnikin
Finance and Administration	Tony Philips	Bob Minnikin
International Participation	Richard John	Sir Llew Edwards
Marketing	Graham Currie	Bob Minnikin
Operations	Ross Given	Bob Minnikin
Site Development	Peter Goldston	Bob Minnikin
Technology	Ken Pope	Bob Minnikin

Source: BESBRA, *World Expo 88: Media Guide* (Brisbane: BESBRA, 1988), 23.

Peter Goldston credits Edwards's 'magnificent leadership' and talent for 'getting excellent work out of average people' with making the exposition possible.[30] Lady Jane Edwards feels similarly: 'It sounds biased because I'm his wife, but I do think it was the right man at the right moment.'[31] Ross Given acknowledges Edwards's personal and political nous: 'What a wonderful man he was, and what an ideal choice he was for the position – a senior politician who knew his way around political life and how to play off all the players in what was quite a complex, difficult political situation.'[32]

Given considers Edwards and Minnikin to have been 'a great team' even though 'they didn't see eye-to-eye on everything', with Edwards's skills and high profile complementing Minnikin's strength as 'the engine-room man'.[33] Barbara Absolon recalls benefiting from Minnikin's expertise from her third day with Expo, when her high-profile Entertainment Division director, Ric Birch, told her, 'I'm going overseas for five weeks – you keep working'.[34] Shortly thereafter, BESBRA's finance department turned to her for the division's six-month cash flow: 'What the hell is a cash flow? Bob Minnikin taught me all those sorts of things. He taught me the business side of business – he was the day-to-day. Sir Llew was sort of the [high-profile] Ric.'[35]

Irrespective of the diversity that world expositions sought to present, Expo's organisational structure reflected the disparities of the day (or, for that matter, of any day). Men considerably outnumbered women in Expo's managerial hierarchy, and the representation of other minorities was poorer still. Even women who were highly positioned had prejudices to negotiate; Absolon recalls that she and Lady Edwards (who had not yet become director of the Communications Division) struggled to secure invitations to division meetings even when operating at a deputy level: 'Every Monday morning at 7 am, there was a meeting of the managers of different divisions, so after about two or three months where Ric had been away – he would be in for some of them – I said to Llew Edwards, "Look, I'm around and available if you need me to represent the Entertainment Division," and I still remember Llew saying "Oh, thank you very much but we might be skipping it next week," or whatever the excuse was.'[36]

Eventually, both women did receive invitations to division meetings. Many months later, Absolon discovered the reason for

Edwards's early reticence: 'We were all having drinks together and it was Peter Goldston who said to me, "I have never worked with women before in roles other than secretaries. In truth, we never thought that women could keep secrets" – which was obviously why Jane and I were not invited along to the management meetings … women could not *possibly* keep management secrets. So it was a real education I think for some of those guys; it was the first time in their lives that they'd ever worked with women in senior decision-making – equal sort of decisions – and the preconceptions that men had back then … when you look at things like *Mad Men* [the television series], that's what it was like. The chicks were out there being secretaries and gasbagging amongst themselves and they *obviously* couldn't be trusted with sensitive corporate information.'[37]

Expo Awareness

The international response to Expo was initially muted, with only three countries (Britain, Tonga, and New Zealand) committing to the event prior to the establishment of an International Participation Division in June 1985.[38] While the situation was disturbing, Lady Edwards believes such reticence was understandable: 'They knew where Australia was, but they certainly didn't know where Queensland was, and they didn't know where Brisbane was – and you were trying to entice them to spend millions and millions of dollars on this faraway place they'd never heard of – so there was a lot of education to do out there.'[39]

Education was also required at home, as there had not been a world exposition in Australia for nearly a century. Absolon recalls she almost turned down her position with Expo as she had no idea what a world exposition was.[40] To properly understand what would be required of them, key Expo personnel visited world expositions in New Orleans (1984), Tsukuba (1985), and Vancouver (1986), along with entertainment meccas such as Disneyland. 'We can all Google things now,' says Absolon, 'but back then there was no way of finding out information about expos.'[41] There were also obstacles to relaying exposition information to the public. 'We're talking about something that was completely unknown,' recalls Absolon, 'when people who had visited expos were talking about the pavilions, goodness knows what pictures were raised in peoples' minds. Pavilions? What are pavilions?'[42]

Demystification efforts included distributing thousands of pamphlets to local residents and schools, and holding multitudinous town-hall-style seminars. Growing public and media scepticism was nonetheless evident in newspaper pieces such as 'Local Apathy Haunts Expo Officials' and 'Where's Our Expo Enthusiasm?', in which Expo's then marketing director, Mark Cassidy, nervously insisted, 'I don't think people realise how big this is going to be. This is going to be a once in a lifetime event.'[43]

Controversies

Approximately half the forty hectares required for Expo was already in the possession of various levels of government (including five hectares of parkland purchased and restored by BCC under Jones); the remainder was composed of light-industrial businesses and ware-houses in various states of repair, a few low-cost boarding houses, and some Aboriginal meeting spaces. Musgrave Park – historically recognised as a site of Aboriginal ceremonial, planning, and social activity – was transferred from BCC to BESBRA for space contingency purposes, though it was eventually released before Expo as surplus to needs.[44] Valuations were frozen in the area to allow properties to be resumed with 'fair compensation' (generally twenty-five per cent above the valuation) by a Land Commission created by the state government for that express purpose.[45] Landowners could challenge the valuation in court (and some did) but could not prevent the resumption.[46]

Sir Llew Edwards credits the Bjelke-Petersen government's infamous lack of accountability with making such an exercise possible: 'It was easy to do in those days with no CJCs [Criminal Justice Commissions] and things – and it had its faults, as we know, where ministers went where they shouldn't go, when they broke the rules – but it was a fascinating period of time when you literally could resume a block of land and resume a whole street ... and have action. There's a bit of communism in it. Nobody minds – provided they're compensated for it.'[47]

This was not uniformly the case. Local business owners surveyed by *The Courier-Mail* in 1983 resented the government engaging in resumptions for inessential entrepreneurial activity, with one claiming, 'This is an infringement of our liberties – coming from a Government which is supposed to be pro private enterprise. All this Expo is a glorified property development exercise.'[48] Labor's Jim Fouras took particular exception to section 30 of the *Expo '88 Act*, which denied landowners the option (under section 41 of the *Acquisition of Land Act*) to buy their property back at market value if it was resold within seven years of resumption; Fouras felt this proved the exposition was an excuse for the government to set up 'prime real estate sites for its development friends'.[49]

Academics also questioned the government's underlying motives. Tony Bennett speculated that the exposition was designed to train the public in consumption styles required by comparatively sophisticated new developments such as QCC and the Myer Centre.[50] Tony Fry and Anne-Marie Willis noted that the 'Leisure in the Age of Technology' theme excluded 'the enforced leisure of the unemployed as it cannot be harnessed to the generation of profits', and functioned 'entirely within the context of the developing end of uneven development', reducing leisure 'to that which can be purchased by a tourist'.[51] Jennifer Craik believed Expo was purely 'an excuse to redevelop the South Bank site' and that it proved 'business rhetoric has skilfully re-written the notion of public good in terms of principles of user pays, de-regulation, private funding and "visions" of development, all of which translate into practices which further disadvantage those with fewest means and no public voice'.[52] Craik also expressed concern that the pro-private enterprise Bjelke-Petersen government was bearing the entrepreneurial risk for Expo, while government-preferred contractors enjoyed the benefits, freedoms, and protections of the statutory authority created to manage it.[53]

Queensland's entrepreneurs had reason to baulk at financing Expo – many recent host cities had failed to break even on their expositions, some incurring significant public debt: $1 billion in Montreal, $76 million in Knoxville, $100 million in New Orleans (the organising body of which went bankrupt during the event), and $400 million in Vancouver.[54] Expo's finance and administration director Tony Philips's responsibilities were dubbed 'an accountant's nightmare' by industry magazine *Australian Accountant*, as they entailed 'running a $460 million business founded on borrowed capital and making sure there is neither profit nor loss when it shuts down for good exactly six months after opening'.[55]

Coordinator-General Sir Sydney Schubert and Under Treasurer Sir Leo Hielscher were placed on the BESBRA board to protect the government's significant investment. Hielscher reveals they made up the rules and regulations for government conduct in relation to Expo 'as we went along'; 'It was new ground – we'd never had a government instrument trusted with a thousand million dollars overdraft. But of course that thousand million dollars was our cash – which we would normally have had on the money market – so that's the interest we charged them [BESBRA].'[56]

Finance in the vicinity of $100 million was initially sourced (at market interest rates 'plus a bit') from the Queensland Government Development Authority, which operated through the state government.[57] 'The way we funded it,' says Hielscher, 'I'd just run it into debt into an overdraft in the government accounts; we didn't have to go and raise a loan before we could spend it, because in overdraft you just kept building up the deficit.'[58] He says that government accounts for areas such as Main Roads, Health, and Public Service Superannuation were in the positive at the time, 'so all the other accounts were running along nicely in front, and the Expo was going down ... it was as simple as that'.[59]

BESBRA planned to repay the loan through multiple revenue avenues: ticket sales, fifteen per cent of gross revenue from Expo's food and beverage outlets, twenty per cent of merchandise sales, thirty per cent of ticket sales from rides, and a 'land-banking exercise' in which it would acquire the site for approximately $80 million and then resell it to developers post-Expo for $180–$200 million.[60] Minnikin lent credence to accusations that the government was sponsoring property development through forced resumptions when he conceded that 'acquisition purely for redevelopment purposes was probably politically unacceptable, however, the added benefits of World Expo to the community generally tipped the balance in favour of acquisition of this complete area'.[61] The sentiment was not shared by many of those living in close proximity to the event.

Exposés

A report into the social consequences of Expo, *The Big Party Syndrome* (directed and coordinated by Phil Day and Tony Kelly), found that the event 'had widespread, well documented, if not readily quantifiable, negative personal and social impacts on the people of South Brisbane and West End', that 'hundreds of households were evicted from their homes and hundreds more were subjected to substantial rent increases', and that 'no studies of its likely impact were undertaken' beforehand.[62]

Countless stories emerged of landlords evicting vulnerable tenants to capitalise on increased rental opportunities. 'Change at my age is very hard,' said single pensioner Charlotte Carney, then eighty-eight, whose weekly rent in Yeronga increased from $55 to $100 prior to the exposition's opening. 'If rising rents and forcing people on to the streets is what Expo is doing for this city, I think we can do without it.'[63] War widow Elizabeth Rowland, eighty, was not given an option to remain in her West End flat:

'The eviction notice says they want to renovate and refurbish the building but why can't they just do it up and let us pay extra for it? They must want to charge the Expo people a lot of money.'[64] Poppy Takis, sixty-five, had lived in a West End flat with her daughter for twenty-five years before receiving a similar notification. 'There is nothing we can do,' she said. 'We must go but we do not know where.'[65] Graffiti spotted near the exposition site in 1987 read, 'No food, no home, no Expo'.[66]

Queensland Greens co-founder Drew Hutton and his peers fought an intense campaign to stop tenant evictions in the lead-up to Expo; many of them also squatted in old houses under threat by developers seeking to maximise Expo rental opportunities by replacing them with apartments.[67] 'West End was still a gem then,' Hutton says, 'cosmopolitan but not wealthy except for Dornoch Terrace ... an old working-class suburb, with significant Greek, Vietnamese and Aboriginal communities, and a large population of itinerant workers.'[68]

One of Hutton's peers, Ken Butler, was instrumental in forming the Southside Urban Research Group (SURG), which comprised residents and social workers concerned about the impact of Expo. SURG estimated that the event precipitated rent increases of sixty-two per cent for nearby apartments (against thirty-four per cent for Brisbane), and documented 605 people displaced by it (while estimating the true number at closer to 2000).[69] The state government belatedly established the 'Expo Housing Hotline' prior to the event's commencement, but this action was dismissed as 'shallow window dressing' by Labor's Henry Palaszczuk when the government refused to disclose how many – if any – callers the hotline had assisted.[70]

Expo also inspired resistance from activists predisposed to scepticism about Bjelke-Petersen initiatives. Journalist David Monaghan knew a number of students evicted from properties near the site, and recalls, 'There was smoking and chair dancing with the Expo coming as the Anschluss – where the National Party was going to show the world it ruled.'[71] He says social expectations were overwhelmingly grim:

> The whole mood was one of impending doom from a
> behemoth of cultural trickery, Joh installing a giant Potemkin
> village to cover his dictatorship, where his grinning visage
> would be projected above like the green face of the Wizard in
> the Expo Oz.[72]

Film director Debra Beattie collaborated with Bjelke-Petersen impersonator Gerry Connelly on the protest short film *Expo Schmexpo* in 1985. Connelly delivered his dialogue in the 'stumble-bum' manner of Bjelke-Petersen, set against hazy footage of a Brisbane in the process of being lost: 'Expo 88 will be taking place, now, in 1988 – as we all know and understand – and this whole area, now, that we see before us will be opened up, and redeveloped for this purpose, all this area, all this region, all this regard, now, of, er, Expo 88, we hope to be able to raze it, uh, to raze it to the ground, from the river – as you can see – from the river – up and down from Brisbane – right through, right through to Musgrave Park; now Musgrave Park, of course, they talk about their rights, their rights, their rights, their rights, they're black. It's all over. We just go ahead and do as we please.'[73]

Beattie made the film to draw attention to the places and ideals being forfeited in the name of development: '*Expo Schmexpo* comes at the end of the destruction of the Bellevue and of Cloudland [demolished overnight, without permit and to great public outcry, by the Deen brothers in November 1982]. All the hype about what Expo was going to be – for us it destroyed a lot of things.'[74] The film's message, says Beattie, was that 'Brisbane is beautiful, and Bjelke-Petersen is in danger of destroying it completely. You couldn't have any trust in what he was going to do to South Bank.'[75]

Brisbane punk band Choo Dikka Dikka metaphorically turned this destruction upon the exposition with their song 'Cyclone Hits

Expo', which contained lyrics including 'Cyclone hits Expo – hits the very spot – cyclone hits Expo – and destroys the fucking lot!'[76] Co-writer Adam Nash says the song was born of frustration with the lack of public consultation for projects such as Expo: 'Just using the same heavy-handed tactics that that government had used for, well, for the whole time we were growing up.'[77]

The Cane Toad Times had a similarly adversarial take, producing 'Wrexpo 88' T-shirts (depicting a giant toad destroying the site) in honour of 'a sham of a mockery of a farce of a World Exhibition', and publishing articles likening the event to 'walking around inside a giant ad'.[78] Editor Anne Jones says 'the essence of our objection to Expo was essentially that so much land was reclaimed ... the local community was a bit disrupted by it; particularly Aboriginal people'.[79]

Activists and residents groups won a concession from Edwards in 1984, when he committed BESBRA to restoring and preserving buildings of historic significance on the site; this came to include the South Brisbane Municipal Library, Collins Place, the Allgas building, the South Brisbane railway station, the Plough Inn, and the Ship Inn (restored by eminent architect Robin Gibson, who also designed the Queensland pavilion).[80] Edwards nevertheless dismissed as 'ridiculous' concerns that the exposition would adversely affect rent or destroy the character of West End, retorting, 'I don't believe that the area has much character to destroy.'[81] Protest actions delayed construction 'to the point where schedules will be tight' but failed to secure a desired six-month public discussion period when Bjelke-Petersen reportedly 'hit the roof', telling Schubert, 'I want all that land by next week.'[82]

The most difficult resumption negotiation involved the heritage-listed Collins Place (formerly known as Byanda) on Grey Street, one of the few remaining stately homes in the area built in the late 1800s. Peter Goldston says the owner (Lynette Bloss) was a 'clever little politician' and the only business owner to vigorously contest the offer of twenty-five per cent more than the land value.[83] Edwards confirms, 'we had to finally pay her a sum of money that was totally unreasonable'.[84] By June 1985, BESBRA had purchased properties from over sixty registered owners for close to $65 million (a figure that was to surpass $90 million in acquisition and land holding costs by the conclusion of Expo).[85] It then sealed off major south-side streets, including Grey Street (from the Performing Arts Centre to Vulture Street) and Stanley Street (between Russell and Sidon streets); the South Bank site was closed to the public on 30 June 1985.[86]

The Master Plan

Bligh Maccormick 88 (a company formed for the purposes of the exposition by established architectural firm Graham Bligh and early Expo advocate James Maccormick) became master architects of Expo in June 1984.[87] Their plan prioritised outdoor spaces with extensive landscaping, shade structures (the sails of which were originally designed to be flat but eventually took the form of the iconic tent-like structures), river views, and winding walkways that revealed eclectic items of interest along the way.[88]

Australia, Queensland, and participating corporations could design their own pavilions, but – in keeping with the exposition's specialised status – international participants and the other Australian states were restricted to standardised temporary modular designs that could be individualised with graphics and modifications. The size of a country's pavilion was determined by how many 'modules' it purchased.[89]

Bligh Maccormick 88 oversaw designs (prepared by consulting architects) for the exposition's restaurants, monorail stations, entrance gates, information centres, restrooms, parade routes, merchandise stations, boardwalk, and entertainment venues. A $9 million landscaping program headed by landscape architect Lawrie Smith incorporated over 72,500 plants, trees, and shrubs, and contained features such as cascading water, the Epiphyte Forest, and the Pacific Lagoon.[90] The architects receded into the background when Expo's construction phase commenced and attention shifted to Thiess Watkins – the company controversially appointed its project manager in an act of cronyism that Labor's Tom Burns deemed so scandalous it 'sealed the commercial fate of Queensland as a respectable place to do business'.[91]

New Controversies, Old Tricks

Nearly thirty companies tendered for Expo's site development contract in 1984, with costs estimated at $50,000–$100,000 per submission.[92] A committee comprising BESBRA executive and board members sent a shortlist of three to Cabinet – at which point they were instructed to add Thiess Watkins (a company represented by Bjelke-Petersen's old friend Sir Leslie Thiess) to their list. The committee acceded, but declined to champion Thiess. Cabinet requested a revision, but Thiess still failed to attain the committee's support. When the recommendations next reached Cabinet, Bjelke-Petersen reportedly searched through a pile of twenty-seven contenders – ranked in order of suitability – until he reached Thiess Watkins (ranked seventeenth), then said, 'this one's my choice'.[93]

In an interview some twenty-five years after the controversy, selection committee member Bob Minnikin revealed that Civil and Civic was the committee's preferred tenderer under the original guidelines, but that Bjelke-Petersen insisted the guidelines be rewritten until the lead candidate was Thiess Watkins. 'I've never been as careful about the wording of anything as I was about that particular piece,' says Minnikin, 'of both the recommendation and of the criteria for the selection – and I thank God I was, because that ended up as a court case.'[94]

Edwards says he sent for Thiess Watkins's management when confronted with this fait accompli and warned them, 'I don't like this. It's not the way we're going to do business at Expo. But you've been appointed. If you go near the premier again – or any minister without my authority – you're fired.'[95] In this way, Edwards began to enforce a 'separation of powers' between BESBRA and the state government in a bid to avoid being placed under further pressure to accept suspect practices. He says his warning 'worked dramatically well', and that 'we could not have asked for a cleaner relationship'.[96]

When asked if cronyism of the Thiess Watkins variety could have been conceived of at the time as beneficial to Expo in any way, Site Development Director Peter Goldston gives an insight into business relations in 1980s Queensland: 'Thiess Watkins had been inculcated by Les Thiess that they had to do a good job for Queensland. So the site team came with that attitude – and it didn't then matter that Les disappeared over the horizon [Thiess sold the business and retired in 1987]. They believed they had a commitment to do a good job – and they did a magnificent job. So while Llew didn't like what Joh did to him then – or many other things Joh did to him over the years – it was the right decision for the wrong reasons.'[97]

Concerns were raised in parliament and elsewhere about the number of Expo contractors and appointments with National Party links, including an insurance contract awarded to a relation of Brian Austin; a National Party identity receiving the VIP catering contract for the Queensland Pavilion without due process (the pavilion's commissioner was Fred Maybury, a media executive and white shoe wearer who had married Sparkes's secretary, replaced Mike Evans as National Party director, and directed Bjelke-Petersen's ill-fated federal election campaign); and the percentage of government-aligned directors and board members overseeing the exposition itself. Labor's Jim Fouras declared that 'the Expo Authority has been filled with National Party cronies' and that 'Joh and his Ministers have dined out long enough on Expo 88'.[98]

Goldston agrees that many of the exposition's appointments were vulnerable to criticism, but he says the process was typically more practical than unethical in intent: 'Expo was built on trust. They wanted people for Expo that they could trust. So there was no formal advertising for Expo or anything like that. They just got a group of mates together. My father had been the commissioner for railways for a few years before that, and he was one of the trusted people. [Goldston gestures wryly towards himself.] Good stock. Llew liked me. I had many contacts in the public service, and they wanted someone with extensive management experience of construction [as a civil engineer, Goldston had worked on major international projects and coordinated construction of the Wivenhoe Power Station]. I, of course, had no prior experience of expos – pretty well none of our staff did. We were all new.'[99]

Lady Edwards says that hiring protocols were effective, if unusual: 'Llew has had the most amazing ability to suss out talent where it's not obvious – the people that he chose to put this thing together were in a lot of ways kind of mavericks and rule breakers, but they were get-things-done people.'[100]

Operations Manager Ross Given offers a small example of the way BESBRA's mavericks mobilised their connections to 'brend' (rather than bend or break) the rules for Expo: 'Don Lane was a friend of mine. He was the Transport minister at the time. I had to see him a few times – for example, when I went to Expo 86 and saw the pedicab that drove around the streets of Vancouver with people in the back. I thought they were a great idea – so I went and saw Don, and he thought they were a great idea – so they were introduced for Expo. Probably not completely ideal for Brisbane roads, but we got away with it – there were no accidents – and they were a lovely carnival thing to be happening there.'[101]

Some protocols were also 'brent' – at the further expense of Sir Edward Williams – when BESBRA's International Participation Division moved to address the slow pace of overseas commitments. Williams's liaison efforts had been hampered by risk-averse federal authorities loath to authorise invitations that would have to be rescinded if the (then financially tenuous-looking) exposition failed; he was also effectively in competition with Mark Cassidy, whose BESBRA marketing contract incentivised the recruitment of international participants.[102] BESBRA's dissatisfaction with both parties was signalled when Cassidy Management was released from its marketing contract in September 1985 (which became a source of controversy when the media and Opposition sought to establish the settlement terms), and when the Authority attempted to have Williams removed from his position.[103] The Commonwealth instead agreed to reduce Williams's role in international recruitment and give BESBRA more substantial support.[104]

Lady Edwards says the Hawke government was 'very, very helpful enabling the Expo Authority to use its framework – i.e., embassies and trade infrastructure around the world – to go out and recruit countries', which enabled BESBRA representatives such as Edwards and International Participation Division Director Richard John to travel the world in a 'barrage of enthusiasm' and secure commitments from wavering countries – including an organisation that they hoped would provide a truly unique display: 'Llew actually had an audience with the Pope [John Paul II] ... I think they [the Vatican] said something like, "We've been a bit worried about the Catholic faith in Queensland, in Australia; you're getting a bit secular – so perhaps it would be good for the Vatican to have a presence there." And so they took all these priceless, priceless treasures – which had never been out of the Vatican before – diamond-encrusted Papal crowns, robes from the Christian martyrs covered in blood ... It's that kind of thing which I think you can't do if you necessarily go through the system – if you go through the Department of Foreign Affairs, there'd be so much protocol and so many hurdles.'[105]

Edwards says he 'consistently' exceeded his authority to avoid 'bureaucratic bottlenecks' but advised his mavericks 'You can bend the law' for Expo 'but you've got to tell me', and 'if you break the law, watch out'.[106] He strategised what he termed the 'short-circuiting' of bureaucracy in order to authorise contracts, replace staff, and bring in new systems 'on the spot', rather than 'under the best system of government', as 'we otherwise would not have opened until the year 2088'.[107]

Minnikin says it was exceedingly difficult to manage Expo within a government accountability framework, as the event's creatives 'found the concept of procurement procedures totally foreign' and resisted attaining 'three proposals and three sets of prices from three different consultants' when they knew who and what they wished to engage; he considered it most fortuitous that the state government held similar views: 'At the time Joh Bjelke-Petersen was the premier. He was a strong supporter of the event and was never one to be too concerned with the intricate niceties of government accountability.'[108]

When asked if what might be termed 'the Queensland method' effectively enabled the exposition to take place, Goldston readily agrees: 'It was a child of its times. It would have taken a lot longer to develop under more conventional administration than it did. The only way it *could* have developed in that time space would have been if the government had completely contracted it out to a private party and said effectively, "We'll pay you whatever it costs." Certainly within a post-Fitzgerald Inquiry environment – and the checks and balances that have been instituted – the government processes have changed completely. I used early on in my conversation the word "trust". We were trusted people. If we said we wanted something, it was presumed that we were honest, and that it was a warrantable request – and people would do it. I'm talking about people in the government. We had trusted relations – which are presumed not to exist any longer – and so to that extent it was a child of the times. Now, is there something intrinsically Queensland in that? I like to think there is.'[109]

Unlikely Alliances

Early controversies over forced resumptions, due diligence, parochialism, cronyism, and lack of consultation did little to disabuse critics of the notion that Expo was a 'Joh Show'. The next phase in Expo's evolution – industrial agreements between BESBRA and various unions – was so emphatic a departure from Bjelke-Petersen's rhetoric as to provoke howls of disbelief from the Opposition.

World expositions were extremely vulnerable to industrial action by virtue of their fixed operation dates. Edwards was reluctant to commence construction before securing a 'no-strike agreement' between BESBRA and related unions, 'because otherwise we might have been sitting there with the site half-built'.[110] Minnikin and Ross Given negotiated these agreements in 1984 to cover the construction period, and again in 1987 for the final stages of construction and to cover approximately 5000 workers during the exposition's operation. Edwards admits such contracts were an awkward imperative with 'Joh belting the unions'.[111]

Bjelke-Petersen's position on unions was notorious prior to the 1984 union agreement with Expo, but he attained industrial infamy in 1985 when he declared a State of Emergency to sack 920 striking SEQEB workers who were protesting erosions of their workplace rights (and who lost long service leave, superannuation, and other benefits as a result).[112] The government directed police to disrupt picket lines and arrest sympathetic protesters, ordered a shutdown of power stations to exacerbate consumer discomfort, threatened power station operators with $50,000 fines for showing worker solidarity, forced a bill through parliament that prohibited electricity workers from striking (penalties included confiscation of their homes), and established a tribunal for electricity disputes (headed by Judge Eric Pratt, chairman of the suspiciously ineffective Police Complaints Tribunal).[113] This is the environment in which Minnikin and Given negotiated what was 'effectively one of the first enterprise bargaining agreements' with Queensland Trades and Labour Council executive Ray Dempsey, who considered the result 'one of the best industrial agreements ever negotiated for any Expo in any country'.[114]

Years later, Minnikin revealed it had one major flaw: 'We negotiated that agreement with the Trades and Labour Council and the unions on the basis that we had the power under the Expo Act – but after we got it all signed, we then thought, "We'll just get it formalised as a regulation as well", and Crown Law then advised us that we haven't got that power. So. I never went back to Ray Dempsey and said,

"Ray. Sorry, mate, but we never actually had that power."[115]

The agreement guaranteed disputes would be settled on site rather than in the courts, and included an awards package in which a higher base rate of pay was accepted in lieu of penalty rates.[116] Labor leader Neville Warburton found the situation wildly hypocritical given the government's ongoing attempts to destabilise such agreements, but praised BESBRA for entering into it 'despite having the Queensland National Party Government looking over the Expo Authority's shoulder in its pursuit of the most objectionable and confrontationist industrial policies and objectives'.[117] Minnikin believes the agreement was made possible through a combination of Dempsey's desire to prove that 'the union movement could deliver outcomes without having to be confrontational', a clear intent on both sides to honour it, and a growing feeling among related organisations that Expo was 'above the politics of the day'.[118]

Another group that Expo's fortunes hinged upon – and that had received antagonistic attention from Bjelke-Petersen – was artists. Early market research showed that potential exposition audiences had little interest in the weightier themes of the bicentenary and instead expressed a strong desire for entertainment.[119] Expo organisers thus found themselves turning to an arts community overtly aware that its sponsoring government condoned police raids on music and arts venues and maintained a Queensland Literature Board of Review known for banning ninety-three publications in a year and a Films Review Board that had banned 120 films in six years; police could arrest an actor for swearing in a play, African dancers could be compelled to wear bras during Queensland performances, and Cabinet ministers such as Russ Hinze could blithely claim that the musical *Hair* (which he had not seen) catered to the 'sexually depraved, or a group of homosexuals, lesbians, wifeswappers and spivs'.[120]

Sir Edward Williams supported Expo's entertainment focus, observing (against BIE dictates) that 'the lofty motives' of early expositions had been supplanted by an economic imperative to draw large crowds through 'an expectation of entertainment, enjoyment and relaxation'.[121] Expo Entertainment Director Ric Birch was well positioned to meet those requirements. He had organised the triumphant opening and closing ceremonies of Brisbane's Commonwealth Games, and executive-produced the opening and closing ceremonies for the 1984 Los Angeles Olympic Games (he would go on to do the same for the Barcelona 1992 and Sydney 2000 Olympics). In addition to overseeing the (Burt Cooper-produced) opening and closing ceremonies for Expo, Birch directed the producers of its major entertainment venues and events:

ENTERTAINMENT DIVISION PRODUCERS (AS AT 30 APRIL 1988)	
Aquacade	Jan Muller
Amphitheatre	Mary-Clare Power
Piazza	David Hamilton
River Stage	John Watson (national and corporate days) Richard East (contemporary music)
Walkways	Barbara Absolon
Parades	Mike Mullins
Lasers	Laurie Plainer
Fireworks	Syd Howard
Queensland Performing Arts Centre	Anthony Steel (World Expo on Stage Consultant Producer with Marguerite Pepper)
Music	Barry Spanier
Water-ski	Fred Hardwick

Source: BESBRA, *World Expo 88: Entertainers' Handbook* (Brisbane: BESBRA, 1988), 21.

Piazza Producer David Hamilton says Birch had an extraordinary gift for finding 'the most unusual group of people with different talents and not worrying that there wasn't a degree behind your name'.[122] Birch did not endear himself to everyone, however. World Expo on Stage Consultant Producer Anthony Steel quipped in his autobiography that the Entertainment director was nicknamed 'rich burke' for his attitude towards all but a small creative and celebrity clique.[123] Amphitheatre Producer Mary-Clare Power recalls intimidating behaviour, and notes (as do Hamilton and River Stage Producer John Watson) that Birch was frequently away on business with his company, Spectac, which increased Barbara Absolon's workload as deputy Entertainment director.[124] 'Barb made it happen,' says Watson; 'that's the truth of it all.'[125]

Absolon demurs: 'Ric's great skill was he was a visionary – and of course he travelled all the time. So people who say, "Oh, really you did the work – Ric was never there," I go, well, you don't come up with great ideas sitting in your office. You get out there – you look at what's around – with a number of Ric's visions, we just had to go "that ain't gonna work", but certainly there might be five ideas and we could make one work.'[126]

Some of those ideas became iconic images of Expo: tap dancers on a pink submarine floating down the Brisbane River; the 2000-piece orchestra at the opening ceremony; an RAAF Hercules aircraft dropping 50,000 balloons; a ten-metre-tall, inflatable, water-skiing version of the event's platypus mascot, 'Expo Oz'; and American-influenced set-pieces such as aquacades, marching bands, water-ski shows, and parades.[127] Birch had access to dozens of celebrities, and could tap industry connections such as Molly Meldrum, Michael Gudinski, and Richard East (producer of contemporary music on the River Stage) to secure major rock acts for Expo. Minnikin conceives of Birch's contribution in terms of contacts and glamour: 'Julio Iglesias flew in with a 747 filled with the most gorgeous array of women you could imagine – flew in, did his concert, and flew out the next day. Ric pulled that off.'[128]

Many of the Entertainment Division producers are complimentary towards Sir Llew Edwards – and appreciative of his connections. Hamilton says he 'was always there if you needed him', and recalls Edwards requisitioning the army to set up tarpaulins and assist with painting when incessant rain in the countdown to Expo became a barrier to completing the Piazza floor.[129] Barbara Absolon, Anthony Steel, Marguerite Pepper, and Mary-Clare Power all remark upon their chairman's preparedness to let them operate with autonomy – and the trust that this managerial style implied.[130]

The unofficial Expo policy of 'brending' the rules was nevertheless used against BESBRA on occasion. In a state where homosexuality was still illegal, Parades producer Mike Mullins circumvented BESBRA concerns that his study visit to the Sydney Mardi Gras would provoke a homophobic reaction within the state government by claiming he was travelling to Sydney 'to meet a designer'.[131] He also 'brent the rules' in the design phase of the parades: 'From Birch I was under incredible pressure to do it the "Disney way", and I wanted to do it the Australian way.' He says that Edwards 'hated the lunchtime parade because they were all nasty insects ... he demanded I redesign the whole thing – which was impossible – it was all in pre-production'; instead, Mullins 'went to Dotdash, a local company, and got all the drawings done in a Disney style – and he [Edwards] approved those; I just went ahead with what I wanted to do – all the nasty insects just had smiles on their faces'.[132]

The Entertainment Division employed thousands of artists, providing Expo attendees with amusement options twelve hours a day, every day, for 184 days. Performance venues and experiences included the 3000-seat Aquacade (at which the comedy *Bligh's Follies* was performed), $7000 worth of fireworks released every night, designated national and corporate days for participating nations and organisations, laser displays, marching bands of up to 349 members, a lunchtime 'picnic themed' parade, an electrical evening parade, the 1000-seat Piazza (with performances ranging from folk-dancing through to orchestras, improvisational theatre, and circus), the 10,000-seat River Stage (for headlining performances), Walkways (for roving performers), and a 360-seat 'Expo Warana Amphitheatre' (featuring smaller scale music, theatre, spectacle, and dance).[133]

The organisers behind Brisbane's long-running Warana Festival (which had relocated in the 1970s to the future Clem Jones Gardens and Expo 88 site) had initially hoped to run the Entertainment Division, and were given the Amphitheatre by way of consolation by Bjelke-Petersen – and against the wishes of Birch, who reportedly regarded them as 'outsiders'.[134] Amphitheatre Producer Mary-Clare Power (who had stage-managed Warana, and who replaced Jane Atkins after the latter had difficulties with Birch) remembers that familiarity with Warana created some awkward programming situations, as there was an expectation from festival regulars – along with 'every dance school in Queensland' and 'every little Betty Ballerina and Betty Ballerina's mother' – that everyone would be booked for Expo. It was not what producers had in mind for a world-class event: 'People would come in and say, "Oh, I'm a juggler," and your head would just hit the table and bang it – because they'd stand there and they could juggle three balls – and they thought that was it. And you'd just go, "Mate – until you can juggle a chainsaw and a live kitten, don't come back."'[135]

'They were terrible,' says Production Coordinator Danny May (himself an internationally travelled performer with many years' experience). 'It was difficult at the time to convince people just how good the talent would be that would come into the country – because I'd been there.'[136] The Entertainment Division strove to deliver new experiences to audiences, which meant getting stilt-walkers to do something other than dress as Uncle Sam and which ensured tense stand-offs with local personalities such as 'Beppo the Clown', who expected an Expo booking by virtue of having been a performance fixture in Brisbane for twenty-eight years (to which Absolon responded, 'That's exactly why we *haven't* programmed you').[137]

Performers from around the world were invited to submit videos of their shows, several thousand of which were viewed by the programming team. Danny May requested that the performance reels also show the applicants engaging with an audience, as he was looking for 'love and heart'.[138] The tapes were of additional assistance to Absolon, who, inspired by the street entertainment at Vancouver's Expo 86, convinced Birch to expand her already weighty workload to include the role of Walkways producer – in which capacity she engaged roving entertainment specialists such as the Natural Theatre Company from the UK (perhaps best remembered for their flowerpot-headed 'people' and the 'businessman' striding through Expo with a leaking briefcase).[139] May says roving Walkways groups of Australian entertainers helped expose those artists to international performance standards, while helping the exposition meet tough quotas imposed by Actors Equity (as the Media, Entertainment and Arts Alliance was then known).[140]

Hamilton says the Expo imperative of booking the finest entertainers in the world caused great conflict with Actors Equity: 'They were just terrible back then – because they were worried about Australian jobs and Australian performers and all that – which I believe in because I'm part of the industry [Hamilton is a well-known puppeteer] – but, you know, you can't give jobs to people if they don't have the act.'[141] Actors Equity actions resulted in several lost programming opportunities for Expo, including the then little-known company Cirque du Soleil.[142] Hamilton found the situation incongruous, as even with the division's heavy emphasis on internationals, Expo was providing 'more work than they'd ever had in their life for Australian performers'.[143]

Absolon says the division spent 'months and months and months' negotiating with Actors Equity, 'trying to convince them that we'd be bringing in people who would then train up Australians', while endeavouring to meet unrealistic quotas from the local talent pool. Eventually, the 'brend the rules' mentality came to the fore: 'From memory, we completely defied the Actors Equity rules, because – stuff it – what have we got to lose? By the time they found out, it will be over.'[144]

Several of the exposition's creatives felt conflicted about committing to a project so closely associated with Queensland's controversial premier. Danny May was warned by Melbourne friends, 'You've come to a police state – watch your back.'[145] Parades Producer Mike Mullins (also a left-wing activist who had devised political performance pieces in Victoria) was acutely aware that 'I was going into enemy territory – which was Joh territory'.[146] Mullins's drive to Queensland when relocating for Expo (in the lead-up to the 1986 state elections) was suitably ominous: 'All along the highway into the city, there was these maps of Australia where everything was red for communists and the only green part, funnily enough, was Joh's land.'[147]

Mary-Clare Power agrees that 'with some people', Expo's connection to the Bjelke-Petersen government was 'a really big issue', but she stresses that there were many less 'socially aware' people in the Entertainment Division who 'really were just trying to put on a good show'.[148] Artists attempting to bridge the gap sometimes experienced a backlash. John Watson recalls, 'I had friends who said, "What the fuck are you doing, John? You've joined the Joh team. You've sold out."'[149] Expo's proximity to the state government was brought into sharp relief for Watson when he received a phone call that 'shocked me to my core': a well-placed person in Bjelke-Petersen's network issued the directive, 'There will be no Aboriginal performers programmed at Expo. Are we clear?'[150]

As a key bicentennial event, Expo was vulnerable to criticisms of its role in commemorating 'the day when the festering vileness of England was first cast ashore to putrefy upon the coasts of New South Wales'.[151] Indigenous singer-songwriter Kevin Carmody encapsulated some bicentennial objections when insisting any festivities be preceded by:

> resolving the questions of our sovereignty, self-determination and self-management … Before White Australia begins to assemble for a piece of the celebration cake it should note that the chief ingredient is blood, our blood, and it will leave an indelible and bitter stain.[152]

The executive officer of FAIRA, Bob Weatherall, equated Aboriginal participation in bicentennial activities with 'asking the Jewish community to celebrate the holocaust', and insisted that involvement in Expo would imply support for 'the fascist regime of Joh Bjelke-Petersen' that 'continually denied Aboriginal people ... basic human rights'.[153]

Weatherall says he and his peers also had more spiritual reservations about Expo: 'There were other issues there in regard to ancestral remains on the South Bank at the same time. People didn't want people going in there around where the ancestors were, because they believe there could have been dangerous things happen; there could have been a catastrophe.'[154]

Queensland state government injustices relating to Aboriginal people did not abate in the years leading up to Expo; one of its most controversial initiatives during this period was the *Queensland Coast Islands Declaratory Act 1985*, which sought to retrospectively abolish native title rights. BESBRA made several attempts to disassociate Expo from the state government's racist paternalism, and Edwards sought the input and support of Aboriginal leaders such as Don Davidson (president of the Aboriginal and Islander Legal Service) in the planning phase – although Weatherall later disputed the legitimacy of this support, claiming in 1988 that Edwards lacked the knowledge to discern which Aboriginal representatives he should be dealing with.[155] Edwards countered that an Aboriginal liaison committee was established to negotiate with BESBRA in 1986 and that he had 'no intention' of listening to a new spokesman who appeared 'out of the blue.'[156]

Relations reached an appalling low in November 1987 when Minister for State Prisons Don Neal decided to reopen the underground cell block known as the 'Black Hole' at Boggo Road jail (declared inhumane and closed by previous Minister for State Prisons Geoff Muntz in 1984) specifically to hold Aboriginal Expo protesters.[157] Neal had lamentable timing as well as appalling judgement, as the news broke just before the Royal Commission into

Aboriginal Deaths in Custody commenced in Canberra – prompting Labor's Neville Warburton to ask, 'Is it to be assumed that, while the rest of Australia seeks an answer to the alarming problems of Aboriginal deaths in custody, this Government is set to throw Aborigines indefinitely into unlit, unventilated cells?'[158] Edwards swiftly distanced BESBRA from the controversy, declaring himself 'distressed' and 'absolutely amazed' by it, and calling upon the government to reverse the decision.[159]

Relations disintegrated further in March 1988 when the police shooting of an Aboriginal man mistakenly thought to be in possession of a gun prompted Don Davidson to warn of a 'bloodbath' if police acted in a similar fashion during Aboriginal Expo protests. He also warned of extreme racial tensions in the lead-up to Expo: 'The signs are already going up around Woolloongabba here "kill a nigger for Expo" and I've heard black fellows saying the (hanging) rope should be brought back for coppers.'[160]

There was considerable division within the Aboriginal community over whether Expo could – or should – be differentiated from other bicentennial events. Weatherall insisted, 'Aboriginal culture hasn't died' and 'we don't have to prove that to the rest of the world' or 'to white people, and we don't have to get their endorsement.'[161] Poet and playwright Oodgeroo Noonuccal (who had changed her name from Kath Walker to her tribal name prior to the bicentennial in protest at '200 years of neglect') believed that participation presented her people with a unique opportunity for international exposure.[162] Over 800 Aboriginal groups and individuals were consulted in the making of the Dreamtime Theatre for the Australian Pavilion at Expo, which featured *The Rainbow Serpent* (co-scripted by Noonuccal and her son, Kabul) as its centrepiece.[163]

Noonuccal's participation was not without frustration: at a press conference to promote the production, she was asked the meaning of the rainbow serpent, to which she responded, 'This is not a surprising question you ask me – because I'd say that eighty-five per cent of the Australian people would ask the same question – because after

200 years they haven't even bothered to find out about our beautiful spiritual way of life.'[164]

In an interview nearly thirty years after first stating his position on Aboriginal participation at Expo, Weatherall offers an insight into the thinking behind it: 'Our view at that particular time – the people and communities – was that we didn't want to be looked upon as being hypocritical. One minute we're trying to expose the government and what have you … so if we took on what Oodgeroo was doing – and some other artists who believed that a message could be brought through their artistic ability – then *our* message – that Aboriginal people didn't have basic rights and freedoms – could get lost.'[165]

Minnikin says the National Party minister for Aboriginal Affairs, Bob Katter, 'pushed very hard' for Aboriginal inclusion at Expo.[166] Katter organised artefact sales and demonstrations of traditional Aboriginal activities such as rock-flaking, corroborees, fire-making, and spear-throwing, and said he could name 'half a dozen' businessmen of Aboriginal descent who expected to profit from Expo – though such participation, as noted by essayist Ian Gill, 'if not token, certainly won't qualify it as an Aboriginal event'.[167]

Key figures within Expo's Entertainment Division also worked behind the scenes to increase Aboriginal representation. Mike Mullins secretly incorporated the Aboriginal flag into the eyes of a model of the sun (harnessed to a performer) that led the Expo parade every day.[168] John Watson strategically defied the disgraceful instruction he had been given about Aboriginal performers: 'Being a dangerous leftie, I thought, "Well, I'll just bide my time on this" … and as soon as I could see the writing on the wall [the beleaguerment of the Bjelke-Petersen government], I began programming Aboriginal entertainment.'[169] David Hamilton convinced BESBRA to let Circus Oz fly the Aboriginal flag during their performances as a political statement.[170] Circus Oz performer Anni Davey says the show contained overt political statements in the form of the 'Bicentennial Rap', and concluded with an appeal for Aboriginal land rights.[171] The piece was written and performed by Guy Hooper (accompanied on stage by a clowning Stephen Burton with frequent interruptions by the 'Bicentennial inspector for gasbagging and self-congratulation', played by Matt Hughes). The inclusion of the 'Bicentennial Rap' in Expo 88 festivities marks a stunning departure from the constraints on expression under Bjelke-Petersen (see appendix for the lyrics).[172]

Hamilton says that Edwards, Minnikin, and Birch had initial reservations about programming Circus Oz, as its performers were 'known for their collective politics', but that those concerns were dispelled once the company took to the Expo stage: 'the Rap was fantastic and nobody complained as Circus Oz was just so well received – so much so the Chairman requested I get them back for the last week of closing celebrations'.[173]

Another complication for BESBRA was the Queensland Government's fraught relations with the Commonwealth and other Australian states. Edwards and Minnikin had the considerable task of communicating messages of collegiality and togetherness while Queensland's high-profile premier was at his belligerent best. Attempts to coax additional Expo funding from the Commonwealth continued to be resisted by Federal Minister John Brown, who said it had already spent more on the exposition than intended, including hosting and security responsibilities and a $3 million grant (federal expenses would eventually expand to include $400,000 towards overseas promotion, $600,000 towards interstate participation, and $2,030,000 towards the participation of developing countries); Brown added that the Commonwealth had bicentennial funding obligations in other states to which it must tend, and that BESBRA would be in less need of financial assistance if the Queensland Government had guaranteed low-interest rates on its loans.[174] Bjelke-Petersen was characteristically rambunctious in his reply, accusing the Commonwealth of expecting credit for Expo while 'sitting back like a jibbing horse in the breeching letting everybody else pull it along', suggesting it had imperilled Brisbane's chance to host the 1992 Olympic Games (by declining to fund a permanent

Queensland–Australia pavilion that could be converted into a media centre for that event), and declaring, 'I'm only sorry that Canberra is prepared to sell Australia short.'[175]

Vintage Bjelke-Petersen vitriol was also dispensed to the states, each of which had declined to commit to the exposition – forcing BESBRA to issue a series of increasingly embarrassing deadline extensions. Responses were generally dismissive and mundane: Premier Brian Burke claimed Western Australia needed no further exposure after the success of the Grand Prix and the America's Cup, NSW premier Barrie Unsworth said the money would be better spent on the Darling Harbour redevelopment, Victorian premier John Cain found the proposal from Bjelke-Petersen 'very unattractive', and Premier John Bannon of South Australia (the first state to formally reply to the Expo invitation – two years after it had been issued) said, 'There are better ways of spending our money.'[176] Bjelke-Petersen accused them of refusing to 'help Queensland look good', and of 'playing politics' because the event was being hosted by a non-Labor state. 'I've already told South Australia I'm sorry they're so poverty-stricken, and too poor to come,' he said, while insisting that the states' collective absence would not affect the event: 'They'll be the losers.'[177]

'The states didn't want to come into "Joh's country", as they called it,' says Sir Llew Edwards.[178] This was problematic, given that Edwards hoped to court international participants with an assurance that all Australian states and territories would be present. 'It's not a Queensland event, it's an Australian event,' Edwards told *The Weekend Australian Magazine* in June 1986, while conceding, 'I think the Queensland Government sees it as something that will be a political winner.'[179] His interviewer suggested Expo could 'out-dazzle' Wran's Darling Harbour redevelopment and make Brisbane 'the place to be in 1988' – if it could shed its image as a 'Joh Show'.[180] This prospect was not aided by the premier's bellicose omnipresence, or by protocol breaches in Expo publicity materials in which Bjelke-Petersen's image preceded – and dwarfed – that of Prime Minister Bob Hawke.[181]

The states' recalcitrance drew criticism from ABA Chairman Jim Kirk (John Reid's successor), who said, 'No doubt it is political.'[182] Bob Hawke assured Edwards he would 'put a rocket up' the states, and said he risked 'personal embarrassment' if they refused to participate.[183] Some Queensland Labor representatives also attempted to assist the exposition, with Opposition Leader Neville Warburton telling interstate colleagues, 'Don't listen to this guy [Bjelke-Petersen], he doesn't talk for the people of Queensland.'[184] The premier and his allies had cause to feel differently: Bjelke-Petersen had become so synonymous with the National Party – and its success – by the early 1980s that posters for the 1983 state election featured just his portrait with the words 'Joh' and 'Queensland'.[185]

(Dirty) Business as Usual

Bjelke-Petersen, the National Party, and Police Commissioner Terry Lewis continued to exhibit Teflon-like qualities in response to corruption allegations. Following the publication of an article on male prostitution by Tony Koch in *The Courier-Mail*, Des Sturgess (a member of the 1977 Lucas Inquiry, who had become director of prosecutions) released a report in 1985 on sexual offences against children, in which he found an alarming incidence of minors being lured to work in brothels, identified key figures behind illegal casinos and prostitution, and noted that they were curiously free from punishment.[186] Sturgess believed the situation 'smacked of organised illegality', and wrote to Attorney-General Neville Harper to inform him that the Licensing Branch remained in the control of suspect police, against the recommendations of the Lucas Inquiry; the branch was headed by Allen Bulger, who pleaded guilty to perjury and official corruption in the aftermath of the Fitzgerald Inquiry.[187]

The National Party's exit from the Coalition seemed to streamline certain aspects of corruption, as there were fewer checks and balances on the government. Political scientist Paul Reynolds observes that between 1983 and 1987, increasing numbers of 'businesspeople, politicians, judges, senior public servants and high-ranking police officers judged it expedient to gravitate towards Bjelke-Petersen's circle, thereby predicating their continuing political and personal fortunes upon his maintenance of power', and creating a situation in which the premier was 'increasingly influenced by informant "courtiers"'.[188]

One of the most notorious of these was 'Top-Level Ted', Sir Edward Lyons, described by Labor's Bob Gibbs as having an 'unnatural, almost demon-like influence over the Premier'.[189] Lyons reportedly endeared himself to Bjelke-Petersen by writing him a series of flattering letters and lingering near his office to facilitate 'chance' encounters.[190] By 1978, Lyons had been knighted and made a National Party trustee, and his influence was on a par with that of Sparkes.[191] Lyons leveraged this to be appointed chairman of the Queensland TAB (over objections from Edwards, who favoured Sir Gordon Chalk), where he doubled his salary, betted illegally on credit, and pressured the board to invest millions in the suspect operations of Rothwells investment bank (of which he was also chairman) and to buy a building from another company of which he had been chairman.[192] He also attempted to use his influence to have a drink-driving charge dropped (reportedly with the aid of Terry Lewis), and convinced Cabinet to grant East–West Airlines (of which he was chairman) freehold title to land on Lindeman Island – including two-thirds of the national park – which drew resistance from Sparkes and Queensland National Party vice president Charles Holm, resulting in the proposal being withdrawn.[193] In addition, Lyons was a director of Kaldeal Pty Ltd, a private company that accepted donations for Bjelke-Petersen's various campaigns (including a 1987 attempt to oust Sparkes as party president), and that seemed to play a role in the attainment of government contracts for donors.[194]

The *Today Tonight* team broke the story of the TAB scandal on Channel Nine – despite Lyons being deputy chairman of Nine's local board and attempting to have the segment pulled.[195] Lyons was also accused of offering $250,000 in government contracts to *Today Tonight* producers to withhold a 1983 segment criticising Bjelke-Petersen's business dealings.[196] The report claimed a Singapore bank had been pressured to provide a loan for Ciasom Pty Ltd (a trustee company for Bjelke-Petersen) for a property managed by the premier's son. The bank's representative told his superiors there was insufficient information to assess the loan, but that failure to do so 'would affect negatively our business in this state', and that 'we think we have to go along as this would open up further avenues in Queensland. I am told we will always be approached first for Queensland Government and semi-Government finance requirements.'[197]

When the allegations aired, Bjelke-Petersen responded with a writ that was not expected to be successful. Two years later, new station owner Alan Bond controversially settled it for $400,000 – ten times the highest possible jury award for defamation in the state.[198] When *Today Tonight* broke that story as well, Bond terminated the program's contract.[199] He later confessed to Jana Wendt on *A Current Affair* that Bjelke-Petersen 'made it under no doubt' that the writ had to be settled 'if we were to continue to do business in Queensland'.[200]

The wealth available to Bjelke-Petersen's courtiers was evident in flourishes such as Rolls-Royce limousines favoured by Lyons and Sir Fred Maybury, and the Robin Gibson-designed home of Terry Lewis; the premier's preferred luxury vehicle was a Jaguar limousine.[201] Political scientist Rae Wear notes that the boundaries between public and private finances had blurred, with extravagant government office parties billed to the public, and Cabinet ministers receiving a wide range of goods and services as a matter of course.[202] The boundaries also blurred for Bjelke-Petersen allies such as Allen Callaghan and his wife, Judith, who were found in 1985 to have misappropriated significant government funds in pursuit of luxurious goods and personal pleasure – which also raised questions about government accountability and public service audits.[203]

In 1986, Queensland Government policy experts Roger Scott, Peter Coaldrake, Brian Head, and Paul Reynolds wrote that 'the Queensland parliament has become a steadily less well-equipped and increasingly impotent and irrelevant institution. The parliament still legitimates government activity, but as a watchdog over that activity it has become absurdly tame.'[204] Corrupt behaviour linked to the National Party was so prolific prior to the 1986 election that National Party trustee Sir Roderick Proctor (who revealed to reporter Quentin Dempster that he had essentially purchased his knighthood from Bjelke-Petersen with a donation of $100,000) felt compelled to address it on the ABC's *Carleton-Walsh Report*, where he accused the state government of cronyism and making 'a charade' of public tendering.[205]

Police corruption also proceeded apace, with protection fees from prostitution and casinos netting an estimated $1.2 million annually in the mid-1980s.[206] While police were engaging in carnal congress at parties thrown for them by brothel owners, Bjelke-Petersen and his more conservative ministers rejected a parliamentary select committee recommendation (led by Ahern) that sex education be taught in schools, and ordered that condom vending machines be torn from the walls of university toilets (at the height of the AIDS crisis).[207] Corruption within the state was so prevalent that journalist Evan Whitton began the preface to his book *Can of Worms: A Citizen's Reference Book to Crime and the Administration of Justice* (first published in 1986) with the sentence: 'It has been said, and not entirely in jest, that Sydney is the most corrupt city in the western world, except of course for Newark, New Jersey, and Brisbane, Queensland.'[208]

Honours amassed by Terry Lewis while corruption thrived included an OBE in 1979, Father of the Year in 1980, and a knighthood in 1986.[209] Bjelke-Petersen received his knighthood in 1984, and an honorary doctorate from UQ in 1985 (against the wishes of many students and staff).[210]

Much to the dismay of the Liberals, the National Party continued to present itself as a good business leader and economic manager – despite evidence of cronyism, high levels of public debt, higher-than-average unemployment, and lower-than-average income in the state.[211] There was little substance to the government-sanctioned boast that Queensland was the 'low-tax state' (a claim linked to the abolition of death taxes, which, until implemented at a national level, prompted a surge of interstate retirees to the Gold Coast that caused the city to be dubbed 'God's Waiting Room'); costs simply shifted to constituents through other measures, such as the highest electricity and car registration fees in Australia.[212]

Joh for Canberra

With the aid of a stealthy 1985 redistribution, the National Party materialised enough safe seats to win the November 1986 state election in its own right – nullifying Bjelke-Petersen's threat to hold another election if he wasn't satisfied with the result.[213] The Liberal Party's failure to return to Coalition government prompted the resignation of Sir William Knox (who had succeeded Terry White as leader) and was received as a dark portent for Federal Opposition Leader John Howard's election chances, with one reporter musing, 'The voters have shown they won't accept a boring little turd as leader and Bill Knox is just an older Johnny Howard.'[214] In jubilant scenes after the 1986 election, Alan Jones (former football coach, speechwriter for Malcolm Fraser, and radio commentator) praised Bjelke-Petersen as a man who 'gets things done', declaring, 'Look out Canberra. Here he comes. Joh is saying the things people want to hear.'[215]

Some people were also saying things Bjelke-Petersen wanted to hear. Gold Coast entrepreneurs Brian Ray (an associate of Kerry Packer) and Mike Gore (a white shoe developer who parlayed access to the premier into permission to build his Sanctuary Cove resort in the face of local council objections, and then secured an unorthodox government loan of $10.16 million when that development was in disarray) were in the vanguard of 'courtiers' encouraging

Bjelke-Petersen to extend his political career into the federal arena.[216] In a surreal interview for *The Sydney Morning Herald*, Gore detailed a scenario in which Bjelke-Petersen replaced Federal National Party Leader Ian Sinclair, defeated the (unpopular at the time) Hawke government, became prime minister at age seventy-seven (with John Howard as deputy), and then stepped aside for Andrew Peacock (who would defect to the National Party) in 1990.[217]

The capacity for delusion fuelling such speculation presumably also allowed Bjelke-Petersen's advisers to ignore the untransferable nature of his state-based political advantages, such as the electoral malamander, weak Opposition, and parochial populism. There was speculation that the move was actually an initiative of Russ Hinze, who fancied himself a contender for the position of premier.[218] The 'Joh for PM for Australia's sake' (later the marginally less ambitious 'Joh for Canberra') campaign was launched in February 1987 with the lukewarm support of Sparkes, who was reportedly appalled by the situation.[219]

There followed a divisive campaign in which Howard and Sinclair were undermined by Queensland's Federal National Party MPs withdrawing from the Coalition – which was damaging to the electoral chances of all.[220] A *Sunday Sun* article warned that it 'would be better if Premier Sir Joh Bjelke-Petersen was not devoting so much of his time to his Canberra ambitions', and linked the campaign's 'wishful thinking' to the perceived failings of BESBRA – while warning that both camps needed to face 'reality'.[221]

A Confluence of Critics

In addition to negative coverage on social and political aspects of Expo, BESBRA endured multitudinous critiques on more prosaic matters, such as the Leo Burnett logo design (a globe and two boomerangs placed back to back – which, it transpired, was an insult in Aboriginal culture); Walt Disney Enterprises' early mascot concept ('an unfortunate chubby dingo'); its later design, Expo Oz ('a hairy Donald duck'); the sunshade structures ('the result of the mating of the Sydney Opera House with a circus big top'); and suggestions the proposed $100 cost for a family of four to attend the event was too high.[222] Sir Llew Edwards replied to this last charge with strained candour:

> There is no doubt there will be a few people who will not be able to come. Similarly, there are people who can't afford to eat fillet steak and have to make do with sausages ... It saddens me but it is a fact of life.[223]

As early as March 1985, the fog of negativity had so obscured any positive aspects of the event that there were rumours 'senior State Government figures' would terminate Expo unless fifteen countries had committed to it by September, and that key BESBRA board members were preparing to oust Edwards.[224] This troubled period also saw Cassidy Management released from its marketing contract, the attempted removal of Williams, and Sir Frank Moore's resignation from the BESBRA board (which may have been motivated by a desire to avoid a direct conflict-of-interest scenario in relation to his site redevelopment ambitions).[225] Minnikin claimed the move to replace Edwards was aborted when it was established that BESBRA was actually in a reasonable position.[226] Goldston says much of the media coverage on the exposition's presumed failures merely demonstrated an ignorance of event milestones – and that the supposedly poor interstate attendance estimates being quoted were twice what BESBRA was predicting, which inspired him to take 'a major decision that my wife praises me for ... I said we're going to double the women's toilets. That decision was made on the basis of a newspaper poll that said Expo was a failure.'[227]

'You expect it at the beginning,' said Edwards, in a 1986 interview, of the exposition's capacity to attract criticism, 'but when you have proved what an exceptional event it is going to be, you do think they should stop.'[228]

Carol Lloyd was joint creative director (with Garrett Russell) at George Patterson Advertising when the firm secured the Expo account. Lloyd was no stranger to Queensland political characters. As frontwoman for the iconic 1970s rock-blues outfit Railroad Gin (and arguably the first woman to front a successful Australian rock band), she had given a number of concerts at UQ: 'All the big Labor boys were students, and they'd be sitting cross-legged in the refec making quite extraordinary comments – Peter Beattie and all those boys, they were kids. They'd be sitting there in their hair and their moustache, [calling] "Show us your tits".'[229]

Lloyd recalls one performance at Mayne Hall being interrupted by police sirens as vehicles with flashing blue lights disgorged 'this bunch of students masquerading as police', demanding the show be shut down so they could address the captive audience; the fake police were led 'by a very fuzzy-haired man with a fuzzy voice; his name was Wayne Goss.'[230]

None of Lloyd's encounters with Queensland political aspirants prepared her for Bjelke-Petersen. Her introduction to the premier was at once highly – and not remotely – informative: 'I remember I had to go and pitch to Joh – the first creative meeting [for Expo]. It was just me and him. I fronted up to the executive building up in the lift, and through security and all that stuff, and I get ushered in, and Joh's sitting behind his desk: "Come in, come in." I didn't even get to open the folder. He rambled off about what he was going to do on the weekend and how he's put this new tree in and it's really lovely and the chooks love it, and "Why don't you come up, yes come on up – look, Flo will be quite happy with that – and you come up and visit us all right?"'[231]

'Mad as a cut snake', says Lloyd of Bjelke-Petersen. She deflected the premier's Kingaroy overture, but could not avoid wondering what she had got herself into.[232]

BESBRA created a Communications Division in 1986 to address

low national and international awareness of the event, along with poor media reports. Absolon recalls, 'I was very aware through the Communication Department that Jane ended up running that there was just a big black hole in the interstate media ... back in those days, anything in Brisbane was just considered parochial – and what point of interest could that *possibly be* to people interstate?'[233]

From mid-1986 to mid-1987, interstate ambivalence evaporated – to BESBRA's detriment – when the national media feasted on another vexed period for the event. In the *Time* magazine piece 'Expo Exposed', by Queensland Newspapers editor-in-chief Harry Gordon, ex–International Participation director Greg Lund (who had been fired by Edwards, and who was an associate of Gordon's) criticised the Commonwealth for its lack of support for Expo, and BESBRA for failing to effectively market the event internationally – accusing the management of having 'no idea what they were getting themselves into when they took on Expo'.[234] The piece critiqued the limited international promotion budget allocated for the event, which was based on 1983 research suggesting there would be a poor return on investment, as sixty-five per cent of visits would come from Brisbane; Gordon claimed this failed to anticipate the international success of *Crocodile Dundee* and the 'Paul Hogan shrimp-on-barbie ads', or 'terrorism in Europe and the Middle East, the shrunken Australian dollar and intense six-way airline competition across the Pacific' – and that it ignored the essential fact that Expo was supposed to be an international event.[235]

Lund also aired his grievances on national television over several *7:30 Report* segments after his dismissal in May 1987. The program cited a 'long list of former employees' associated with a stream of bad publicity that was 'putting the ex in Expo'.[236] Documents leaked to the program indicated strong international concern with the direction of the event: a Foreign Affairs report from November 1986 stated that Canadian and British representatives were 'aware of our internal problems' and urged resolution 'in the interests of the success of Expo'; a communication from Ian Fraser, commissioner-general of the New Zealand Pavilion, in February 1987 warned, 'We are far from confident that Expo will achieve its projected visitor numbers', and threatened 'a token commitment' from his country; BIE delegate Marcel Galopin stated in January 1987 that Expo promotion, publicity, and financial matters 'haven't been taken on in a satisfactory way'.[237]

A leaked BESBRA internal report marked 'read and destroy' offered a dire assessment of the exposition's prospects: 'There are no theme pavilions or plazas. Few, if any, newsworthy phenomena. No Eiffel Tower monumentality. No firsts. No startling curiosities.'[238] The report's author, Ron Woodall, had been creative director of Vancouver's popular 1986 world exposition. He came to the attention of key BESBRA members during their fact-finding tour of the Canadian event, and was invited to assess Expo's strengths and weaknesses.

Goldston recalls his excellent – somewhat brutal – advice: 'Ron said to me, "What you've got to remember about these expos is that the pavilions are boring. They're all just bloody travelogues. If you saw 'em on television, you'd change the channel. What you've gotta do is you've gotta cut 'em up in the aisles." And what he meant by that was you've got to have quirky streetscaping and lots and lots of street entertainment. And you've got to do something to entertain the people outside the pavilions. He said, "You gotta sack the architects at a certain stage and you gotta get people from the movies in."'[239]

Absolon believes Woodall 'might have been a bit jaded' by this time, as when she and her fellow Expo organisers visited Vancouver in 1986, the pavilions 'blew our minds'.[240] Nevertheless, Woodall's 1987 report warned there was no 'cohesive essence' for Expo and that a 'rescue mission' was required in the form of 'a crack creative team' and a large injection of funding and content. A separate leaked document linked to Woodall nominated John Truscott (an Australian actor, designer, and artistic director, and two-time Academy Award winner for art direction and costume design on *Camelot*) as Expo's arts saviour, and suggested that the services of elite designer Ken Cato could be secured if Truscott was 'on board'.[241]

Woodall and Minnikin appeared on the *7:30 Report* to address the leaks and concerns raised by Lund. Woodall said his assessment of Expo was very critical as his task had been to play 'devil's advocate', but insisted that even if his recommendations were ignored, there was no need for concern: 'Brisbane's Expo is a virtual no-lose situation. This is a city that gets kind of quiet at 4:30 in the afternoon. I think that for 180 days [*sic*] you're going to have lights across the river. You're going to have music. You're going to have a place to go that's going to be fun. I think the city will respond to it. I think if Expo did nothing more, it would be a success.'[242]

Edwards declined to comment on Lund's sacking when he appeared on the show, but said the leaks were 'ill-informed' and that the treatment of BESBRA was unfair: 'It's about time the people of Queensland and Australia and the media recognised this is one of the most complex tasks that any Authority in Australia has ever undertaken ... let me assure you that 396 days from today there will be many people seeking credit for the most successful event in Australia's history.'[243]

Goldston says Lund was released from Expo for leaking stories and 'internal turf wars' – behaviour counter to the expectations of fealty within BESBRA.[244] Minnikin assured *7:30 Report* viewers that BESBRA accepted Woodall's recommendations and had sourced additional funds (courtesy of the Queensland Treasury) for entertainment, streetscaping, and theming.[245] A creative team headed by Truscott was duly appointed. He commissioned such iconic Expo features as the eighty-eight-metre-high 'Night Companion' (aka the 'Sky Tower', aka the 'Skyneedle', aka the 'Stefan Needle'), the playful 'Human Factor' sculptures, glass-pyramid-encased animatronic robots positioned at the entry gates, and hundreds of engaging artworks and novelties strategically placed around the site.[246] 'He lived and breathed it,' says Hamilton of Truscott; 'it practically killed him.' (Truscott died five years after the exposition, age fifty-seven.)[247]

Absolon recalls that his exacting standards encompassed million-dollar installations and the minutiae of sticky tape: 'John Truscott said, "We must never see a sign up at Expo – even if it's a temporary sign for an hour that's stuck up with sticky tape." Everything just had to be professional, and that's stuck with me to this day. Those sort of things – it lifts the quality – it lifts the expectations – it lifts everything.'[248]

Truscott's dislike of signage frequently brought him into conflict with BESBRA – especially when the signage was for big sponsors. 'He was an unbelievable character,' says Edwards. 'Some used to say John was mad, bad, and indifferent – but he would ring me up and call me unbelievable names.'[249] Goldston recalls that when the Marketing Division accepted a Telstra (then Telecom) proposal to float mini-balloons, including logos, over information screens at Expo, Truscott stormed into Edwards's office, leapt onto the desk, raised his hand in the air and said, 'I put a curse on this site! If you don't remove them, I curse this site!'[250] That same day, the exposition's purportedly cyclone-proof $6 million shade complex was shredded in a rare 'black roll-cloud storm', causing an estimated $250,000 worth of damage.[251]

Minnikin says that Truscott won most of his battles with the Marketing Division, as he had 'the best contacts book of anybody I've ever known. He was unbelievable – particularly in the entertainment field ... Jack Warner was a producer on that [the film *Camelot*, for which Truscott won his Academy Awards], so Truscott came from that era'.[252] Minnikin recalls 'a hell of an argument' between Truscott and representatives from British Petroleum (BP) who insisted that large corporate signage appear on the site: 'The next day, Truscott said, "It'll all be fixed tomorrow." I said, "How do you bloody know that? Those guys were adamant." And sure enough, the next day the guys from BP came back in – tail between their legs – and said, "Yeah, we accept your proposal." I said, "How the bloody hell did you pull that off?" He said, "I know Lord-so-and-so who's the chairman of BP. One phone call to him last night and I got it fixed."'[253]

Goldston says Truscott had a gift for extracting budget increases from the BESBRA board – quite a feat, as it included Coordinator-General Sir Sydney Schubert and Under Treasurer Sir Leo Hielscher: 'I knew they were both real hard guys – they were Joh's enforcers. Joh would waffle on, and they would get things done. And Leo in particular as under treasurer was a demon on money.'[254] Goldston says the site-scaping budget was gradually increased from less than $10 million to $45 million largely as a result of Truscott's dynamic presentations to the board: 'Hielscher was entranced – he said, "Yes, spend the money" – Truscott was incredible. A quantum leap different from other people that I've ever met.'[255]

Minnikin recalls considerable rivalry between Truscott and Birch – 'very talented guys, completely different ends of the spectrum' – and says Birch successfully campaigned to keep the entertainment budget on a par with that of site-scaping (and vice versa).[256] Amphitheatre Producer Mary-Clare Power remembers talking with Barbara Absolon about the resources available to Expo years after the event's conclusion: 'Barb said to me one day, "Love, we'll never have a budget like that again to do anything," and she was absolutely right.'[257]

Absolon says the creative budget's exponential growth required a fundamental shift in the board's perception of entertainment: 'There is a story that I tell – I heard part of it second-hand, but I fully believe it – the original budget for entertainment was $8 million. And we got that up to $45 million – part of it before Expo, through Ric's persuasiveness, et cetera, but then during Expo – when the Authority saw the value of the entertainment program. But the story that I heard was at the board meeting: before Expo, the entertainment budget in most organisations meant the chairman and directors and general manager, or whatever, taking people out to lunch – back in the eighties – when you never ate without drinking and all that sort of stuff. When the entertainment budget was $8 million, one of the board looked at it and said, "Eight million dollars? How many fucking lunches are they gonna have?"'[258]

When asked to confirm this story (and his suspected centrality to it), Hielscher grins mischievously and says, 'I cannot recall the details.'[259] The situation at the time was more grim. A sharp rise in interest rates caused interest on BESBRA's loan to rise from twelve to twenty per cent, because the government had not guaranteed the low rate.[260] 'We were up to a billion dollars,' says Hielscher; 'that's a big overdraft.'[261] Lack of expected financial support from the Commonwealth and the private sector had forced BESBRA to seek private bank loans to replace the Treasury loans in 1986 – and prompted Hielscher to take some financial risks: 'We borrowed – temporarily – we borrowed in yen, for example, and didn't convert it to Aussie dollars. It was cheap money, but if you lose your value, you pay dearly for it. It's the only time I've ever done it. Whenever we borrow now – or even then – we always swap it into Australian dollars: we don't take any currency risk.'[262]

Academic Peter Carroll noted that some of BESBRA's currency experiments were unsuccessful, including the decision to move the debt into US dollars in the expectation that it would appreciate before being switched back into Australian currency – which resulted in significant losses when the manoeuvre was undone by the 1987 stock market crash.[263]

Hielscher reveals some Expo debts were ameliorated through unconventional measures, such as accommodating the chairman of Credit Suisse (with which the debt was so significant that 0.1 per cent of it 'was a lot of money') and his echelon on the Gold Coast during Expo, and escorting them to the event by hovercraft. They were also given access to a dining room otherwise reserved for the Queen and taken to the Great Barrier Reef for a sightseeing tour on the premier's jet: 'The next day, it [the interest rate on the loan] was a quarter of a per cent less.'[264]

BESBRA's massive funding injection and the commensurate flurry of activity seemed to placate international participants. A few months after Lund's allegations aired on the *7:30 Report*, New Zealand commissioner-general Ian Fraser (also vice president of the Steering Committee of the International Commissioners-General) declared himself astonished by the relentlessly grim exposition portrayals in the media – while blithely ignoring his own cameo appearance in this – and insisted that 'all we countries recognise Expo is going to be a knockout, not that that is thought in Australia'.[265]

All that remained was to convince nearly everybody else.

5

We'll Show the World

From the local community that didn't want the site there,
out in ripples to the general sort of Brisbane community that
just thought it was nonsense, and then out around the rest
of Queensland – you know – 'why should we be spending
money in Brisbane when it should be in Rocky or Cairns or
whatever', and then, of course, the rest of Australia and the
rest of the world – I think we all got a bit angry. Here was this
thing which had a lot of opportunities for a lot of people – and
the more you learned about it the more you thought it would
be a great catalyst for Brisbane – and it just began to annoy a
lot of us that when you'd go to Sydney and Melbourne to talk
to the media, you had to step across the barbed wire of 'Oh,
it's Queensland' and 'Oh, it's Joh' and 'Oh, it's Brisbane and
what a dump' and 'It'll never work' ... and so it was a sort of a
motivating and energising feeling – we just thought, 'Well, to
hell with this.'

Lady Jane Edwards[1]

AT THE HEIGHT OF THE Expo lows, Sir Llew Edwards says he
took comfort in a letter he had received from the chairman of the
1986 Vancouver exposition that urged him to persevere; it also

warned him that there would be a period when he would wish he had 'never heard of Expo'.[2] The Vancouver exposition had been plagued by criticism, including jests that it was a 'McExpo' (a reference to the event's sponsor, McDonald's, and the perceived business focus of its organisers).[3] Setbacks were so frequent, Vancouver's exposition authority recommended the event be cancelled just fourteen months before it was due to open.[4] Some of its major pavilions were also confounded by historical events: the US space program display had to be updated with a tribute to the crew of the *Challenger* after the space-shuttle disaster, and the Soviet Pavilion closed a tribute to Kiev (which focused on that city's perennial ability to rise from ruins) when the Chernobyl disaster occurred two days before the exposition opened (the radioactive detritus of the tragedy 'drifted over the North Pole in time to settle on the first week's festivities').[5]

Edwards says the Vancouver chairman's letter helped him withstand the period of leaks, firings, resignations, terminated contracts, and attempted coups against himself and key staff, but that the onslaught had a dispiriting effect on the managerial team – many of whom were working eighty- to a-hundred-hour weeks: 'There were times when we felt it wasn't worthwhile to work so hard with so little positive response ... but we stuck to our strategy.'[6] That strategy was 'like a massive, massive election campaign', he says. 'I was very lucky – I'd worked with politicians a lot. We understood the need to go in at the grass roots.'[7]

The Communications Division's formidable efforts encompassed a Speakers Bureau (in which speeches were delivered throughout Australia by Toastmasters and ITC), a Preview Centre (a sixty-six-seat theatre, video facilities, and a model of the Expo site to inform and impress representatives from travel agencies; government agencies; and business, community, and school groups), an Education Programme (including student booklets, schools updates, and essay competitions), and regular publications such as *Travel Industry Update, School Students' Update, Community Connections, Corporate News Update, Government News Update, Club 88* (for the exclusive business club of the same name located at the top of Expo House, with a joining fee of $5000 for individuals or $8000 for corporations), *Neighbourhood News* (delivered to 7200 residents in suburbs surrounding the Expo site), and *Entertainment Update* (distributed to national and international entertainment writers).[8]

The division also produced brochures, souvenir guides, press releases, and videos; provided media facilities for television, press, and radio; organised direct marketing promotions such as 'Expo Invites the World' and 'Queensland Invites Australia' (competitions that encouraged people to invite overseas or interstate relatives to the event); and coordinated public relations activities such as Expo Oz appearances, the launch of Expo uniforms (designed by Prue Acton), theme weeks, occasions such as '500 days to go', and even the release of Expo car number plates.[9]

The Marketing Division focused on advertising, sales promotion, travel marketing, and corporate participation. Expo proved more successful than many other bicentennial events at attracting corporate sponsorship, with signings including IBM, Qantas, Cadbury, Australia Post, Australian Airlines, and SGIO Building Society.[10] The Marketing and Communications divisions were ably assisted by Expo's television partner, TVO. The O-TEN network agreement with Expo was signed by the station's owner, entrepreneur Christopher Skase (whose previous dealings with the state government included obtaining permission to build his Mirage Resort on prime beachfront land at Port Douglas), in 1985; the relationship continued after Skase sold the network in 1987, as the new management considered Expo a way to get 'that parochial link' in the style of Channel Seven's 'Love You Brisbane' station advertisements.[11]

Expo also – eventually – benefited from favourable local press. After countering Harry Gordon's early negativity towards the event with paid advertorials, BESBRA finally persuaded him of its potential.[12] Local coverage of Expo became significantly more optimistic when Queensland Newspapers and Queensland Regional

Dailies became the exposition's official city and regional newspaper groups in 1987 – *The Courier-Mail* becoming Expo's joint 'official newspaper' with the *Sunday Mail*.[13]

Goldston says the exposition's 3000 enthusiastic volunteers (managed by Lorraine Martin Personnel) were also a valuable marketing resource: 'We heavily concentrated on volunteers, and that was brilliant. And we got that from the Commonwealth Games – and everybody does it now – but a volunteer is worth ten clients. If you know a volunteer at Expo, ten of you are going to go to see what they are on about. And that really adds to the feeling of "it's ours" and "we can enjoy it".'[14]

Carol Lloyd's contributions through George Patterson Advertising included suggesting that Expo's soon-to-be-iconic shade structures be called 'sunsails' rather than 'tension membranes' ('I won that one,' she says, 'thank Christ'), and sidelining the solemn globe and boomerang design by designating it a 'corporate logo' – which created space for a more festive 'marketing symbol' by Ken Cato Design Studios, based on the exposition's sunsails.

Perhaps most significantly, Lloyd devised the campaign line 'We'll show the world'. The motive and meaning of this campaign have been much speculated upon by journalists and academics. Lloyd reveals its true intent: 'The campaign line was deliberately quite parochial. It was there to band us all together with pride in what we had to offer the world and showcase for Queensland and Australia and all that stuff – "*We'll* show *them*" – there was a bit of that in it. Bit of attitude – which it needed. And it also appealed to the underdog thing – you know, Aussies love an underdog, and Queensland was the underdog in Australia.'[15]

Edwards says he liked the campaign line, but he worried that it reinforced the parochialism he was striving to coax the event away from (partly as it would repel interstate participation). Then, 'one night, in the middle of the night, I woke up and said "We'll reword that – *Together* we'll show the world" – *together* wasn't in it'.[16] When advised of the change by Marketing Division Director

Graham Currie, Lloyd remembers thinking, 'Well, it's not as neat an advertising line if I've got to add that on, but I'll do it if you like.'[17]

Lloyd worked separately on a pitch for the music for Expo. The result was the popular and pervasive theme song 'Together We'll Show the World' (co-written with Frank Millward), the success of which Lloyd only partially enjoyed: 'The downside of it was the guy who was the commissioner for the Queensland Pavilion, Fred Maybury – who had a media group at the time – drove a very ruthless deal on the publishing and ended up making us sign over the grand rights to the song ... We got a crappy little fee for composing it [and no profits on the sales] ... So you learn by these things, but there are times when you just can't beat City Hall – there is so much bloody power bearing down on you, you just can't fight it. You gotta go, "Okay, you win – take it away."'[18]

Unbeknown to Lloyd and 'City Hall', new contenders were entering the fight. Since late 1986, *The Courier-Mail* reporter Phil Dickie (with encouragement from the newspaper's new editor, Bob Gordon) had been collating data on brothels based on property records, his own observations, and the 1985 Sturgess report.[19] His January 1987 article 'A Year after Sturgess, Sex-for-Sale Business Thrives Unchallenged' claimed there were up to sixty illegal prostitution outlets in Brisbane; named key operators, such as Hector Hapeta, Anne Marie Tilley, Vittorio Conte, and Geraldo Bellino; and noted they had been largely untroubled by police.[20]

ABC reporter Christopher Masters and the *Four Corners* team arrived in Brisbane in March 1987 to investigate links between police and organised crime.[21] Both Dickie and Masters consulted with Sturgess.[22] In April, Dickie's article 'Brisbane's Casinos Flourish Despite Gunn's Vow to Close Them' revealed that casino numbers had risen since Minister for Police Bill Gunn had ordered them closed the previous August, detailed illegal casinos operated by the Bellino family, and noted that Bjelke-Petersen had officially opened a marble mine for the Bellinos in 1983.[23]

The premier seemed untroubled by these revelations as he presided over an altogether different opening in the Queen Street Mall on 30 April 1987, when he became the first person to purchase a season ticket for Expo – a year out from opening day. Next in line were Lord Mayor Atkinson and Sir Llew Edwards's then wife, Lady Leone Edwards (who died from a suspected asthma attack just weeks before Expo opened).[24] Season ticket prices commenced with an early-bird incentive of $99, which rose every three months to peak at $160.[25]

The Moonlight State

On 11 May 1987 – less than two weeks after the Expo ticket launch – the *Four Corners* documentary 'The Moonlight State' (produced by Masters) screened throughout Australia. It contained lurid images of Brisbane's illegal sex and gambling industries, and sensational claims about police corruption made by current and former officers.[26] The following day, Bjelke-Petersen assured viewers of the Ray Martin *Midday* program that there was no need for an inquiry into issues raised by the *Four Corners* team.[27] Within an hour, Bill Gunn contradicted him, saying 'a series of Police Ministers have had these types of allegations hanging over their heads. They are not going to hang over mine.'[28]

Journalist Evan Whitton suspected the lewd content in 'The Moonlight State' forced the government to take action or risk alienating the 'Bible belt', and that Bjelke-Petersen believed he would escape any fallout – which prior events suggested would be negligible – upon entering the federal arena.[29] Indeed, Judge Eric Pratt was initially considered for the role of commissioner – which would have placed history at almost unbackable odds of repeating itself.[30] Des Sturgess was so alarmed by the prospect that he had meetings with Chief Justice Sir Dormer Andrews and former Attorney-General Harper (the Cabinet member with whom he was most familiar) to urge a different selection.[31]

Bjelke-Petersen was evidently so unperturbed by the pending inquiry, the 'Joh for Canberra' campaign, and the alleged state of Expo that he flew to Los Angeles after a premiers' conference on 25 May to open a trade office and visit Disneyland.[32] Bob Hawke reportedly gave him a warm farewell and wished him success in promoting Expo.[33] Two days later, Hawke called a surprise federal election for 11 July 1987 – before Bjelke-Petersen had even nominated.[34] In his autobiography, Hawke writes of Bjelke-Petersen as 'a lonely and irrelevant man' in his dealings with state premiers and the Commonwealth, who nevertheless precipitated a crisis in the Federal Coalition 'with a bid to make his eccentric brand of flat-earth, [twenty-five per cent] flat-tax politics an Australia-wide phenomenon'.[35] Hawke judged that the Liberal Party was in disarray, with ideological 'wets' such as Andrew Peacock 'falling like ninepins as Howard sought to make his party drier than a bone', and recounts his amusement when the 'rock-solid Coalition which Menzies had founded was being riven and thrown into turmoil' as the junior partner spurred by Bjelke-Petersen 'acquiesced in a death wish for the party to go its own way'.[36]

Bjelke-Petersen's campaign quickly collapsed. Central figures (such as National Farmers Federation Leader Ian McLachlan) chose not to run; the promised campaign funding from Gold Coast developers failed to materialise; and John Howard, Ian Sinclair, and the NSW National Party ran a joint Senate ticket to keep the Queensland aspirant out.[37] Bjelke-Petersen withdrew from the election on 3 June, returning his attention to a premiership suddenly as precarious as John Howard's 1987 election chances – and to a disintegrating relationship with Sparkes, whom he irrationally blamed for the implosion.[38]

Bjelke-Petersen's losses may have been assuaged by gains in other areas; a *Courier-Mail* piece published less than two weeks after the federal election declared that 'the doom and gloom merchants have been proved wrong – not only has Expo steadfastly refused to sink it is moving full sail for next April at an impressive rate of knots'.[39]

The assessment was based upon the phenomenal public response to the release of Expo season passes, with 192,000 sold in the first ninety days – almost the total number forecast for the event. The announcement was made by a smiling Sir Llew Edwards while the exposition mascot, Expo Oz, performed a jig to the recently released theme song, 'Together We'll Show the World'.[40]

Less family-friendly matters were also afoot. Gunn had been persuaded to overlook Judge Eric Pratt in favour of appointing Tony Fitzgerald QC – who had been a justice of the Federal Court and was considered incorruptible – as commissioner of what was to become the Fitzgerald Inquiry.[41] The proceedings were expected to take six weeks and be constrained by limited investigative and judicial powers and tight terms of reference relating to claims made in 'The Moonlight State'. But with cooperation from Gunn and Attorney-General Paul Clauson, Fitzgerald adroitly obtained the power of extradition, the ability to offer cooperative witnesses indemnities, the power to resist restrictions on reporting, and consent to twice expand the terms of reference – which came to include police connections with prostitution, gambling, drugs, and 'any other matter or thing appertaining to the aforesaid matters … in the public interest' dating back to 1977 – thus setting the stage for a comprehensive almost two-year-long investigation of long-term systemic corruption and abuse of power in Queensland.[42] 'This inquiry,' said Des Sturgess at its outset, 'will decide whether organised crime has a future in Queensland.'[43]

The prevailing view was that no matter what strengths Fitzgerald, Council Assisting Gary Crooke, and their associates brought to the inquiry, the alliance between police and the state government was stronger still.[44] On 31 August, Police Commissioner Terry Lewis eviscerated that alliance under questioning at the Fitzgerald Inquiry by alleging that Bjelke-Petersen and five successive police ministers (Tom Newbery, Ron Camm, Russ Hinze, Bill Glasson, and Bill Gunn) had instructed police to tolerate prostitution. The next tectonic shift in the inquiry came when Detective Senior Sergeant

Harry Burgess traded information and his resignation for indemnity for past crimes, admitting corruption and naming twenty police in association with it. 'That was incredible,' recalls Goldston. 'I'll never forget the day that that police sergeant rolled over and said "I'll tell you everything" – nobody ever believed that would happen.'[45] This precipitated a fusillade of police confessions and the implosion of corrupt networks within the force; on 21 September, Gunn directed Terry Lewis to stand down.

The revelations did little for Expo's fledgling public relations campaign. The general manager of Von Roll in Queensland (the company responsible for Expo's $12 million monorail and the Swiss Pavilion ski lift) Wayne McCamley recalls a thwarted attempt to stage an 'announcement day' when the monorail became operational: 'We thought, "Well, we'll get all the media on board and they can give us some very positive press with regards to that," and we catered for it, and the train went from what was called the north station down to the south station and Joh Bjelke-Petersen would hop off, having driven the train from one station to the other – for the media throng that was waiting at the end, and they were all going to say, "What do you think about the train? What do you think about Expo?" et cetera – none of which was raised. The only question they pushed into his face was, "What are you going to say with this Fitzgerald Inquiry?" ... The media was really the tail wagging the dog.'[46]

It might have seemed to Bjelke-Petersen that the tail was also wagging the dog in relation to his political life. At a National Party State Council meeting in October 1987, it was resolved that ministers would be required to step down from portfolios a reasonable time before retirement – a measure seemingly aimed at the premier.[47] To pre-empt the decision being made for him, on 8 October Bjelke-Petersen announced he would retire on the 8th of the 8th, 1988 – twenty years since he had become premier, and in the middle of Expo.[48] Political scientist Paul Reynolds – who has a very close knowledge of parliamentary politics in Queensland – posits that this would have given him time to undermine Sparkes (who had instigated the State Council meeting), purge critics such as Ahern from Cabinet, halt the Fitzgerald Inquiry, and receive Queen Elizabeth II when she opened Expo.[49]

Towards the end of October 1987, the 'bellwether' states – NSW and Victoria – finally committed to Expo (swayed, in part, by financial inducements from the Hawke government) – three years and four deadline extensions after the invitation had been issued. The remaining states and territories followed suit.[50] Goldston enjoyed witnessing some fortuitous interstate rivalry when showing NSW delegates around the Expo construction site while Edwards escorted representatives from Victoria. After NSW committed to a module-sized pavilion, Goldston phoned Edwards with the good news, whereupon he was informed that Victoria had just committed to a larger space; Goldston turned to the NSW representative and said, 'Oh, by the way, Victoria's just agreed to two modules,' to which the delegate replied, 'You bastards' – the end result of which was that 'the big states took two modules and the rest of them took one'.[51]

On 11 November, BESBRA staged a handover of sixty-two pavilions to corporate, national, and international participants a record six months before opening; officials jocularly dubbed the comparatively struggling Darling Harbour redevelopment 'First Aid 88'.[52] At the handover, Edwards censured the 'experts, cynics, doubters and public in general' who had criticised the project over the years, noting, 'everything has gone ahead on budget and on schedule, thanks to a lot of hard work from a great team of people'.[53]

A team of people had also coalesced against Bjelke-Petersen and his courtiers. At the National Party Annual Conference in November, the premier suffered a string of losses: condom vending machines were endorsed, sex education was permitted in schools, Sparkes was re-elected party president with eighty per cent of the vote, and the Foreign Land Register declined to grant trusteeship of land initially proposed as a national park to the Iwasaki Company.[54] The Fitzgerald Inquiry was also circling some of Bjelke-Petersen's closest advisers. On 16 November, TAB General Manager Arthur Harriott testified that Ted Lyons had pressured him to recommend Rat Pack member Tony Murphy for a TAB agency on Stradbroke Island.[55] Lyons reportedly met with Bjelke-Petersen within days of this revelation in a bid to stop the inquiry.[56]

Another of Bjelke-Petersen's questionable entanglements then came to the fore. The iconic Canberra Hotel (opened in 1929 as the Canberra Temperance Hotel) near Brisbane Central Station was to be demolished to make way for an office tower; tenders had been called for the project, and the Interdepartmental Committee's preferred operator, Seymour Group, was before Cabinet when Bjelke-Petersen reportedly produced – without warning – a proposal from one of his 'courtiers', John Minuzzo, to build the 'world's tallest building' on the site.[57] Town-planning experts warned that such a construction would be able to contain the equivalent of the population of Warwick (approximately 10,000 people), and place enormous stress on existing infrastructure.[58]

BCC Lord Mayor Sallyanne Atkinson offered considerable resistance to the premier's plan. 'I had a huge shrieking with him over the world's tallest building,' she recalls. 'He went a bit odd after Flo went to Canberra [as a senator] – he lost his bearing somehow, and he was then cast about on a sea with people, and he was getting older, and when people have been in power for a long time … people become stars and they start to lose their sense of reality … and believe they can do things that twenty years before they wouldn't have done – and I think that's what happened to Joh.'[59]

At the last Parliamentary National Party meeting over which Bjelke-Petersen was to preside, Russ Hinze recommended passing special enabling legislation (in the manner of Expo) to usurp BCC's authority in the Minuzzo matter.[60] Such action required a compliant Cabinet, which was not forthcoming. The world's tallest building might have seemed a natural fit in the state of 'big things', but the proposal also had a whiff of Big Corruption about it. National Party backbencher Huan Fraser claimed to have sighted letters in which the government secretly committed to occupying twenty-one floors of the building and providing $5 million towards outfitting.[61] He reportedly referenced the rumoured $20 million bribe the premier had been offered to get the project through Cabinet when denouncing him to the party room: 'I know there is a bloody big pay-off to you coming as a result of this. You're a corrupt old bastard and I'm not going to cop it.'[62]

On 23 November, Bjelke-Petersen took the extraordinary action of visiting Governor Sir Walter Campbell to sack five senior ministers he suspected had conspired with Sparkes to force his retirement date: Bill Gunn, Geoff Muntz, Mike Ahern, Brian Austin, and Peter McKechnie.[63] Campbell suggested he seek their resignations instead. All objected, with Gunn alleging the premier intended to seize the Police portfolio and end the Fitzgerald Inquiry. The following day, Bjelke-Petersen asked Campbell to sack Ahern, Austin, and McKechnie, and call an early election. Campbell consented to the first request only, and three backbenchers were duly sworn in – prompting Labor's Keith De Lacy to quip that it was the only time in history when rats swam *towards* the sinking ship.[64]

At a meeting of the Parliamentary National Party (organised by Sparkes) on 26 November, Ahern and Gunn announced a motion for a leadership spill, for which each would be a candidate (along with Hinze). Ahern won the vote, ousting Bjelke-Petersen as the National Party leader, and Gunn became deputy leader.[65] Bjelke-Petersen refused to concede defeat, or to leave his office – leading to a tragicomic scene in which a tearful Hinze reportedly called through the premier's closed door, 'Come out, Joh, it's over, mate.'[66]

Bjelke-Petersen turned instead to his old political enemy: Labor. At a clandestine meeting (orchestrated by Lyons) with then state secretary Peter Beattie, Bjelke-Petersen suggested they unite to form a caretaker government. Journalist Tony Koch speculated that this extraordinary proposal (which Labor declined) revealed the extent of Bjelke-Petersen's desperation to officiate at Expo.[67] Having exhausted all other options – including an appeal to the Queen – Bjelke-Petersen formally resigned on 1 December 1987, almost six months after the instigation of the Fitzgerald Inquiry, and approximately five months shy of Expo's opening.

Ahern then turned his attention to two of the most significant events in Brisbane's recent history: 'One of the big problems I had was World Expo 88 – which was a big job to do. It wasn't the biggest. The biggest was the Fitzgerald Inquiry, which was running at the same time. It [Expo] was obviously something very big that I had to do – and do well – but I knew what had to be done, which was to roll out an international-standard program as well as we could.'[68]

There was naturally some overlap between the two events in the countdown to Expo. Ahern recalls meeting with Bob Hawke at Expo House to discuss the safe return from London of corrupt police 'bagman' Jack Herbert (whom Lewis and Lane had reportedly advised to 'disappear' before the inquiry); Herbert had turned witness for the state in exchange for indemnity. 'Nobody wanted him on an aircraft because there was a price on his head,' recalls Ahern; 'he [Hawke] met me there [at Expo House] and he agreed that Herbert should come home on an RAAF aircraft'.[69]

In the lead-in to Expo, the new premier embarked on a series of actions that inched Brisbane towards the modernity expected of an exposition host city, including closing the 'Black Hole' prison cells earmarked for Aboriginal people protesting Expo, and overseeing the liberalisation of food and drinking laws required for the event. Ahern's efforts inspired one commentator to credit him with 'dragging Queensland into the 20th century when that century is almost passed'.[70] His modern policies and support for the Fitzgerald Inquiry were so well received by the public and media that Queensland Labor operatives grew concerned that their party – especially under the leadership of respected but staid Neville Warburton – seemed lost in the past.[71]

The state government, BCC, and private business also aided Brisbane's dilatory journey into the twentieth century (with various degrees of cooperation). A number of major developments were completed in time for Expo, including double-lane highways to the north and south coasts, the Queen Street Mall extension, QCC, the Chinatown Mall, the extension of Anzac Square, the Myer Centre, and the Gateway Bridge ('They've got a better name for it now,' says a smiling Sir Leo Hielscher, after whom the bridge was renamed in 2013).[72] Ahern reveals that some of the last-minute modernisations were decidedly 'old school' in execution. When a contractor made construction errors and 'went broke' before completing a de-tensioning process for the Myer Centre car park, the centre's quest to be open in time for Expo was placed in doubt: 'I said, well, what happens if you don't de-tension? They said sometimes someone will come along and dig up the street there, and the whole car park will fall in.' Ahern held a series of tense meetings with the works department in relation to this cosmopolitan quandary. 'One of the toughest decisions I had to make was we'll go ahead with it. I said, "Carry on."'[73]

BCC had also wrangled some heritage victories over the construction-centric state government, including a control plan to preserve important buildings and workers' cottages in Spring Hill (over Hinze's urging that the area be opened for 'gracious high-rise residential development'), and the establishment of a Heritage Buildings Advisory Committee to protect structures such as the Old Windmill and Reservoirs in Wickham Terrace, and the old School of Arts in Ann Street.[74] Another BCC contribution to the looming festivities was its 'Image '88' campaign (in the style of its 'Shine On Brisbane' variant that preceded the 1982 Commonwealth Games), which urged residents, businesses, and community groups to 'Look Great' for 'A Brighter Brisbane'.[75]

As Expo's opening date loomed, the 'agent of change' responsibility passed from development and planning to the event that proponents claimed would not just 'show the world' but also deliver a 'coming of age'. In the yearlong countdown to Expo following the release of season passes, local media and much of Brisbane's formerly sceptical public exhibited a willingness to be swayed by the marketing rhetoric. By opening day, an anticipated nine million exposition visits had been sold – eclipsing the total official target of 7.8 million before the event had even begun.[76] But the pressure on Expo organisers and those encouraged to conceive of themselves as the 'we' in 'We'll Show the World' was considerable. The feeling was artfully captured by one of those best positioned to enjoy it should Brisbane stumble – a writer of the southern press:

> Forty-eight hours before the opening of World Expo 88,
> the atmosphere in Brisbane is a peculiar mixture of pleasant
> anticipation and sick-in-the-stomach apprehension. The
> city is like the scene of a meticulously organised party in the
> desperate half-hour before the guests arrive, when you wonder
> if you should put even more champagne on ice and whether
> you remembered to post the invitations. The decorations are
> up, the preparations almost complete, but will people enjoy
> themselves? After all this time and effort, will the celebration
> be a success?[77]

6

Brisbane Comes of Age – Again

It was a season of love, and the Queenslanders were in love
with their state, their gleaming capital city, in love with their
entrepreneurial Expo, themselves, everything except the corrupt
Brisbane partment.

Alfred Heller[1]

AMPHITHEATRE PRODUCER MARY-CLARE POWER vividly
recollects walking through the Expo site an hour before the
opening day festivities. After years of controversy, building, and
bustle, the area felt strangely quiet. As she reached the Queensland
Performing Arts Centre (QPAC) end of the site, she was stunned
to behold thousands of people amassing outside the entry gates. A
co-worker turned to her and said, 'We're about to lose our place.'[2]
The crowds waiting at the exposition's four public entry points were
entertained by street performers, brightly uniformed volunteers and
staff, costumed characters, and animatronic robots housed in clear
pyramid cases, the programmed repertoire of which included the
greeting: 'Well, you're here at last. I thought you'd never come. My
friends have already welcomed you, so now I can tell you: you're in
for the time of your life.'[3]

Open for Business

World Expo 88 opened to the public at 10 am on 30 April 1988 – approximately fourteen years after the Whitlam government proposed hosting an exposition to mark the bicentenary of European settlement in Australia, and ten years after the Bjelke-Petersen government commenced the labyrinthine process of securing the event for Brisbane. Its opening was preceded by an otherworldly parade through the city from King George Square and across Victoria Bridge to the exposition site, helmed by the event mascot, Expo Oz, seated astride a golden horse. A *Weekend Australian* article christened the spectacle a sign of change:

> In the old days, under the former premier, Sir Joh Bjelke-Petersen, anyone who marched through the streets of Brisbane ran the risk of being arrested. If more than three people stopped to chat in King George Square, they were liable to be deemed an illegal gathering.[4]

The Melbourne Street exposition entrance was opened to the public with a ceremonial ribbon-cutting by Sir Llew Edwards and Expo Oz. Ribbon duties at other entrances were performed by contemporary public figures such as Diane Cilento, Grant Kenny, Lisa Curry-Kenny, Dawn Fraser, Jeannie Little, Bill Collins, and *It's a Knockout* star Billy J. Smith.[5] Expectant crowds joined an estimated international television audience of hundreds of millions to watch Her Royal Highness Queen Elizabeth II – the great-great-granddaughter of a key instigator of the very first world exposition, in 1851 – as the *Royal Britannia* sailed up the Brisbane River towards the Expo site.[6]

Opening day speeches from Queensland politicians inclined – perhaps forgivably – towards the triumphal. Lord Mayor Sallyanne Atkinson declared the event a coming of age for Brisbane, and evidence – in tandem with the 1982 Commonwealth Games – that the capital was more of a 'can do' city than the 'large country town' the Queen had encountered on her first visit, in 1954, when 'Southerners called Brisbane a cultural desert'.[7] Premier Mike Ahern deemed it a proud day to be a Queenslander and invited the world to 'take a look at Queensland and all it has to offer'.[8] Prime Minister Bob Hawke was less geographically specific, claiming that 'Australians have worked hard to make Expo 88 a success', and 'for Australians, Expo presents us with a very significant opportunity to show the world what we are capable of'.[9] Sir Llew Edwards recalls that after Hawke's speech, 'in his way, as only he could do – tears ran down his face – he said to me as we walked off the stage, "I am the proudest man in Australia today."'[10]

Former Australian prime ministers Gough Whitlam and Malcolm Fraser also attended the opening ceremony, Fraser reportedly telling Edwards, 'This is going to be a great success and I will come back' (which he did).[11] The opening speeches studiously overlooked Bjelke-Petersen, who was reportedly disgruntled when told that BIE rules prohibited him – as a non-government representative – from opening the event.[12] The former premier responded to rumours that the federal government had pressured BESBRA to seat him away from the Queen by saying, 'If they are small enough to want to put me behind some boxes, then that's their problem.'[13]

Edwards says Bjelke-Petersen never forgave him for the opening day snub: 'I think the premier wouldn't like me saying, but he gave that radical view, and we wanted to make everybody feel Expo was the happiest place on earth – the safest place – and we just didn't want anybody to be the star. The star was to be Expo itself, and that's why – whilst I had a profile in a sense – I really wanted to be part of a team totally. He claimed that he was the father of Expo. I think he thought that he owned Expo, but when I said, "I'm sorry, Joh, but we cannot [permit you to open the exposition], but we can have you on the stage" ... "No, no," he said, "I was the brains." Yes, you were the brains, but the *rule* – he would not accept that he could not open Expo.'[14]

This was not the only protocol tested by the lure of a VIP-laden opening ceremony. Atkinson recalls that 'both the governor-general and the governor were there, and I said to Lady Campbell [wife of Sir Walter Campbell, then governor of Queensland], "I thought if the governor-general was here, the governor couldn't be here," and she said, "We weren't going to miss out."'[15]

Peter Goldston's recollections of the opening ceremony are tempered by a potential protocol breach of unpalatable consequence: 'We were all sitting on the artificial grass in front of the River Stage for the opening ceremony. I was sitting in the middle – two or three rows back from the front – and sitting in the front row was the Queen and the Duke; and running down underneath the artificial grass, I knew, was a sewerage line. And that came to my mind because I could see a damp patch developing underneath the Queen's seat. And I was afeared that what we had was a leaking sewerage pipe underneath the Queen.'[16]

The patch grew darker and wider as Goldston made frantic mental calculations pertaining to the likelihood of the sewerage pipe bursting open directly beneath Her Royal Highness Queen Elizabeth II before a potential viewing audience in the hundreds of millions. A quarter of a century later, Goldston's relief is palpable: 'We got through the opening ceremony without it bursting.'[17] Her Majesty remained peacefully unaware of the threat, delivering a convivial speech that included the line 'I am told you like to call your state the sunshine state – but I prefer to think of it by its original name: Queen's Land' before concluding, 'I now declare World Expo 88 well and truly open.'[18]

An average of 120,000 people a day were then made welcome – from 10 am to 10 pm, for six months – to be resident at 'the happiest place on earth'.[19] Attendees strolled through millions of dollars' worth of landscaping and public art while immersed in displays and activities on a scale never before seen in Brisbane. Entertainment options included roaming street performers and myriad scheduled events at the Piazza, Amphitheatre, Aquacade,

Riverside Stage, and the Brisbane River; visitors could also immerse themselves in the World Expo on Stage program at QPAC (offerings included Kabuki, the English Shakespeare Company, the Philip Glass Ensemble, David Byrne, Roger Woodward, and the first staging of *Strictly Ballroom* outside of the National Institute of Dramatic Art), or view 'blockbuster' Expo-aligned art exhibitions at the Queensland Art Gallery (QAG) featuring Aboriginal art, Japanese ceramics, masterpieces from the Louvre, and drawings from the royal collection at Windsor Castle. Dedicated 'National Days' showcased the culture and/or technology of participating nations, while special theme weeks explored subjects such as travel, communications, and circus. In a single day, attendees could experience space-themed thrill-rides at World Expo Park (the five-hectare brainchild of Dreamworld investor Ken Lord); view fireworks, parades, water-skiing, marching bands, and rock concerts; indulge in then-exotic refreshments such as sushi, kimchi, and green tea; and engage with the dynamic, static, and interactive pavilion displays of participating nations, governments, and corporations.

Pavilion offerings included the popular 'sensation theatre' (New Zealand), in which visitors sat astride sheep-shaped stools to watch roller-coaster footage while mechanised floorboards moved beneath them; demonstrations of traditional dance from Tonga, Vanuatu, and the Cook Islands (Pacific Lagoon); Kitt the talking car from the television series *Knight Rider* (Universal Studios); bricks from the Great Wall (China); original paintings by Dalí, Miró, and Picasso (Spain); and video of Soviet children moonwalking (at the last world exposition for the USSR). Interactive displays invited attendees to try lifting a bar of gold (Western Australia); test their speed, reflexes, and agility (Canada); take a gondola ride (Switzerland); and join a one-hundred-person game conducted within a room-sized computer (British Columbia).

As opening day eased into opening night, Goldston felt some operational anxieties easing alongside it: 'We were building a temporary circus, and I was frightened people wouldn't come – that they wouldn't like it; but, just before closing time, you could feel the atmosphere – people were so happy.'[20] Barbara Absolon's 'proof-positive that Expo would be a great success' was when her mother, on her first visit, asked for a season pass: 'I thought, "Crikey, if my mother is enjoying this, everyone is going to enjoy it," because she was a hard woman to get out of the house.'[21]

The front page of the *Sunday Sun* the following day reflected this optimism (though it might have been expected to, as an event sponsor), announcing – with parochial flair – 'We Showed 'Em', accompanied by the dazzlingly unrestrained sub-header 'The World Bows to Expoganza' and the joyful declaration 'Yes! We DID show the world.'[22]

Expo also extracted backhanded praise from national newspaper *The Australian*, which dubbed the event a world-class attraction, and proof that its host state was 'no longer a tropical backwater inhabited by cattle, cane toads and bushies in wide hats'.[23] Similarly qualified affirmation appeared in the *Weekend Australian* piece 'Brazen Brissie Joins the Big League', in which 'Brisbane's big moment' was touted as a 'much-appreciated boost to morale' after decades of 'waiting in the wings' and being 'dismissed as a slow-moving country cousin of Sydney and Melbourne'.[24] Quite unexpectedly, *The Australian* also acknowledged Queensland's increasingly out-of-favour entrepreneurs:

Much has been written – not a little of it unflattering – about Queensland's so-called 'white shoe brigade', but it is those often unpolished entrepreneurs who have often been the driving force behind the State's development. Theirs is a frontier mentality, where the seemingly outrageous – drain a swamp, move a mountain – becomes the commonplace. It is this spirit that has marked Expo 88 from the start.[25]

Newspapers also gave front-page coverage to the *other* opening day march, in which Aboriginal activists, including Michael Mansell and

Bob Weatherall, led more than 1000 supporters in a peaceful march from the Roma Street Forum to Musgrave Park to highlight issues such as Aboriginal deaths in custody, land rights, and the tastelessness of celebrating the bicentenary of European settlement in Australia.[26] Slogans sighted at the event included 'Cook came 40,000 years too late' and 'Expo 88 Celebrates White Invasion'; some protesters chanted 'Expo sucks'.[27] After the march, Aboriginal demonstrators and supporters – including Labor Member for South Brisbane Anne Warner – were denied service at the Melbourne Hotel, prompting her to remonstrate, 'We are playing host to the international community and this sort of thing happens to our own people.'[28] Placard-waving protesters the next day shouted, 'Shame, Australia, Shame' outside St John's Cathedral as the Queen attended mass.[29] Twenty Aboriginal people were subsequently arrested while shouting, 'You call it suicide, we call it murder' and 'Let's tell the world at Expo our story' during what was labelled an 'illegal' land rights march near the Grey Street Expo gates.[30] Tensions escalated in the afternoon when a hundred Aboriginal protesters stormed the Melbourne Hotel – reportedly unsettling staff and causing minor damage – after receiving word that an elderly Aboriginal woman had been refused a glass of water.[31]

Queensland politicians – presumably alert to the prospect of negative national and international media attention after successful Aboriginal protests during the 1982 Commonwealth Games – were united in their condemnation of these events.[32] Lord Mayor Atkinson stated, 'Protests do not achieve what they set out to do.' The new state Opposition leader Wayne Goss – an architect of the Aboriginal Legal Service (ALS) in the 1970s – said that 'while the Aborigines have obviously got a grievance and are entitled to put their case, I would have to question some of their activities today'.[33] And Premier Mike Ahern claimed:

We are not going to allow them to disrupt our Expo and make
an exhibition of themselves before our international guests
[or] allow a festering sore to run during Expo. If they want

to continue some reasonable demonstrations over in a corner somewhere, that's fine ... They've had a fair go by a factor of five, and the people of Queensland have had enough.[34]

Townsville Aboriginal and Islander Community spokesman Wayne Wharton said Aboriginal people were not surprised by Ahern's comments but were appalled by those of Goss, and suggested Aboriginal groups dissociate from Labor until he was 'brought into line'.[35] Don Davidson took a more conciliatorily approach, presenting BESBRA with an Aboriginal flag to fly at a ceremony in which the Aboriginal and Islander Legal Service (formerly the ALS) – of which Davidson was president – became an Expo sponsor.[36] BESBRA was persuaded against flying the flag when Aboriginal elders convinced Edwards it was contrary to the community's wishes.[37]

Despite such controversies, Expo festivities were less ethically awkward than the 'Celebration of a Nation' activities overseen by the ABA. The bicentennial authority had been buffeted by staff changes and the fluctuating social and political objectives of myriad governments and pressure groups, resulting in a pastiche of contested bicentennial themes ranging from the self-aggrandising 'The Australian Achievement' to the more conciliatory 'Living Together'.[38] In a doomed attempt to be uncontroversial and inclusive, it pursued a strategy dubbed 'tactical pluralism', which celebrated almost everything in wilfully imprecise detail.[39] The ABA's much-criticised bicentennial program included the nationwide Australian Travelling Exhibition (essentially an oversized tent replete with unlabelled paraphernalia such as immigrant baggage, Christian iconography, Ned Kelly's armour, an Aboriginal canoe, and a dingo trap), and *two* maritime tributes: the First Fleet re-enactment (originally cancelled to avoid offending Aboriginal people, then reinstated to avoid offending monarchists) and the Tall Ships (ridiculed for sailing into Sydney Harbour bearing the Coca-Cola flag).[40]

Early efforts on BESBRA's part to exclude the ABA inadvertently shielded Expo from some ideological conundrums. The willingness of many Aboriginal people to participate was predicated on the fact that the event barely addressed the bicentenary it ostensibly existed to celebrate. Expo's 'Leisure in the Age of Technology' theme offered whimsical speculations about the future in place of sombre ethical deliberations, and was, in the words of one critic, 'commemorative of nothing at all'.[41]

Aboriginal culture was central to the popular Australian Pavilion at Expo, in which Oodgeroo Noonuccal's special-effects-laden Rainbow Serpent Theatre taught attendees about the Aboriginal connection to the land (exemplifying BIE education ideals in the process).[42] The pavilion also indulged in some stereotypical 'Australian lifestyle' imagery by way of beer-belly competitions, cane-toad racing, lamington tossing, and damper making – prompting one attendee to speculate that the Rainbow Serpent Theatre formed the pavilion's centrepiece, as Australia 'has no culture of its own'.[43] International guests such as British prime minister Margaret Thatcher and Japanese prime minister Noboru Takeshita were prevailed upon to indulge Australian stereotypes by holding koalas or wearing Driza-Bones during awkward-looking photo sessions, and the Queen was briefly confounded by the pavilion's Bluey the robot spouting colloquialisms such as 'Any excuse for a barbie', 'How yer goin?', and 'The billy's on the boil and so am I'.[44]

The Queensland Pavilion presented the state as predominantly white, male, and rural – though bikini-clad women promoted tourist attractions, and blonde-haired hostesses (this hair colour being an employment requirement) led attendees to a 'people mover' imported from Japan that steered them through business- and tourism-imbued visions of Queensland.[45] Representations of the state included an outback pub where blue-singlet-wearing 'Aussie types' (mannequins with televisions for heads) had a 'yarn' to visitors about primary industries, and some 'loveable larrikins' engaged in whip-cracking and gumleaf playing. The pavilion also boasted an 'entrepreneur's entrance' and executive suites; 'We aim to woo business and industries to Queensland as well as looking at business opportunities for

Queensland on the international map,' said the pavilion's National Party–aligned commissioner, Sir Fred Maybury, of his profoundly anti-BIE objectives.[46] The contradictions between Edwards's vision of Expo as a modernising force for Brisbane and the dominant rural image projected by the pavilion were explicable in terms of the 'city versus country' divisions between the former Coalition partners.

Expo protests continued, but in comparatively muted fashion. Some took the form of arts protests, as with the play *Under Wraps* (held in the Paint Factory), which critiqued 'The Imposition' or 'Impo'.[47] There were also community initiatives such as the West End Street Festival, founded during Expo as 'a celebration of our unity' and proof that 'we don't need large-scale high-technology' for a 'participatory and affordable festival'.[48] Musgrave Park was transformed into a 'tent city' during Expo (as it had been during the 1982 Commonwealth Games protests) for an alternative cultural festival called the United Indigenous Cultural Survival Gathering, in which evenings 'were spectacular affairs, with bonfires blazing from tin drums, and performances both traditional and contemporary lasting into the early hours of the morning'.[49]

Bob Weatherall says the Aboriginal protests were not intended to run beyond Expo's media-saturated first few days, as there were other high-profile campaigns to focus on: 'We knew we wouldn't be able to stop them [BESBRA or Expo], but we knew that we'd be able to utilise that period of time to expose the Queensland and the Australian governments' inability or unwillingness to address Aboriginal concerns.'[50]

Other Expo protests dwindled for a range of reasons, including the simple fact that some battles (such as land resumptions and forced evictions) had already been lost. For many, a barrier to enjoying Expo had been removed with the fall of the previous premier and the event's relative depoliticisation. One attendee, when asked what he loved about Expo, replied, 'Bjelke-Petersen didn't make a speech claiming all the glory.'[51] Absolon believes that some Expo objections dissipated through demystification: 'I think people often protest against the unknown. Once it began, people could actually see it there – they could understand it, they could enjoy it – there was pretty much nothing to protest about.'[52]

Cane Toad Times editor Anne Jones agrees that 'there really wasn't much negative protest once it got going'.[53] She and her colleagues secured press passes to appraise the event they had been so sceptical about, 'but we didn't see a lot because we were all rather unwilling to queue – and if you didn't want to queue, there wasn't much going on'. Jones was unmoved by what they did see: 'It was a kind of gloss mainstream culture that we didn't feel comfortable with.'[54]

That same culture was heartily embraced by that same mainstream. Within the first nine days, nearly three-quarters of a million people had passed through Expo's gates – an average of 80,000 a day against the projected 44,000.[55] The breadth of experiences available prompted something of a lifestyle change for mainstream Brisbane – significant enough at the time to merit the headline 'City Stays Up Late' for an article conveying surprise at the number of people still on site at closing time.[56] The excitement filtered beyond the exposition environs and across the river to the Queen Street Mall, the area 'coming alive' after Expo's 10 pm nightly finish, when crowds gathered at street-side eateries and were entertained by 'some of the worst street musicians anywhere'.[57] Bob Minnikin observed that it was 'no longer true that somebody could fire a cannon through the city after dark and not hit anyone'.[58]

Newspaper interviews conveyed the excitement emanating from the exposition grounds. 'There's such a hype around the city,' said an Expo volunteer, 'it's like we're all having a big party and everyone's in a holiday mood.'[59] Local commentators began to search for significance beyond the exuberance:

> Six weeks into the festivities, Expo 88 is in danger of becoming
> not just a laughter-filled frolic, but an addiction ... the success
> of Expo, coming on the heels of the Commonwealth Games
> in 1982, already has inspired a conviction in the community

that it can host just about any type of world event. But it has also awakened appetites for new experiences; most notably in food and entertainment, but also in building bridges to a global community becoming acutely aware of what the city, State and nation offer. The days in Brisbane of settling for the comfortably familiar or playing second fiddle to bigger, richer and more glamorous southern capitals are over.[60]

Some Expo celebrations took place behind the scenes. Mary-Clare Power recalls that the Entertainment Division 'worked hard and played hard ... we used to hop on the intranet [Expo 88's internal communications system] and go, "What are we doing tonight? Oh, look, Canada's having a party."'[61] Sometimes Expo continued informally after-hours at various rental houses through which the Entertainment Division rotated national and international performers. Power recalls – with obvious conviction – that 'there were some *great* parties at those houses'.[62] David Hamilton believes that Expo's behind-the-scenes moments contributed greatly to the overall environment: 'To see the joy of the Aussies and other nationalities in the Entertainment House [performer] area where they were sharing their talents and communication and language – that part was a magic that the public never saw, but we got to see that wonderful exchange ... which was brilliant.'[63]

Some key Expo staff worked eighty- to a-hundred-hour weeks throughout the event – a bonding experience Absolon likens to 'how army buddies must feel'.[64] Hamilton says members of the Entertainment Division often slept on site, 'because it was open from 10 am to 10 pm, so rehearsals were from midnight onwards, so you'd have international acts arriving and that's when you'd bump in all the props – from their visas to Actors Equity, props clearing customs – spending twenty minutes repainting the floor to get rid of an extra dot [stage positioning mark] for the marching band'.[65] He is convinced that 'the incredible staff, and the dedication every member gave – you can only get that from staff who know that there's a start and there's a finish; and on the 30th of October you didn't care that you hadn't had sleep for six months'.[66]

Expo had unusually low staff turnover for a world exposition.[67] Significantly, the union agreements negotiated prior to Expo were honoured on all sides, and not a single day was lost to industrial action.[68] The agreements were described in *The Australian Financial Review* as being similar to the 'Japanese employer–employee relationship', in which workforce loyalty is to the company before the trade, and were credited with inspiring an extraordinary level of 'courtesy, helpfulness, happiness and efficiency' that constituted a public relations triumph.[69]

Edwards concedes that, away from the public eye, BESBRA's relationship with various unions was not seamless: 'There was a lot of blood on the floor in my office, I might say, where we'd run into a problem ... I was called names I'd never heard of ... but it worked; it was a good relationship. I could not pay a higher tribute for the cooperation we had from the trade union movement.'[70]

The social aspect to Expo positively influenced the work environment of many employees; one craft shop assistant spoke of it as 'the most fantastic opportunity to meet people', and some exposition employees found themselves in 'Expo love'.[71] An Expo Oz souvenir shop supervisor conceived of the event as 'one big family – we're all sharing this together', and said, 'it's hard to be unhappy in a place like this'.[72]

As the sense of euphoria grew, the concept of 'change' – once the promissory domain of the exposition's spruikers – was increasingly invoked by columnists to denote the present:

> When visitors enter Expo they are transformed. Hardened
> cynics babble like excited children as they compare pavilions
> and plot which to visit next. The average person in the street
> begins chatting like an experienced jet-setter: 'We'll go to
> Canada and meet you up at China – oh, Russia was great ...'[73]

Criticisms

Visitors were encouraged to foster the illusion that they were 'seeing the world' by obtaining Expo 'passports' that could be stamped at the counters of various pavilions. Exposition veteran Alfred Heller challenged the validity of this notion, arguing that most of the pavilions were miniaturised, 'Disney-ised' versions of participating countries, and that Expo hardly represented a completist's idea of a world trip:

> A bit of the globe was missing: India, for example, with a sixth of the people alive today; Saudi Arabia, Israel, Iran, Iraq, Brazil, Argentina and all the other nations of the South American continent. Except for Kenya, the African countries were absent, as were Turkey, Mexico and the countries of Eastern Europe and Scandinavia.[74]

Academics also critiqued the event. After examining its visitation profile and finding that ten per cent of attendees were from overseas, twenty-five per cent from interstate, fifty per cent from Brisbane, and fifteen per cent from other parts of Queensland, Jennifer Craik concluded that the exposition – like many before it – was a mere 'fantasy of internationalism and otherness', while participants were 'rubbing shoulders with fellow citizens' and experiencing a 'reaffirmation of self' more likely to inspire parochialism than reduce it.[75]

Tony Bennett detected an echo of the racial theories central to earlier expositions in the Pacific Lagoon, which 'provided an imaginary retreat from the Expo sea of modernity, one in which, in however idealised and romanticised a fashion, Pacific Islanders were assigned the role of representing the backwardness from which progress had progressed'.[76] He also observed that entertainment, once relegated to the periphery of such events, was now central, while corporations such as IBM and Fujitsu continued to displace national pavilions as the epicentre of technology and 'progress'.[77] In assessing that technology, Bennett found support for Umberto Eco's theory that countries increasingly sought to demonstrate their global standing through the technology used to present their displays, rather than the actual content.[78]

Much of Expo's technology existed behind the scenes, and was headed by the former director of the State Government Computer Centre Ken Pope.[79] The 'Exponet' database and communications system linked BESBRA with government departments and major Expo participants; its centrepiece – the host machine for 220 computers – was the IBM System 38, with its then formidable 32 Mb of storage.[80] Coupled with relevant IBM software, it provided contemporary cutting-edge services such as online searchable databases; rostering and scheduling systems; calendar features and reminders; software for preparing and distributing memos; 'electronic mail' exchanges between users and groups; the ability to monitor the frequency of VIP, staff, and season-pass-holder visits through their barcoded passes; and a 'Lostots' audiovisual communications system for reuniting lost children with their carers.[81]

Expo's public-facing technology included touchscreen displays with information on scheduled events, and computer terminals that could be utilised for activities such as booking seats at Expo restaurants or viewing laser-disc video of potential holiday destinations.[82] The division had been advised that the public's understanding of technology was commensurate with that of a child, and to focus on the 'fun' aspects of the technology available to it rather than 'frighten the uninitiated'.[83] Had BESBRA chosen differently, it might have bolstered the event's 'education' and 'progress' credentials, and helped to dilute claims that it offered little more than consumption. One writer perceived the evolution – or devolution – of the entire world exposition concept in its Brisbane incarnation:

When world's fairs began, they convened in great cities and functioned to send out sweeping statements to the world at large of empire, industry and cultural refinement. Today, as often as not, they're likely to be held in some abandoned railroad yard or rundown dock area in a once-great or never-was community that most people would never otherwise go near. And their messages – to the extent that they have any at all, have become internalised – they speak to the population of the host city of urban redevelopment or regeneration of the local economy, rather than exhibiting any grander impulse toward world peace and progress. In this respect, Brisbane's World Expo 88 may be the quintessential modern fair.[84]

Anne Jones marvelled at the level of 'fakery' inherent in celebrating Expo while the scandalous practices of the state government were being exposed by the Fitzgerald Inquiry: 'Here we are, going, "Aren't we great?" – glossing over the fact that you had a very repressive government that was in many ways a police state – and you're celebrating it.'[85]

Many of Expo's key contributors were associated with the increasingly tainted Bjelke-Petersen government, including early instigator Sir Frank Moore, Minister for Expo Bill Gunn, Premier of Queensland Mike Ahern, Australian Commissioner-General Sir Edward Williams, Queensland Pavilion Commissioner Sir Fred Maybury, and Expo Chairman Sir Llew Edwards. One can imagine these gentlemen checking the daily news with mixed levels of anxiety. The Fitzgerald Inquiry was certainly not the party Edwards had in mind when planning Expo: 'It was a little sideline that I didn't need ... here's the state falling apart ... Fitzgerald was on, and during the Expo I had to give evidence – and I got three days of belting from the prosecution – but it did give me a great deal of pleasure to be able to be cleared and so forth.'[86]

Edwards's early efforts to insulate the exposition from felonious practices almost certainly helped shield it from the inquiry's fallout: 'There was a lot coming out about corruption, and fortunately from day one I said to our team, "Everything's above board. There's no expense allowances," and we paid them very poor salaries. I think I was paid $80,000 a year for chairman, whereas in parliament I think I was getting that as a minister. I just said to them, "We can't have one smelly event – if we have one smelly thing during the Expo preparation, or in Expo – we're dead."[87]

River Stage Producer John Watson says he and his peers appreciated Edwards's anti-corruption directive, but that the exposition faced an uphill battle against place and time: 'You've got to remember that Expo ... it was the '80s. We had Christopher Skase and we had the white shoe brigade and we had Bjelke-Petersen – corruption was everywhere; and there are stories I won't tell you that even shocked me – the learning curve I went on about all of that stuff – stories like having to sack security companies because of all the thieving that was going on after hours and all of that sort of stuff.'[88] Nevertheless, Watson is cogent in his conviction that 'there was time and opportunity during Expo for idealism to triumph despite all the other crap'.[89]

Edwards suspects his repeated insistence that Expo was a national rather than a state event may also have protected it, to a degree, from the adverse publicity flowing from the inquiry: 'Not that we were ashamed of Queensland, but it was a difficult period for us to suddenly appear to want to show the world – 'We'll show the world' – when technically people were getting ready to go off to jail.'[90]

Balancing Act

As premier, Mike Ahern performed the delicate task of welcoming the world gaze to Brisbane for Expo while the state, its police, and its politicians faced the most intense scrutiny in Queensland's history. Ahern appeared privately at the inquiry 'to clarify a point', but he is pragmatic about the degree to which Fitzgerald focused on the state government: 'If someone says to you in politics, "I didn't know that was happening", I, ah, I smile, because not only do you know what's happening, you're hearing it too loud. It's being shouted at you.'[91]

For this reason, Ahern prioritised the less pleasurable of these momentous events: 'The Expo was a good job to do. We knew what had to be done, and we were able to get good teamwork going ... I didn't like the Fitzgerald Inquiry process. Who would? But my commitment was that if the state was going to put itself through such persecution – it would only hurt because it had to – then it was my duty to see that it got the benefit from the process. And that was extremely tough ... so the two were running side by side. There was nothing I could do to stop the Fitzgerald Inquiry – didn't want to – I felt there was so much problem there it had to be exposed and rectified. That just had to be done; and we had to do as good a job as we could with Expo.'[92]

Expo Parades Producer and political activist Mike Mullins and his then partner, British painter Margot Hutcheson (who had been harassed by Queensland police while living in an alternative community in Yandina with her previous partner, Peter Carey), took an active interest in the inquiry, with Hutcheson completing the painting 'Wasn't the Fitzgerald Inquiry Fun?' after attending some of the hearings. 'It would be very interesting to speculate,' says Mullins, 'where Queensland and Brisbane would be today if they were just dealing with the Fitzgerald Inquiry at that time – i.e., they didn't have the diversion of Expo.'[93]

It would certainly have been difficult to extract the Fitzgerald Inquiry from the consciousness of many Expo attendees. *Sydney Morning Herald* cartoonist Alan Moir encapsulated the level of public interest in both events with an illustration of crowds lined up behind two signs – one marked 'Expo', the other 'The Inquiry'.[94] Sallyanne Atkinson says the dramas unfolding in the courtroom were a popular subject during Expo's numerous VIP functions: 'My favourite story is at one of those lunches for a visiting dignitary. It was just when Bill Hayden [former policeman and former federal Labor leader] had been announced as the governor-general, and Gough Whitlam was at the lunch, and somebody said to Gough, "So what do you think of Bill Hayden's appointment?" and he went, "Hmm. Well he is that rare phenomenon: an honest cop from Queensland."[95]

For some, the Fitzgerald Inquiry contributed to the party-like atmosphere emanating from the exposition grounds through its role in the long-awaited exposure of corruption. The alleviation of the 'police state' mentality – coupled with the provision of a cultural space where residents were encouraged to gather in their tens of thousands to celebrate – provided some of the conditions for the long-prophesied change that beguiled Brisbane. One commentator credited the initial excitement with catalysing Expo as a seismic event:

> It's this very sense of a never-ending party, the release that
> comes with kicking up one's heels and doing things the Sir Johs
> of the world never approve, that infected Brisbane in those first
> weeks of Expo 88 and fed the fair's success.[96]

Showing the World

For Atkinson, the glamorous VIPs drawn to Expo were integral to Brisbane's changing psyche: 'We had the King and Queen of Spain, the President of Romania – God help us. Margaret Thatcher came – all of a sudden we were the centre of the universe. And people from around Australia came and said, "Wow, this is happening in Brisbane. How amazing."'[97]

Visiting royalty and heads of state included Japanese prime minister Noboru Takeshita, President Francesco Cossiga of Italy, the Duke and Duchess of York (colloquially known as Andrew and Fergie), the Duke and Duchess of Kent, Prince Edward, British prime minister Margaret Thatcher, and West German chancellor Helmut Kohl (whose role in the reunification of Germany helped to ensure this was the Federal Republic of Germany's last appearance at a world exposition).[98] Sir Llew Edwards says BESBRA was advised that American president Ronald Reagan was likely to attend, but that 'unfortunately there was some major crisis about that time'.[99] Prior to Expo, Edwards was quoted saying he hoped that the president of the Soviet Union, Mikhail Gorbachev, would also visit; years later, he confides that this was just diplomacy: 'Gorbachev was never a goer. There was a lot of talk that he would come, but it wasn't our belief ever that he would.'[100]

The least welcome visiting head of state was almost certainly the genocidal dictator Nicolae Ceaușescu, the last Communist leader of Romania, who had notoriously instructed security forces to fire upon his starving countrymen during unrest he himself had caused by exporting much of his country's food. The Expo appearance of Ceaușescu and his wife, Elena, was the final chapter in a graceless venture begun by Bjelke-Petersen's friend Lang Hancock (the iron ore and asbestos magnate and a Queensland National Party donor), who persuaded the 'kitchen cabinet' of Hielscher, Schubert, Bjelke-Petersen, and Beryl Young to visit the dictatorship in 1987 about a possible coal deal; upon arrival, it became clear that the coal was to be exchanged for old Romanian technology. At the end of this unsuccessful trip, Bjelke-Petersen invited the Ceaușescus to visit Queensland – presumably as a diplomatic courtesy. As they departed, Hielscher recalls Bjelke-Petersen saying, 'You wouldn't know he had blood on his hands, would you?'[101]

Ahern remembers Ceaușescu as an 'obnoxious character' who required the air-conditioning to be turned off during a dinner held in his honour at the Parliamentary Annex in case poison gas was fed through it, then insisted upon using food testers and avoiding all elevators for fear of assassination.[102] During the celebration, tense Romanian security guards drew their weapons on the drunkenly exuberant member for Southport, Mick Veivers, who reportedly cried out, 'Fuck! I nearly got shot!'[103]

The head of QAG during Expo, Doug Hall, recalls escorting the Ceaușescus on an excruciating gallery tour during which the couple frequently baulked at winding staircases that might conceal assassins; Elena also required a private opening of the Myer Centre after-hours in order to shop.[104] The couple's paranoia was justified – after a revolution in 1989, they were found guilty of genocide and gathering illegal wealth and were executed on Christmas Day.

The Arts End

Arguably of greater excitement to Expo attendees than most of the political VIPs was the line-up of local and international celebrities participating in or visiting the event, including Tony Curtis, Arnold Schwarzenegger, Danny La Rue, Phyllis Diller, John Farnham (at the height of his *Age of Reason* powers), Jason Donovan, Kylie Minogue, Wally Lewis, John Denver, Dick Johnson, Jimmy Barnes, Dick Smith, Rolf Harris, the Hoodoo Gurus, the Divinyls, Kids in the Kitchen, Yothu Yindi, Mondo Rock, The, the Little River Band, James Taylor, the Village People, Joe Cocker, Sir Edmund Hillary, Max Headroom, and Dexter the robot from Network Ten's *Perfect Match*.[105] Superstar musicians Crowded House charmed the already rapturous crowd with deft changes to the lyrics of 'Mean to Me': 'She came a long way. A long way to Queensland. She came a long way. A long way to Expo.'[106]

Walkways Coordinator Ian Williams recalls 'a lot of policy on the run there', as word spread and increasing numbers of artists tried to get booked for Expo, since their peers 'were all having a good time'.[107] The exposition also provided some quirky behind-the-scenes celebrity vignettes. Williams says that when Bryan Ferry reached Expo's Media House for promotional photos after a long flight, the star-struck staff were dismayed at being unable to meet his simple request for hair gel: 'He just said, "Tell you what, don't worry about it. Have you got a coffee cup?" We went, "Yeah, yeah. How do you take it?" He went, "Na, na," then mixed sugar and water into a slurry in the cup, and slicked it all through his hair in time to meet the press.'[108]

With more than 25,000 performances scheduled over the duration of the exposition, Absolon correctly claimed that 'People could come here every day for 184 days and only see entertainment, and still fill every day.'[109] Williams credits the quality and variety of the performances, along with the wealth of international headlining acts – 'no one had ever seen that sort of thing before' – with leaving 'a positive indelible mark on so many people'.[110] Many of the performances were once-in-a-lifetime opportunities for attendees.

Hamilton recalls some personal highlights from his venue, which hosted a range of events from sumo wrestling through to tap dancing, fashion shows, BMX demonstrations, and, his favourite, the world ballroom dancing championships: 'Some people didn't leave all day – the best of world ballroom dancing with a symphony orchestra – I stood and thought, well, you'll never see anything like this ever again.' Another Hamilton favourite was a reunion concert for acclaimed opera singers Donald Smith and June Bronhill – the last time they ever performed together. 'The Piazza was packed,' Hamilton says. 'There was a standing ovation. You can have the big shows, but sometimes it's just a little moment in time that you think, well, thank goodness I thought to do that. They've passed away, both of them.'[111]

Not all entertainment associated with Expo was well received. Anthony Steel and Marguerite Pepper, Consultant Producers of the World Expo on Stage program at QPAC (for which they curated over 500 performances by artists from thirty countries), freely concede that attendance figures were poor, which they attribute to people's reticence to leave Expo – especially when doing so entailed paying additional fees.[112] The turnout was certainly not an indicator of quality. In an interview a quarter of a century after helping to curate it, Pepper mused, 'That program, even today, would be very contemporary and relevant, I think.'[113]

Mike Mullins thinks it provided an entry point to Expo for those who may not have been enamoured with its other charms: 'One of the big bridging elements for those sort of left-wing artistic creative people was Anthony's program, because they got to see – literally – Expo [performances] from the world; that program was quite extraordinary.'[114]

Barbara Absolon concurs: 'Really great artistic directors – they're few and far between. And Anthony is one of them.'[115]

The curatorial decision to 'stimulate as well as to entertain, to provoke as well as to divert' caused some consternation among the mainstream public. Steel recalls placating audience members after productions that contained swearing, or that were alleged not to have made sense.[116] He also remembers encountering an irate woman after the experimental *Cosmic Odyssey Nippon* who 'absolutely let me have it … said it was the worst thing she'd ever seen in her life and how dare we bring it to Brisbane, et cetera'.[117] Towards the end of Expo, Steel experienced the 'change' being spoken about in relation to the event, when the same woman made 'a beeline' for him in the foyer after another show:

> I couldn't escape so smiled encouragingly and waited. She had come, she said, to apologise and to say that the whole season had opened her eyes to theatrical possibilities of which she had never dreamed. She wished, she added, that she had the chance to see *Cosmic Odyssey Nippon* again now, for she would certainly watch it with completely fresh eyes. It is reactions like this that make such jobs worthwhile.[118]

Too Popular for Comfort

World Expo Park was also adversely affected by the popularity of Expo – and by attendee unwillingness to pay an extra entry fee for entertainment similar to that on offer at the annual Ekka. Poor visitation figures necessitated reducing staff, removing the separate entry fee, and extending operating hours.[119]

Local businesses suffered too, especially those in rival service industries. McDonald's Coorparoo takings fell by $500 a day, its licensee speculating, 'Parents seem to be saying to their kids that if the family goes to Expo there is nothing left in the budget for a Big Mac.'[120] While Expo's Munich Festhaus was selling 130,000 litres of beer a month (making profits estimated at $1.5 million a week), a Spring Hill publican lamented, 'I had 14 people in here Friday night. They didn't pay the wages of the two girls behind the bar.'[121] Expo-induced downturns in the local entertainment industry were of sufficient magnitude that a coalition of strippers announced they would 'bare their wares' in the Queen Street Mall to protest.[122]

The anticipated flow-on effect for tourism operators within Queensland largely failed to eventuate, with one northern Queensland resort operator claiming a fifty per cent downturn, and the Queensland Hotels' Association Townsville president announcing multiple tour bus cancellations because 'people are only going as far as Expo'.[123] Rival tourist locations also suffered, as people engaged in destination switching to Brisbane, prompting headlines such as 'Brisbane's Expo Joy Becomes NT's Woe', 'Expo Hits [Gold] Coast Business by up to 30 Per Cent', 'North Hit as Tourists Rush Expo', and 'NSW Hit as Expo Attracts Tourists'.[124] NSW was particularly unsettled, as there had been an expectation of a bicentennial 'boom'.[125] A commentator visiting Sydney during this time noted that 'not one word of Expo 88 appears anywhere in public there. But a clerk will often ask under his breath how things are going in Brisbane, with the air of someone looking over his shoulder to see what's gaining'.[126]

There were some positive figures for related businesses during Expo: Ansett and Australian Airlines announced a twenty to thirty per cent increase in flights to the city, and international tourism consultant Horwath and Horwath predicted an additional $54 million in profits for Brisbane's hotel and motel operators.[127] Australian Bureau of Statistics figures showed a 1.1 per cent increase per month in retail sales for Queensland – almost twice the national average – which *The Australian* dubbed an 'Expo binge'.[128]

Expo attendance figures continued to exceed expectations: by the midway point, there were 7.4 million recorded visits, just shy of the 7.8 million predicted for the entire event.[129] These numbers were partly attributable to the popularity of season passes, many of which had been pre-purchased at the discount price of $99. Mary-Clare Power believes the passes generated significant goodwill towards the exposition, as 'people forgot they paid for it ... Expo gave them something – to their mind – free to do every day'.[130] Goldston says BESBRA recorded twenty instances of people who used their passes more times than the exposition was actually open, and one attendee who passed through the gates 365 times: 'He worked near the site and used to go there for lunch and dinner.'[131]

With queue waiting times approaching five hours for popular attractions such as the New Zealand Pavilion, stories emerged of people feigning illness and borrowing wheelchairs to avoid the line-up.[132] Absolon says Expo's planners sought to mitigate such delays with the help of roaming entertainers and the design of the queue itself: 'They adopted the Disney style of queuing. All that kind of stuff was new to Australia. Before Expo, if there was a queue to go in to anything, it just went in a line. That zig-zaggy way of queuing was designed by Expo because people were entertained by walking past each other – whereas if you're in a straight line, you're just seeing the back of someone's head the whole time.'[133]

Some critics were flummoxed by the extent of the queuing – and by what people were queuing for. The predominance of video displays in many pavilions drew the charge: 'It doesn't matter what the signs outside a particular pavilion promise – a trip to the moon or a balloon ride over Kenya – what you're going to get is another piece of celluloid.'[134] Other Expo targets included the popular 'Human Factor' sculptures, which were labelled 'a shameless adaptation of a device that worked well in British Columbia', and the sail-like structures that had come to symbolise Expo, which were dismissed as too similar to the Federal Republic of Germany's pavilion at the 1967 Montreal exposition.[135]

Goldston recalls some prescient advice from Edwards: 'He said, "Run your life as though everything is going to be on the front page of the newspaper" – and it often was.'[136] Negative media coverage detailed war veterans traumatised by the nightly fireworks, beer costing $1.60–$2.40 a pot ('For that price,' said a despondent attendee, 'you'd want to keep it forever'), the accidental destruction of the 'pink submarine' during repairs, the ten-metre-high inflatable water-skiing version of Expo Oz sinking without trace after becoming unbalanced by a wave, the million dollars of Expo-related parking fines issued by BCC, passengers trapped on the monorail and Titan roller-coaster during mechanical breakdowns, construction accidents and fatalities, the Night Companion bursting into flames, the destruction of the Alien Encounters ride after two separate fires, a food-poisoning death following a meal at a Sri Lankan restaurant (that aroused xenophobic suspicion of 'exotic eating'), links to road deaths on the highway between Brisbane and Sydney, and Amnesty International's attempts to deliver dossiers to twenty-five participating countries detailing their violations of human rights (an action Edwards declared 'illegal').[137]

The Expo bubble was also popped, on occasion, by its official guests. During a speech for Sri Lanka's National Day, Prime Minister Ranasinghe Premadasa reminded the crowd that the 'leisure' celebrated by Expo was a distant dream for many in poorer countries.[138] Some school principals were also censorious, one bemoaning a rise in absenteeism during the event, another warning that it 'encouraged self-indulgence and materialism with little concern for those less well off in the age of technology'.[139]

The media was fortuitously absent or circumspect during some potentially calamitous moments, such as when the King of Spain was almost killed on Australian soil. 'Somebody forgot to lock off the podium,' recalls River Stage Producer John Watson, 'and when King Juan Carlos stood up, the podium moved, and he fell over and nearly died.'[140]

Watson and Hamilton say Barbara Absolon was the 'go-to' person when problems arose in the Entertainment Division.[141] Challenges ranged from locating a missing piece of Circus Oz equipment (accidentally taken to a dump at Darra) and restoring it moments before the performance, through to serious police and legal affairs.[142] Walkways Coordinator Ian Williams describes Absolon as 'a wonderful woman in a linen suit who didn't sweat', and who 'without yelling and screaming created a base of such professionalism' that whatever crisis emerged, 'she could get people to remember what their job was' so that the show could go on.[143]

In an interview nearly thirty years after first convincing BESBRA that women could keep secrets, Absolon only discreetly alludes to the litany of challenges that were faced: 'There were disasters on a daily basis – from things that were so serious I could never reveal them through to light-hearted things. In that year, Bobby McFerrin's song "Don't Worry, Be Happy" was released. I got one of my staff to dub it onto an audiocassette again and again and again. In my office was a lounge suite. The really big ones [disasters] I'd just go, "Sit down", press the play button, and just listen to Bobby McFerrin singing "Don't Worry, Be Happy" three or four times, turn it off, then go, "Okay. So what the hell are we gonna do about this?" Move on, because tomorrow there's going to be another drama.'[144]

This 'show must go on' mentality prevailed across BESBRA's divisions, and helped deliver a mainstream utopia capable of eliciting acknowledgement from unexpected quarters. In *The Big Party Syndrome* (a report that strongly criticised the lack of social planning prior to Expo and its effect on the local population), the author concedes some stark factors in the event's success:

> It is possible to be cynically disparaging about much of Expo's stage set-type gimmickry, the plaster and plastic, and some of the more crass manifestations of commercialism ... But the essential message is that Expo clearly enabled vast numbers of people to experience simple, basic, relatively unsophisticated pleasures which they do not normally experience in a modern urban environment ... out-of-doors eating, drinking, walking, talking and resting. It offered the possibility to see and be seen. It provided entertainment and educational and multi-cultural interest.[145]

Local citizens were certainly encouraged to enjoy being watched – in the article 'We're the Envy of Expo World', the *Sunday Sun* reported that 'foreigners manning the pavilions have been looking at us' with approval, concluding that 'we are laid back, comfortable with ourselves and our capital city, and friendly'.[146] Expo prompted a surge in civic pride that would surely have satisfied that grand master of parochialism, Sir Joh Bjelke-Petersen – had he still been involved. Many respondents to a *Sunday Mail* readers' poll listed the Queensland Pavilion as their favourite Expo venue, with accompanying comments such as 'I am proud to be a Queenslander'.[147] State pride was also available for purchase as a single release, with 'I've Been to Expo Too', based on the popular Redgum song 'I've Been to Bali Too' (the flipside featured the 'Festhouse Chicken Dance'); it was produced by radio station FM 104 as 'a dig at the southerners and whingers who all said Expo would be a flop'.[148]

The pro-Brisbane and Queensland hype may have helped ignite simmering intergovernmental tensions when the state venue (the *only* pavilion through which the popular monorail was routed) came into open conflict with the national venue after Prime Minister Hawke appeared at the Australian and Victorian Pavilions during Australia's 'National Day' celebrations in June. This prompted the front-page story 'PM Snubbed Qld Pavilion at Expo: Spokesman', in which Hawke's action (or lack thereof) was excoriated as a 'great breach of protocol and a slight on the pavilion'.[149] The improbable response from Hawke's camp, that he had merely passed through the Victorian Pavilion on his way 'to view the parade', proved insufficient, and the prime minister was compelled to reschedule his itinerary to include the Queensland venue.[150]

In his *Commissioner-General's Executive Report*, Veivers identified this incident as one of the exposition's 'low points', and claimed that international participants were 'bemused at the continued efforts by some Queenslanders to "upstage" the Commonwealth and the other Australian States'.[151] Veivers also lamented the Commonwealth's 'lack of commitment to the project in the early days', which allowed

Sir Llew Edwards (left) and Sir Joh Bjelke-Petersen with an early model of Expo, circa 1985. Some details changed prior to Expo, including the shade structures, removing a space shuttle model in the wake of the *Challenger* disaster, and the premier himself.

The Clem Jones Gardens, 1985. The gardens were part of the five hectares of Brisbane City Council land resumed for the forty-hectare Expo site.

The Expo construction site, 1986. The two lonely buildings near the centre of this image are the Plough Inn (right) and the Allgas building. Other historic buildings such as the Ship Inn, Collins Place, and the South Brisbane Municipal Library skirt the edges of the site.

The Titan roller-coaster at World Expo Park.

Dancers light up the Brisbane River on a pink submarine.

Expo 88 guides staffed booths at the entrances, escorted VIPs, and helped the public with everything from locating restrooms to knowing which venue hosted 'the chicken dance'.

The monorail passing beneath the iconic sunsails.

The 'BP Waterski Spectacular' – one of the few Expo entertainments with naming rights, another being the evening 'Qantas Light Fantastic Parade'.

Some of Expo's popular 'Human Factor' sculptures, several of which have been preserved and can be found dotted around Brisbane today.

A concert at the River Stage, with the Brisbane River and CBD as a panoramic backdrop.

Much of Expo's entertainment took place after dark and included lasers, fireworks, fluoro art, the 360-degree Night Companion searchlight, and the electric night parade.

Wrexpo 88, *Cane Toad Times*, Autumn 1988. This protest illustration by Michael Barnett could be purchased from the magazine in the form of a T-shirt.

A political cartoon by Alan Moir depicting queues for Expo 88 and the Fitzgerald Inquiry.

The South Bank Parklands canal, 1995. The canal was one of several parkland features razed in a redevelopment that introduced the Grand Arbour pedestrian walkway.

The prize feature of the South Bank 'people's playground' is the artificial beach formerly known as Kodak Beach (presently Streets Beach), pictured here in 2015.

The former Night Companion being refurbished in readiness for the SkyNeedle Apartments development, 2017.

Expo to be promoted as a 'Queensland affair', and claimed that its Operations and Communications divisions prioritised the state over international participants, which 'failed to appreciate the true meaning of an Expo'.[152] In his report for the BIE, Dr Damaso de Lario (chairman of the Committee of Commissioners-General for Expo) also faulted the Commonwealth for treating Expo as a Queensland matter until it 'appeared to be on the road to become a national and international success', by which time BESBRA had so much power that internationals felt compelled 'to just play along'.[153]

The late commitment to Expo from other Australian states was believed (certainly by Queensland newspapers) to have led to their 'big yawn' pavilions, which were deemed likely to inspire a visitor 'exodus':

> The sorry circumstances that caused the other states to delay
> their decisions to take part in Expo clearly left them with too
> little time to prepare competitive exhibits. Most are pretty
> dull – perplexing, in the case of Victoria, which puts you
> inside a human lung for no apparent reason, offers a few other
> random exhibits, and then has a wine bar at which they hope
> you will forget the entire, sorry mess.[154]

The states nevertheless claimed satisfaction with their Expo experience – and with the merchandise, tourism, and business opportunities that ensued; some speculated about participating in the exposition scheduled for Seville in 1992.[155] NSW premier Nick Greiner favoured an Expo 2000 bid. 'Sydney needs a great event,' he said. 'The most noteworthy impact of Expo on Brisbane is that it has changed the whole culture and atmosphere in Queensland and the people of Brisbane ... Sydney and New South Wales could well do with something like this.'[156]

The Queensland National Party was stymied in its ability to capitalise on Expo's popularity, as the 'father of Expo', Bjelke-Petersen, was no longer in power. His replacement, moreover, had

had so little to do with Expo prior to becoming premier that attempts to associate him with it were vulnerable to criticism. Labor's Keith De Lacy took gleeful aim at an advertisement featuring Ahern and the Expo site:

> Every time people see that advertisement they say, 'Fancy Mike Ahern taking credit for Expo.' I was never a supporter of the former Premier … However, I must say that Expo is the kind of project that honourable members have always associated with the former Premier, Sir Joh Bjelke-Petersen. He liked the big-headline glamour projects, the ones that would cause people to clap their hands … I can tell honourable members that the current Premier, with his reputation for being a wimp … would never have accepted Expo being held in Brisbane. The people of Queensland treat that advertisement as a joke.[157]

The premier was largely absent from mass-produced publications such as *World Expo 88: The Official Souvenir Program*, which has a greetings page featuring Edwards and Williams and an acknowledgement of Bjelke-Petersen's founding role, and *World Expo 88: Brisbane – Australia*, which has a foreword from Hawke and an introduction from Edwards. Given Bjelke-Petersen's prominence in pre-1988 Expo materials, it is difficult to imagine such omissions occurring had he still been premier.[158]

With Sallyanne Atkinson's high visibility at Expo as mayor, her central role in the site's redevelopment debate, and her preternatural knack for publicity, her exposition exposure was arguably greater than that of the premier, potentially linking her with the instigation of Expo in the public consciousness (though she herself never made any such claim); this may have amused BCC instigators of the 1982 Commonwealth Games who were subsequently media-gazumped by Bjelke-Petersen. It certainly bemused Expo organisers such as Peter Goldston, who had been privy to heated clashes between BESBRA and BCC: 'Mike Ahern – who was a lovely man – never got the political advantage out of Expo that he could have, and, I dare say, should have done. Sallyanne Atkinson is believed by many people to be one of the progenitors of Expo. She's not. She's far from it.'[159]

Expo was most likely to be associated in the public mind with its upbeat chairman, Sir Llew Edwards, who reportedly made 5200 speeches, thirty-five overseas trips, 147 interstate trips, thirty-one intrastate trips, and attended 11,600 meetings and deputations on behalf of the event.[160] His tireless diplomacy surely played a part in the thirty-seven awards he received as Expo chairman, including Queenslander of the Year.[161]

Bjelke-Petersen and Edwards's relationship never recovered from the former's exclusion at the opening ceremony (and, presumably, from the glory that became attached to an ex-Liberal politician, rather than the Bjelke-Petersen National Party government, in the wake of Expo's success); Bjelke-Petersen testified at the Fitzgerald Inquiry that everyone slept 'with one eye open' around Edwards.[162]

Exposition instigators Maccormick and Moore were also sidelined during Expo's operational phase, though both received media acknowledgement of their respective roles in establishing the event, and Edwards credited Moore in BESBRA's closing financial report.[163] Moore says he was able to accept 'stepping back' after midwifing the event with the aid of some stoic advice he once received from Bjelke-Petersen: 'Joh said to me quietly, "Well, Frank, we've got a lot of friends now, but just remember: in public life, it's not a question of 'what have you done for me?', it's 'what have you done for me lately?'"'[164]

Credit controversies flared when a number of (predominantly Queensland-based) Expo contributors received Australia Day honours, while others – notably, Australian Commissioner-General Sir Edward Williams and Expo General Manager Bob Minnikin – were left out.[165] Sir Leo Hielscher considers Minnikin's to be the gravest omission: 'He was the one that really made it happen. I mean, we were all there, but he was the one that *really* made it happen. And he was the one that would have got the shafts if it collapsed. But he didn't get any handclaps when it succeeded. He was brilliant. And he was the one that was biting his fingernails up to the elbows the night before the opening when he had them out there still painting the footpaths [after an unseasonable amount of rain].'[166]

Ahern says he was ambivalent about publicly associating himself (and, by implication, his party) with Expo, as his priority remained the Fitzgerald Inquiry: 'In my view, the important thing was to get that done correctly … and get the recommendations of the Royal Commission done – that was something that was my legacy. Did I put my name in the paper enough? I don't worry about it.'[167] He did, however, worry about negative reporting in relation to his premiership. Having befriended British prime minister Margaret Thatcher during her Expo visit, he later ventured to ask how she coped with bad publicity. 'Young man,' she replied, 'a conservative never reads the newspapers.'[168]

The Queensland media remained generally supportive of Expo – to the point of tacitly disassociating the troubled state government from its success. 'Realistically, Queensland is no utopia', ran a *Queensland Times* editorial as 'Queensland Day' was celebrated at the exposition (participating nations or governments were allocated a nominal Expo 'day'), since 'the State has one of the highest youth unemployment rates in the country, a high bankruptcy rate and drought problems in the south-west. However, today we celebrate the good things in our State.' The paper nominated Expo as 'one of the best reasons for Queenslanders to be proud of their state on Queensland Day', and credited the population with its success: 'Queensland has never looked better and its citizens have every reason to feel pleased with themselves and their achievements.'[169]

From Infatuation to Love Affair

Expo continued to inspire positive reports from various interstate commentators, but others remained steadfastly unimpressed. One critic at *The Australian Financial Review* charged that the pavilions contained little more than 'trivia and pretty pictures', and declared that 'if Brisbane people are prepared to wait an hour and a half to get in to look at boring pictures of grid iron and baseball players [at the US Pavilion], then there's something wrong with Brisbane people'.[170]

Perhaps there was. Perhaps there was something terribly wrong with Brisbane people. And perhaps it was something that Expo – with all its perceived virtues and vices – was helping to address. Goldston is remarkably candid in his view of Expo's success: 'There were a lot of lonely people in Brisbane. Some people came to Expo just so they could talk to other people. We found many examples of people who used to queue to go into the New Zealand Pavilion, get to the head of the queue and go back to the end just to talk to people … we had reached a catalyst level and they were entertaining each other, enjoying each other's company – because the pavilions weren't all *that* good. Even our streetscaping and entertaining wasn't all *that* good. But people wanted to enjoy it. They had taken the decision, or they took the decision very quickly, that they wanted to enjoy this – and they determined that they would enjoy it – and they did.'[171]

Goldston's observations are strongly supported by vox-pops and surveys of the day. During Expo's closing stages, when asked what they would remember about it, many attendees referenced its social aspects: 'The friendly feeling of the whole thing; whole families from grandparents to babies enjoying days out together'; 'The colours, the sculptures and the feeling that Brisbane was alive'; 'The willingness of passers-by to join when requested by (street theatre) actors'; 'The way people talked to perfect strangers; once through the gates people seemed to lose their inhibitions and become one big happy family'; and the simple fact that 'Sunday's not dead anymore'.[172] One commentator observed, 'It was a great way to forget about the woes of the world'; another praised 'the lack of inhibition so that no one minded or looked askance if you jigged or jived or whistled along with the show'.[173] One person went so far as to say, 'Expo restored my faith in humanity and the possibilities for the future: if we can leave creeds, colours, religions, politics outside the gates and just be humans.'[174] Another was just grateful for the opportunity 'to be among so many people and so much life that loneliness simply vanishes'.[175]

A report on Expo's effect on youth leisure elicited a similarly enthusiastic response. The event was considered so different from existing youth activities such as watching television, reading, listening to music, going to voluntary groups, and playing sport that respondents had trouble finding words that could do justice to their experience. Attempts included 'Expo's so different from anything else like the Mall because it's more exciting; there's more people and things to do', 'Expo gives me more freedom. My parents don't mind if I go to Expo', and 'I feel alive everywhere: I feel happy all the time'.[176]

Behavioural specialists declared the event a 'psychological success' that enriched family life and fulfilled emotional needs.[177] Psychologists and sociologists expressed surprise at the extent to which Expo influenced behaviour: people affected by alcohol were happy rather than belligerent, there was minimal anger at queues or queue-jumpers, and negligible vandalism occurred on the site.[178] One commentator speculated that this geniality might be partly attributable to a sustained public relations campaign urging locals to 'show the world' a happy face, but was nevertheless impressed by the outcome:

> It would be hard to recall any fair that's done more to work a change in its host, instantly, even before the event was fairly under way. Responding to Expo 88's internal message, that defiant rallying cry of 'show the world', Brisbane turned a face toward the incoming hordes it's never shown before.[179]

Exceptionally good weather may also have boosted the general mood, with only eight days of rain during the six-month exposition.[180]

One behavioural specialist suggested that good behaviour at the event stemmed from the perception that Expo was 'ours'.[181] There was also the simple fact that a large number of people had been offered an extraordinary array of experiences at an affordable price and had a wonderful time.

Where else could attendees taste a drink cooled with ice cubes cut from a 10,000-year-old iceberg? Be photographed on a lunar landscape? View a peacock statue once lost in a shipwreck en route to the 1880–1 world exposition in Melbourne? Where could they see mannequins simulating heart transplants and laser surgery? View a pitch experiment, a Michael Jackson impersonator moonwalking on rollerskates, or a lady with a pot plant for a head? Ride a hovercraft, see an artificial lake, an aviary, a rainforest, and a glow-worm cave? Eat a crocodile burger while watching a laser beam etch a koala, then linger over a medieval document – the foundation stone of parliamentary authority – before joining a conga-line led by Expo Oz? Where else offered a chocolate factory, bell-ringers, traditional dancing, music, weapon demonstrations, magicians, muscle men, robots, rollerskating, an earthquake monitor, and its own mint? All of it watched over by the omnipotent Night Companion as it ejaculated beams of light some sixty metres into the air in Expo's own take on the bat signal. In the absence of any logical or cultural consistency, Expo became something other than a place – it was a state of being.

With just five weeks left to run, season passes to Expo were still being purchased at the rate of 600 a week.[182] Goldston says some people even tried to purchase one on the final day of Expo, 'totally illogically'.[183] With less than a month to go, the event was on target to record the highest attendance levels – on a per-capita basis – in the history of world expositions. Attendance figures (bolstered by staff, VIPs, and repeat visits) were close to one hundred per cent of Australia's population – against twenty to thirty per cent for other recent world expositions.[184] There were more than a million visits recorded during its final eight days.[185] Other statistical feats include the sale of over 525,000 season passes and 2.1 million three-day passes over the duration of Expo, the reconnection of 4000 lost children with frazzled guardians, and the consumption of 1.7 million hamburgers, 1.4 million dagwood dogs, eight million hot dogs, five million chicken nuggets, and eight million buckets of chips.[186] Enough beer was consumed to fill 650 family swimming pools.[187]

The unofficial keywords of Expo, 'success' and 'change', continued to dominate deliberations on the event, but there was also a change in tone from the southern press. A writer for *The Australian Financial Review* opined that the Expo 88 'bicentennial highlight' should become a how-to guide for establishing and organising future world expositions.[188] Once-obligatory references to cane toads and cowboy hats slowly dissipated. Where negative remarks were made, qualifications were also offered; one publication acknowledged that 'despite the image, Brisbane had plenty of after-hours entertainment … and cultural activities before Expo, but it involved a narrower base of people than great cities of the world'.[189] The writer credited 'Sir Llew Edwards' crew' with ensuring that 'not just the trendoids and yuppies' were exposed to the cosmopolitan agenda of Expo: 'by marketing Expo to the average Joes and Jolenes of Brisbane', a surprisingly diverse range of people were now embracing the concept of 'change':

> Most significantly, it is a phrase used by what were the most parochial, conservative, inhibited and least proud citizens of a mainland Australian capital. The people who cheered as Sir Joh Bjelke-Petersen used commissioner Sir Terry Lewis' police to bash street marchers are now caught up in the atmosphere of fun and fantasy as crowds swarm through city streets after Expo closes each night. The people who righteously clapped as Sir Joh used special legislation to stamp on buskers in Brisbane's main street and mall now delight in the performances of the wandering entertainers around Expo.[190]

Some things – notably politics – stayed the same. The disgruntled Bjelke-Petersen refused to attend festivities for the final day of Expo.[191] Lord Mayor Atkinson was controversially left off the speakers' list for the closing ceremony (as, initially, was another of Edwards's rivals, Sir Edward Williams).[192] Atkinson staged a deft public recovery by arranging with Expo's television sponsor Network Ten to deliver a pre-recorded speech (along with Minnikin) for its highly anticipated closing special, *The Carnival Is Over*.[193] Judith Durham declined to reunite with iconic band The Seekers to perform their hit song of the same name at the ceremony, stating her reluctance to be associated with a bicentennial event when Aboriginal people had nothing to celebrate (Durham's vocals were sung by Julie Anthony).[194]

The generally adoring crowds turned briefly against BESBRA – and demonstrated a growing sense of ownership over the event – when informed that Expo would be closed to the public at 4.30 pm on the final day (instead of the usual 10 pm), and that the closing ceremony would be restricted to approximately 20,000 accredited personnel, VIPs, and guests.[195] 'The public has been supporting Expo for six months,' said one attendee. 'It's pretty unfair to shut us out for the biggest night of all.'[196] 'It's a big thing the last day of Expo,' noted another enthusiast; 'I think everyone should be able to go.'[197]

The final day of Expo was, nevertheless, a triumphant affair, with attendees sobbing, dancing, having teardrops painted on their faces, jumping into fountains, and cheering as ticker tape descended from above.[198] 'Expo finished when the crowd didn't want it to finish,' remembers Hielscher in an interview nearly twenty-five years after the event. 'That's a good way to finish anything, really.'[199]

At the formal closing ceremony, Edwards and Ahern both acknowledged Bjelke-Petersen's role in Expo, with Ahern urging the crowd to 'join me in giving a pat on the back to Sir Joh for doing this'.[200] Edwards also thanked the trade union movement for keeping the exposition free from industrial disputes, the BESBRA board for its loyalty (despite the fact that some members had attempted to unseat him), and staff and visitors for making it 'the happiest place on earth'.[201] Prime Minister Hawke observed, 'It seems incredible that only a few months before Expo opened it was being written off as an impending embarrassment, even a disaster. Today we all recognise that in every respect it has been a brilliant success.' With typical audaciousness, he then said, 'I am proud the Federal Government was a supporter of a major bicentennial event from start to finish', and claimed that the exposition had 'given us the opportunity to show the world what great attributes Australia has to offer'.[202] Sir Edward Williams thanked the international guests and, somewhat cryptically, said that 'hopefully, through Expo 88, we have acquired just a little more of the virtue of humility'.[203] Ahern's speech proved the stark improbability of this trait at such a time:

> The comment I heard repeated most often during Expo was: 'I can't believe this is Brisbane.' It's certain – the old town will never be the same again. We will never be the same again. World Expo changed our lives in hundreds of little ways … our attitudes … to Brisbane, to Queensland, to Australia, and to ourselves. We're a more confident people now. We know we can do anything. In fact we know we can do everything.[204]

At the conclusion of the speeches, Hawke and Edwards hugged, and, with Ahern, raised their hands in celebration to cheers from the crowd.[205] The television-viewing audience, and the thousands assembled along the banks of the river or watching from boats, were then treated to a grand fireworks display before the moment arrived – fourteen years and myriad struggles in the making – for Expo's lights to be switched off for the last time.[206] Special events technician Sherry Peck had spent the previous six weeks reprogramming the system so that, with the aid of one hundred manual operators, the lights would turn off progressively from the outer reaches of the exposition grounds through to their innermost point. It took sixteen seconds.[207]

7

After Party

Well, I'm sure you're coming to the conclusion – I hope you
are – that Expo was a watershed. Brisbane is a terrific place
nowadays, I think. No one would have called it that twenty-five
years ago, that's for sure.

Anthony Steel[1]

'THE NIGHT AFTER IT CLOSED,' says World Expo on Stage
Consultant Producer Marguerite Pepper, 'it was like the life had
been sucked out of the city.'[2] One hundred and eighty-four days of
'showing the world' later, the carnival really was over. Forty hectares
of yesterday's otherworldly delights lay barren – fenced off and
prepared for demolition. Social opportunities withered overnight:
national and international guests went home, there were fewer
performances and venues, extended licensing hours were retracted,
dining options diminished, and the meeting place was gone. The
worry set in – a sense of unease snaking through the longed-for
feeling of success. Expo's 'coming of age' mantle had been won,
but what was Brisbane growing into? Could adulthood be managed
without the Expo crutch? A spate of existential articles wrestled with
the question 'What does it mean?'

The battle for Expo's legacy took place on several fronts, from finding a cure to the post-Expo blues through to conceptualising Brisbane's post-Expo identity. The most vitriolic of these concerned the Expo site. The redevelopment of Brisbane's South Bank incited bitter debate between public and private interests, between the state government and the BCC, and within the teetering National Party. The outcome provided tangible proof that Expo had changed Brisbane in more ways than its instigators could have imagined.

Withdrawal Symptoms

Dialogue on the meaning and legacy of Expo began years in advance of the event, but intensified as the moment arrived. The exposition was swiftly hailed a success in terms of attendance figures and organisational prowess – which prompted similarly swift ruminations on the meaning of that success. 'The big question,' mused a writer for *The Weekend Australian*, 'is whether Expo will be remembered as a great party for Brisbane or a real boost for Queensland and Australia.'[3] Local newspapers also pondered the legacy's fine print:

> Is the party nearly over, or has it only just begun? The choice is ours. Here we are, more than two months into World Expo 88, and caught up in the wildest and most colourful event in our State's history. But is it really just another party? Or is it an event that will have a profound effect on our lifestyles, our expectations and our futures? Will Expo be remembered only as the fun fair to end all fun fairs, or will it prove to be the moment in history that put our sleepy, sub-tropical backwater squarely on a world map of places not to be overlooked, ignored or underestimated?[4]

At the event's conclusion, another local journalist opined that Brisbane 'will probably never be the same again', then set the city and its population the task of filling 'what for many will be a post-Expo void.'[5] There were grave fears for Brisbane's social future. As the finale loomed, Premier Ahern warned, 'We may find ourselves going cold turkey after October 31 if we don't have some way of sustaining the high.'[6] Newspapers prophesied 'Expo-itis', 'post-Expo blues', and 'Expo junkies' unable to get their daily fix.[7] The Queensland Council of Churches President formed 'Expo Anonymous' to help those struggling with their return to the every day, and suggested that 'symptoms of post-Expo depression will include grief, anger and disbelief ... some people have just lived for Expo. Its closing will be like a death in the family'.[8]

The state chairman of the Australian Psychological Society advised counselling and retraining for Expo staff, a measure backed by a Canadian Pavilion employee with two prior expositions under her belt: 'When you work at an Expo you're special and you belong to a big family. Expo is like a city unto itself. But when Expo ends, it is hard to readjust to not having that status.'[9] Some precautions proved necessary; Ahern recalls, 'We had to engage therapists to help some people who were trying to get into the site after it had closed.'[10] Most Expo enthusiasts proved more resilient – Expo Anonymous was disbanded a few months after its inception due to low participation rates.[11]

The employment movements of thousands of Expo workers (30,000 staff were accredited during the event) were not closely tracked, but a newspaper article the following year observed, 'It appears the bulk of them are now in other jobs.'[12] Lady Edwards says many Expo volunteers 'went on and offered themselves to hospitals as a group, or to kids' sports ... the model for all of that was used by the [Sydney] Olympics'.[13]

Sir Llew Edwards – a fortress of positivity in relation to Expo – admitted to concerns over the capacity of government and business to build on its momentum, warning that if they failed to act swiftly, Expo would just be 'a nice memory'.[14] By way of example, he suggested the city mall could 'become the Expo mall in atmosphere if not in name', optimistically predicting that 'the day of the busker sitting playing a guitar and collecting coins is finished'.[15] Proposals from other parties included a science centre aimed at children (which evolved into the Sciencentre) and a 'big events' consulting group with representatives from government and private enterprise (which became Queensland Events Corporation).[16]

According to Tony Bennett, Expo had been 'preceded by its own bequest' in some ways, as the typical architectural legacy of world expositions (museums, monuments, cultural centres, and arts venues) existed prior to the event with the adjacent QCC.[17] He lamented that Expo's greatest anticipated physical legacy was the World Expo Park amusement zone – the cultural antithesis of traditional exposition endowments.[18] The troubled entertainment venture failed in 1989, and Ric Birch was unsuccessful with his bid (in collaboration with Kern Corporation) to transform the area into an 'Expocity' of artist lofts, studios, and workshops, where visitors could peruse and purchase art en route to restaurants and coffee shops.[19]

Atkinson committed the BCC to preserving some of the event's artefacts by purchasing work from high-profile artists such as Arnaldo Pomodoro, correctly predicting that these would increase in value; the decision was criticised by Alderman David Hinchliffe, who considered it more egalitarian to keep the popular 'Human Factor' collection together – ideally in a dedicated park, as sculptor John Underwood had suggested.[20] Many artefacts were destroyed at the event's conclusion when their preservation proved financially or physically impractical. Some were lost when countries seeking to donate paraphernalia were denied tax exemptions.[21] Other items were sold or donated to public and private interests in Queensland, interstate, and internationally. The whereabouts of many such artefacts is unknown. Some (including an Expo Oz costume) reside in museum environments; others, such as the 'Human Factor' piece *Around the Camp Fire*, are on display in the Brisbane CBD. The Queensland Pavilion houses a church, and the Japan Pond and Garden has been relocated to the Mt Coot-tha Botanic Gardens.[22] Less fortunate works such as the Ken Done–designed 'Australia' lettering and some of the Expo parade floats are deteriorating in exposed or isolated locations.[23]

Several large Expo artefacts were preserved, including the Nepalese pagoda, which was retained through donations spearheaded by Expo enthusiasts Ray Lewis and Myra and Frank Pitt.[24] The tallest Expo landmark, the Night Companion, was destined for Tokyo Disneyland before being purchased by Queensland hairdressing magnate Stefan Ackerie, who relocated it near his headquarters in Manning Street, West End (incurring the original designer's ire in the process by adding multicoloured 'Stefan ring' lights to its crest).[25] Ackerie jocularly referenced his Lebanese heritage when announcing the purchase: 'Expo is a really great success story. And as long as this needle remains in Brisbane, young people will remember how good Expo was. And I think it's better for a wog to leave the needle in Australia – in Brisbane – than for an American or Japanese person to take it away.'[26]

In 2015, it was revealed that the tower and surrounding land had been sold to developers, and that it would form the centrepiece of the new Pradella complex.[27]

Technically impractical hopes that the monorail would be repurposed to shuttle commuters from UQ to South Brisbane or to connect the area with the CBD and Woolloongabba were dashed when its builders exercised a 'right of purchase on resale' clause in their contract, and the monorail cars were removed from Australia.[28] Expo's iconic sunsails were divided and purchased by Griffith University and an overseas buyer.[29] BESBRA received several offers for the rights to Expo Oz but decided against allowing the mascot to represent anything else; Edwards explains, rather gently, 'We decided to send him off to Expo heaven.'[30] For historians, Expo heaven is divided between the Queensland State Archives, where truckloads of records were sent after the event, and the John Oxley Library, which houses items ranging from architectural maps and promotional materials through to dining menus, exclusive Club 88 invitations, and Expo ambassador memorabilia.[31]

The Main Game

For many politicians, developers, and business leaders, there was only one piece of Expo memorabilia of real consequence. For them, Expo had always been about the after party: redevelopment. It had long been public knowledge that the site would be sold to help finance Expo, but the details were rather less public. Minnikin says nascent hopes that a major sports and entertainment complex would be established on the post-Expo site were dashed early on when arrangements were made to build one at Boondall instead.[32] Labor MLA Henry Palaszczuk's 1984 suggestion that the site be transformed into low-cost housing for city workers was roundly ignored.[33]

The potential ramifications of intransparency relating to the site redevelopment only became apparent when Expo's success was all but assured. With the Fitzgerald Inquiry looming in August 1987, Deputy Leader of the Opposition Tom Burns sought to link the Bjelke-Petersen government's secretive redevelopment plans with previous controversies:

> I ask the Government when honourable members are to be
> told what is to happen with the site after the sideshow ends? In
> particular, the Government has still given no guarantee that the
> former public riverside land at the Expo site will be retained for
> public use. The Government will sell it off to Iwasaki, or the
> old bloke will go overseas to sell it to Romania or some other
> place, as he has done with most of our other public land.[34]

Calls for socially minded action grew more urgent as Expo's opening day loomed. In an address to parliament in October 1987, Labor's Terry Mackenroth argued:

> The site represents a unique opportunity to reclaim the centre
> of the city for the people of Brisbane; to reclaim the centre
> of the capital for the people of Queensland ... we urge the

Government not to look for a short-term expedient and not
to think only of next year's Budget and how it would be
good to pull in 10, 20, 30 or more millions of dollars to help
balance the books, but to think of the future, to preserve that
area ... and to enforce a sympathetic development of low-
rise architecture and public open space so that when Expo is
remembered in the years ahead it is remembered not as a fond
thing that drifted away – a nice thing when it happened but
look at what is over there now – but as a lasting legacy for the
future generations of this State.[35]

The National Party was in a difficult position. It had promised Expo
would be run at no cost to the public – indeed, this was a specific
requirement of the *Expo '88 Act*.[36] If it sold the site to keep its
promise, the government could expect to be flayed by the media and
its rivals. If it broke its promise to keep the site ... it could expect the
same treatment. Without electorally awkward promises to negotiate,
it was comparatively easy for other parties to advocate saving the site.

BCC had a strong interest in the fate of the exposition grounds.
When the state government excised the land from its control in
1984, it steamrolled over town-planning functions the council was
democratically constituted to perform. With the council no longer
shackled by the need for intergovernmental cooperation in relation to
the 1987 Student Games or its (failed) 1992 Brisbane Olympic Games
bid, it could more strenuously contest the amount of commercial
development on the post-exposition site; the preference – in keeping
with Clem Jones's policy – was for open riverside spaces with parks
and low-level development.[37] Under Lord Mayor Roy Harvey, such
ambitions had been balanced with the state government's need to
alleviate exposition costs by permitting 60,000 m² of commercial
development.[38] During Atkinson's time as mayor, the land required
by BESBRA to offset rising costs soared to upwards of 250,000 m²,
which threatened to depress CBD land prices and the council's rate
base; a compromise of 100,000 m² was sought.[39]

'I was determined we were not going to have an alternative city as you have in North Sydney,' Atkinson recalls. 'If Joh had had his way, this site would have been covered by buildings, and it would have absolutely killed the CBD; in terms of urban planning, there was a lot at stake … it was just an extraordinary opportunity that we had: that amount of open space within walking distance from the city'.[40]

The BESBRA board established the Post Expo Development committee (PED) in 1986 to assess the site's redevelopment options. PED was advised by Jones Lang Wotton (JLW) property consultants, with whom Edwards later accepted a position; the committee did not include a representative from BCC.[41]

Atkinson says she discerned a lack of preparation regarding the post-exposition site: 'I had been to Canada to have a look at the Expo site there in Vancouver, and I realised then that they [Brisbane] were in a bit of a mess because they had made no plans at all … Stanley Kwok [who successfully redeveloped much of the Vancouver 86 site] came out, and we had a seminar in City Hall and started planning.'[42] It became apparent, however, that BCC would have scant input into the redevelopment process. 'That's when the real tensions started,' says Atkinson, 'because I guess there was an expectation – certainly I had an expectation during Expo – that we would be involved in the post-Expo planning process; but I could see that wasn't happening, so I had to really sort of push my way in.'[43]

Atkinson had several advantages over the theoretically more powerful state government: she was untainted by scandal or corruption; her party had been re-elected in a March 1988 landslide; and, as a popularly elected mayor (rather than one chosen by the majority party), her position was secure. When first elected, in 1985, Atkinson was the unintended beneficiary of National Party amendments to the *City of Brisbane Act* designed to foster that party's urban incursion by helping install popular cricketer Greg Chappell as a National Party mayor; Chappell did not contest the election, and Atkinson became the un-deposable voice of one of the largest municipal governments in the world.[44] She recalls, 'Bob Hawke was fond of telling me that I was the most powerful politician in Australia because I was popularly elected ... a premier or a prime minister can be toppled.'[45]

The More Things Change ...

Increased BCC involvement in the redevelopment process arose through a series of self-administered blows to the National Party's fortunes. The failed 'Joh for PM' campaign and disturbing revelations from the Fitzgerald Inquiry leached much of the goodwill that traditionally accrues to the originators of successful expositions. The party's popularity had been grafted to the former premier for so long that it struggled to detach itself on his way down. After deposing Bjelke-Petersen, Ahern had promised a new era of openness and accountability. His efforts to keep the Fitzgerald Inquiry running, his accessions to requests for expanded terms of reference, and his willingness to introduce a Public Accounts Committee were notable steps in this direction. But much of his party's reputational restoration was undone by its Expo-related manoeuvrings.

JLW had advised selling the site in advance of the exposition to reduce holding costs on the land, and to make it available as one parcel to tempt developers with a monopoly.[46] Calls for expressions of interest closed in March 1987, and were assessed by representatives from the Premier and Treasury departments, BESBRA, JLW, and BCC, then submitted to the Post Expo Evaluation Committee (formerly the PED), consisting of Schubert, Hielscher, Edwards, and the BCC town clerk.[47] Discussions continued beyond Bjelke-Petersen's December 1987 replacement as premier by Ahern and into 1988.

National Party identity Sir Frank Moore was chairman of one of the bidding parties, the River City 2000 consortium. Its proposal was similar to one Moore had floated in 1982 while in the vanguard of Expo enthusiasts. BCC recommended against this proposal as it consumed too much riverfront space and included elements significantly outside the tendering parameters, such as a casino; it also offered less value than some of its rivals.[48] The committee favoured a proposal from Don Cunnington's CM Group that included a world trade centre, an exhibition and convention centre, a boulevard, parkland, a private university, and a canal.[49]

Peter Goldston sheds some light on what happened next: 'We made a Cabinet recommendation that Don Cunnington's group get it. Frank Moore over the weekend got wind of what our recommendation was, worked the Cabinet levers, and Cabinet came back to us the next Monday and said, "We would like you to do some sort of a deal with Frank Moore." So Llew had been bounced twice now [including Bjelke-Petersen's subversion of the tendering process to favour Thiess], so he wasn't real happy ... they did it for what they thought were valid reasons: Frank Moore's a solid citizen ... I eventually asked him, "Okay, give us your price without a casino." He said, "I'll take $20 million off if you don't give me a casino licence." Bang. We had him. We raced out and got David Graham to price a casino licence in Brisbane; he came back and said $150 million. So we went back to Moore and said, "We'll deal with you if you give us $150 million for the licence." Scream, whinge, whine, moan. So this is taking too much time, I'll report to you, some skerricks got into the press. Who would tell the press anything? I don't know [Goldston grins]. And the public went mad: "No, no, no, not our beloved Expo site! We don't want casinos there; we want it to be a tribute to Expo!"'[50]

While there were question marks over the character and capacity of some of Moore's bidding rivals, it was a monumentally inopportune time for Cabinet to award monopolistic control of the South Bank site to a National Party associate with a storied history of alleged preferential treatment, whose proposal emphatically flouted tender guidelines while being financially uncompetitive, and in a semi-secret process that overrode the recommendations of the assessment committee. Labor's Len Ardill swiftly invoked ghosts of the National Party's past: 'Before the Deen brothers move in on the Expo site the

Government should say, "Stop! Hold! Just wait until we think about this."[51] Liberal Denver Beanland (an Atkinson ally and former BCC alderman) predicted 'another world's tallest building fiasco will be in the making', and referenced some of Moore's previous National Party interactions:

> The clock on this development should be stopped, and a
> new start should be made with the community having a
> genuine input into any development proposal ... Should the
> Government need to meet a shortfall in funding, then so be it.
> The people of Brisbane, as well as all Queenslanders, deserve
> something better than just another Toowong Railway Station
> development or a Roma Street Transit Centre.[52]

Labor's Eric Shaw observed that a submission offering $150 million in cash had been overlooked in favour of Moore's offer of $50 million followed by $25 million a year for six years, which effectively turned the government into a finance raiser and guarantor for a private consortium – and that that was a better deal for the consortium than BESBRA had been given to stage Expo.[53] He denounced this along with the National Party's 'Vision of Excellence' campaign:

> The Government's scandalous plan to dispose of the Expo land
> has destroyed this myth – before it even got started! ... The
> National Party Government of Queensland has shown that
> it not only does not have a vision of excellence, but lacks
> any vision whatsoever, beyond seeing the opportunity for
> private profit. The hopes of so many people that Queensland
> had passed into a new era, where fair play and adherence to
> high principles of conduct might prevail, have been dashed,
> ruthlessly.[54]

Sir Frank Moore felt rather differently. He viewed the proposal in terms of keeping a promise he had made as part of his seminal role in convincing the state government to invest in Expo: 'When everyone said how are we going to pay for it, I'd said, "Well, that's how you can pay for it [the sale of the land], and if you can't do it, I'll do it – and I'll do it with private money." Now, when it came to the end of the day, I said, "I'll do it – if you want it, I'll do it" – and so they said, "Yes, okay, we'll do it." And then once the decision was made, they went, "Ahhhhh! Our Expo!" Well, bugger it. If that's what they wanted – they had it – but I'd done what I said I'd do – I'd pay for it. It was as simple as that.'[55]

The controversy had a deleterious effect on Ahern's popularity, which sagged to the level of the National Party government more broadly.[56] 'There was enormous protest going on,' recalls Edwards. 'I think I got over a thousand letters from people who said, "How dare you take down Expo!"'[57] Dissenting groups included the National Trust of Queensland, the Queensland Country Women's Association, the Save Our South Bank Committee, the Queensland Synod of the Uniting Church, the Slack's Creek Progress Association, and the Women's Christian Temperance Union.[58]

American businessman Chuck Sanders was not surprised by the controversy; the twelve-time exposition veteran (including Expo) had 'a history of watching a site used as a political football', and observed, 'it is a game that can go on for months or years'.[59] Expo had once again become a source of protest – but this time many objections stemmed from a love of the event where once there had been loathing, and this time the objections were heard. Ahern tasked Edwards and Schubert with investigating post-Expo alternatives. They concluded that the government could reasonably abandon its vow to hold the event at no public cost if it were in the interest of facilitating greater public use of the site.[60]

Ahern reveals that some responses were more reasonable than others: 'There had always been an argument that we could recover from sales of the site enough money to cover the cost. When it was finished, there was such an emotional wash about it that there was a protest every day about the suggestion that we maximise the money return. They said, "Can't you do something to leave it open for us?" And there was – the lord mayor Sallyanne was "Please, please" – there were proposals coming from developers for putting high-rise and casinos and taking it out of the public arena altogether and putting up a full-on, hundred per cent occupied commercial site. And there was such a revolt about it after Expo that I was persuaded that we wouldn't accept the commercial development. My party were livid. And, uh, Cabinet went "boom".'[61]

Ahern says he made many enemies within the National Party when he withdrew the preferred tenderer status of River City 2000, and that there was 'a revolt in the business community' when he chose to limit commercial exploitation of the site.[62] Given Bjelke-Petersen's history with protest, development, parliamentary proprietary, and Moore, it seems unlikely that the tendering process would have reopened had he still been premier. The Fitzgerald Inquiry and dwindling National Party fortunes also had a bearing on the outcome. A local journalist identified another element in the equation:

> There can be no doubt the Government's decision to re-open tenders for the redevelopment of the site was as a direct result of the effect Expo has had on all of us, and the fire of enthusiasm it seems to have ignited in our collective bellies … Until Expo came along, the inhabitants of this State were inclined to accept having bad government decisions imposed upon them, sometimes at dead of night … But the euphoria of Expo … quickly led to a wave of outrage and dismay over the Government's cavalier decision to accept a redevelopment proposal which seemed to appeal to nobody but the developers themselves and their good friends in Cabinet.[63]

An event intended to bring glory to the National Party had thus midwifed infamy instead, inspiring a wave of self-interest that turned the people of mainstream Brisbane into the 'ratbag communist' protesters Bjelke-Petersen had railed against.

Peter Goldston – who was to become the founding general manager of the South Bank Corporation (with Vic Pullar as chairman) – felt conflicted by the opportunity: 'We'd done our job. We'd wrapped the land up on a nice parcel for the government. They'd stuffed it up ... It so happened that I was one of the people the government turned to to handle it. But, so far as Expo was concerned, we'd done our job. On a personal level ... yes, we loved the fact that there would be – let me call it a memorial to Expo. In our professional lives, that wasn't the case.'[64]

The reopened tendering process was led by BESBRA, but Ahern allowed greater consultation with BCC and the community.[65] Edwards and Goldston were dispatched (with two public servants and two council representatives) on an eight-day study tour of exposition redevelopments in Europe and the United States.[66] Ahern expressed an interest in turning the site into a cultural precinct with significant parkland, but this was financially incommensurate with BCC's stipulated maximum of 100,000 m^2 of commercial space – their combined ambitions risked a revenue reduction of up to $100 million, to which BESBRA could not legally consent.[67]

Atkinson challenged the requirements of the *Expo '88 Act*, the continued lack of transparency in redevelopment deliberations, and the dominance of unelected voices in the debate: 'My main fights were with Llew Edwards ... he did really well at Expo and was sort of the king of Expo; but I think he wanted to be the king after Expo. So we had a few ... yes ... dust-ups on that.'[68]

'Llew and Sally didn't get on,' remembers Ahern. 'There's some history attached to that. I've known Sally since schooldays. They're both very egotistical, those two.'[69] Edwards certainly expresses nostalgia for the previous lord mayor, Roy Harvey, who he felt 'had no interest in the Expo at all – then Sallyanne came and she tried to intervene a lot, and so we said to get out of our way – and it did put a bit of tension between Sallyanne and me'.[70]

Atkinson had the court of public opinion on her side. A newspaper survey near the end of Expo found that sixty-seven per cent of respondents believed there had been insufficient public consultation on the redevelopment, with one adding, 'We have been treated with contempt.'[71] A Harry Gordon *Courier-Mail* editorial argued that the debt should be forgiven so that something special could be achieved with the site: 'Nothing in politics is imperative or absolute least of all the pledge of a politician, particularly a deposed one.'[72] The newspaper also charged that the redevelopment had been a rushed and expensive 'disaster' with a 'cronyistic conclusion', and quested for BCC to have a greater role in the planning process.[73]

Debate over the redevelopment continued beyond the close of Expo and into 1989. Goldston was alarmed by the delay: 'We had read the history of post-Expo developments in many other places, and it's a disaster. In many places – New York – expo sites sit for twenty, thirty, forty years as festering messes while people argue about what should happen to them. I was told by the state government and I was requested by the city council at almost the highest levels to clean down the Expo site and put grass on it, while they fought about what they would do post-Expo. So I knocked down the Expo site and didn't put any grass on it; and it looked terrible. And I came up with all sorts of reasons why we couldn't put grass on it – and that put tremendous pressure on them to accept the ideas we were coming up with for post-Expo development.'[74]

The Price of Success

Goldston had reason for concern: the Expo debt was rising by $500,000 a week through interest rates and holding costs on the land.[75] Deputy Opposition Leader Tom Burns accused the government of expensive 'dithering' over the redevelopment, and of being 'less than honest' about Expo's financial position.[76] A report BESBRA submitted to the BIE in December 1988 claimed the budget was $625 million (including $200 million from corporate and government exhibitors).[77] Expo's economic stimulus was estimated at $1020 million – in addition to approximately $1200 million generated by the Business Visitors Program.[78] In March 1989, newspapers reported that BESBRA had made a $653,000 profit from a $480 million investment.[79]

Jennifer Craik disputed Expo's figures, arguing that millions of dollars' worth of hidden services had been borne by various government departments.[80] Queensland Institute of Technology (later Queensland University of Technology) lecturer Kerry Donohue claimed Expo had made a loss of approximately $120 million, consisting of $77.7 million in services provided by the state government and BCC, between $26 million and $30 million by the federal government, and $20 million in the difference between the site's estimated value and the recent valuation of $178 million.[81] Other hidden costs included $26 million on rail service upgrades, $18 million on the Queensland Pavilion, $9.7 million on police services, and $4 million on the Business Visitors Program.[82]

A follow-up report by Donohue and Peter Carroll noted that the event's cost to the public included stamp duty exemptions, sales tax exemptions, a freeze on city council rates, and a substantial drain on public service resources and staff since 1984.[83] They concluded that Expo's $653,000 book profit was 'basically correct', but only in a choose-your-own-accounting-adventure narrative in which direct and indirect government subsidies were excluded from calculations.[84] The challenges from Craik, Donohue, and Carroll generated front-page headlines such as 'Taxpayers Left with the Bill: Report', '$100m Expo Slug Claim', and 'Secret Study's Shock Finding'.[85] A *Sun* editorial concluded that such financial misdirection reflected poorly on BESBRA and the state government:

> Some of the contributions, such as interest rate subsidies and
> the cost of the Queensland Pavilion, may be seen as write-
> offs. Others, such as relocation of the South Brisbane transit
> centre to Roma Street, are of enduring value. But that doesn't
> alter the fact such items make the Expo statement somewhat
> rubbery and less than useful as an accounting exercise. Most

Queenslanders reckon they received top value from Expo and would accept a reasonable loss ... But, in what seems a frantic attempt to live up to perhaps rash promises of a cost-free world fair, the Expo Authority and some government members are in danger of digging themselves into a monetary mire.[86]

Minister for Finance Brian Austin dismissed the criticisms as a useless academic exercise, arguing that 'if you are going to tally up the general government costs of Expo, then why not also add up the benefits to the economy and the community from the increased visitors and tourism activities?'[87] Carroll was not convinced there were any: 'Although it was a well-managed expo compared with some of the other fiascos, financially and economically its value was questionable.'[88] Carroll and Donohue said it was impossible to accurately determine Expo's impact on tourism, but that it appeared to be limited, redistributive, and temporary.[89] They believed Expo's effect on income and employment was also limited, as the resources could have been used elsewhere, and an estimated $210 million had leaked overseas in the form of profits and wages.[90] Negative outcomes identified by Carroll and Donohue included steep local increases in housing rental costs and reduced trade for rival tourism, dining, and entertainment businesses.[91]

The Opposition continued to make great political capital out of Expo's controversies. Labor's Ken McElligott bemoaned the 'hopeless inability of the Ahern Nationals to provide effective, assertive Government' inherent in the stalled redevelopment's 'inner-city eyesore' status, and in Expo's secretive finances, 'soaring debt', and vulnerability to 'entrenched National Party cronyism' – he concluded the process 'seems little different from the way in which business was done under Joh'.[92]

To resolve the politically damaging stalemate in which the Expo site could not be legally redeveloped in a way that threatened the exposition's bottom line, the *Expo '88 Act 1984* was repealed by the *South Bank Corporation Act 1989* on 28 April 1989. This transferred

BESBRA's outstanding debts and business and legal transactions to the Crown and allowed the South Bank Corporation to start debt free.[93] It also – belatedly – reflected recommendations predating the 1983 dissolution of the Coalition government that Expo's construction and operation phases be managed separately from the site redevelopment.

For Ahern, establishing a debt-free South Bank Corporation meant writing off a great deal of money: 'Llew Edwards is going around saying the good thing about Expo was it cost us nothing. Maybe. Maybe not. With this hand, I wrote off a debt for $150 million to do that. That's what it cost ... South Bank couldn't be started off with a debt of $150 million. That was just not going to work. We needed to say: "Gone. That was what Expo cost us. Now, start to develop a people-precinct in the whole area there that future generations will enjoy ... an arts precinct, open precinct. Beach. All sorts of museums, convention centre." But it costs money.'[94]

Goldston views things differently: 'In the long term, because they'd changed the post-Expo usage of the land, there was a cost to the public – effectively the establishment of South Bank. But so far as Expo was concerned, it handed land back over that balances the books. That's what the land's worth. We're finished. Profit.'[95]

Rather than sell the land in one parcel as originally planned, South Bank Corporation Chairman Vic Pullar announced, 'There will be a structured and very carefully considered progressive release of parts of the site.'[96] Some business representatives were unimpressed; the state manager for Hooker Projects observed, 'My own view is that the Government really has a duty and a responsibility to really just forget about what the site owes them.'[97]

BCC was granted greater input in the redevelopment process than previously accorded, with two of the five South Bank Corporation members nominated by the council; but Ahern baulked at returning jurisdiction of the site, noting, 'If we're paying for that debt, we're going to have to have a say in how it's developed.'[98]

Edwards disengaged from the process at this stage: 'I'd just had enough. I'd worked long years as a doctor and as a politician and then Expo and ... my wife had died and I was making a new relationship with Jane, and I said, "We've just got to get out of all this," and so we changed our lives totally ... I decided to go on boards from then on.'[99]

A competition for the South Bank redevelopment was won in 1989 by architect Des Brooks and his company Media Five; their concept, christened 'Brisbane's Backyard', combined parkland, retail, and residential space in a design reminiscent of a theme park.[100]

Lawsuits

Another aspect of the exposition subject to scrutiny concerned its attendees. Expo's 18.5 million attendance figure was boosted by approximately 2.5 million unpaid visits by staff and VIPs. The remaining figure of approximately 16 million paid visits still vastly eclipsed the number of individual attendees, which was closer to 4.3 million (including single, three-day and season-pass holders).[101] Jennifer Craik noted that season-pass holders made an average of seventeen Expo visits each – a financial loss on the anticipated twelve visits.[102] Repeat visits were advantageous for businesses such as food and drink outlets, but problematic for those such as souvenir shops that could expect reduced sales from returning attendees – a situation that caused a headline-generating lawsuit between BESBRA and TNT Leisure.[103] The company's head, Sir Peter Abeles (a transport magnate later linked with crime figure Abe Saffron and corruption allegations in connection with NSW premier Sir Robert Askin), had negotiated a fee of $6.3 million for the rights to souvenir sales at Expo.[104] In an attempt to hedge his bets, Abeles requested a rebate of $1.50 for every visitor under the attendance estimate of 7.8 million; Edwards agreed, with the proviso that BESBRA receive $1.50 for every person above the estimate.[105] TNT challenged its subsequent $11 million Expo debt, claiming, 'We interpret the contract differently from the authority.'[106] Goldston says, 'We settled for $10.25 million ... which was very good, seeing that we weren't all that sure of our case.'[107]

Debt recovery was critical if BESBRA was to achieve its vaunted $653,000 'book profit'. Approximately a hundred outstanding accounts were resolved, typically for amounts between $50 and $300.[108] Goldston was very pleased with the results: 'There are usually an enormous number of legal cases as a result of an expo. I'm talking about thousands of legal cases ... we did markedly better.'[109]

A Controversy Too Far

The most contentious Expo settlement involved Pennant Holdings, majority owners of the poorly attended World Expo Park. The five-hectare site had been bought from BESBRA for $10 million, of which only $1 million was ever paid.[110] After Expo, BESBRA agreed to purchase the land (that had not been paid for) back for $29.3 million, then lease it to the fun park for a dollar a year while the company traded out of trouble – after which the site would be turned into a convention centre (to be paid for by the sale of a casino licence in the Brisbane CBD).[111] The reasoning behind the ostensibly generous terms was that land value had been added with the construction of a car park, and that a prospective lawsuit over lower than expected attendance figures for the park could be averted.[112]

The Opposition took a dim view of this arrangement. Labor's Keith De Lacy revealed that a subsidiary of Pennant Holdings, John Holland Constructions (which had worked on Expo), was a favoured contractor of the National Party government, and that a director of the company, Brian Holland, was a close friend of one of the deal's key negotiators, Sam Doumany (a former Liberal who had switched allegiance to the Nationals).[113] He pronounced the result 'a deliberate back-room deal between the Government and what appear to be mates of the National Party'.[114]

It was the second suggestion of a major Expo 'back-room deal' under Ahern's promised new model of openness and accountability – a model also straining under challenges to Expo's opaque financials. Ahern's premiership was vulnerable: his disapproval rating had risen from twenty-one per cent in March– April 1988 to fifty-four per cent in July–August 1989.[115] Wayne Goss used the World Expo Park controversy to portray Ahern as a weak premier, torn between kowtowing to select business interests, public pressure, and the power-broking knights of the National Party such as Sir Robert Sparkes, Sir Frank Moore, and soon-to-be 'Sir' Fred Maybury.[116] With a confident glance at the future, Goss suggested that any remaining National Party associates desiring the ubiquitous honorific make their arrangements before the upcoming election, as 'there will be no knighthoods next year'.[117]

End of an Era

The Fitzgerald Inquiry concluded in July 1989 – almost two years after the investigation expected to take six weeks had begun. Numerous police officers were discredited and imprisoned. Police Commissioner Terry Lewis was found guilty of corruption, imprisoned, and stripped of his knighthood. National Party ministers Geoff Muntz, Leisha Harvey, and Brian Austin were jailed for misappropriation of funds, and Don Lane for falsifying expenses.[118] Bagman-turned-star-witness Jack Herbert attested that Lane had also been a direct link between corrupt police and Cabinet. Russ Hinze was found to have received benefits of approximately $4.2 million from developers and other interests, but died of cancer before facing the allegations in court.[119] The inquiry noted numerous instances of Cabinet skewing the tendering process in favour of National Party donors.[120]

Bjelke-Petersen was charged with corruption and perjury in relation to accepting a brown paper bag containing $100,000 from Singaporean businessman Robert Sng, whose company became the preferred applicant for the Port Office redevelopment against recommendations to Cabinet. Bjelke-Petersen avoided judgment courtesy of a hung jury followed by a mistrial when it was revealed that jury foreman Luke Shaw was a member of the Young Nationals and the 'Friends of Joh' movement. There was no retrial. It later emerged that National Party members had sought to discredit a potential police witness against Bjelke-Petersen, and that his defence (led by former police officer Barry O'Brien, who had links with the Rat Pack) had conducted an investigation into the political leanings of potential jurists.[121] A 1991 libel trial found that Sir Leslie Thiess had bribed Bjelke-Petersen 'on a large scale and on many occasions' to procure government contracts for a number of developments, including Expo.[122]

Among the Fitzgerald Inquiry's recommendations was the establishment of an Electoral and Administrative Review Commission (EARC), which was expected to advise ending or severely truncating the zonal voting system. This faced considerable resistance within the National Party, some members of which already viewed the Bjelke-Petersen era with a twinge of nostalgia.[123] Ahern committed the government to key Fitzgerald recommendations in relation to parliamentary committees, the CJC, and the EARC (which was not expected to report until after the 1989 election), but at a cost to his leadership.[124] Parliamentarians he had removed from Cabinet destabilised his premiership while Bjelke-Petersen ran a public campaign against him, offering support to non-National candidates in damaging by-elections.[125] His position was weakened further by an unpopular daylight saving trial and the highly publicised Expo controversies. Ahern was deposed as premier by Russell Cooper in September 1989.

Before his removal, he assured the media that the Fitzgerald Inquiry recommendations would be implemented 'lock, stock and barrel': 'I knew that they were counting heads for an assault on me, and I thought, "Well, you just might be able to do that, but you're going to run into a statement from me that I'm going to implement the recommendations lock, stock and barrel," so I went out and did that. Anyone coming along then ... they had to deal with my undertaking.'[126]

Labor strategists felt the National Party had made an error with Ahern, as they possessed data showing that he was still well liked – and that he was more popular than his deposer in country areas where Cooper claimed support.[127] The National Party ran its campaign – quite extraordinarily – on law and order, economic credentials, and Labor being 'morally soft'.[128] The Goss campaign presented Labor as 'The Only Change for the Better' while striving to convince business of its economic credentials.[129] It also courted Brisbane's post-Expo entertainment addicts with a pledge to bring an arts festival to the city.[130]

Russell Cooper was premier of Queensland for seventy-three days before Labor surmounted the zonal system to win the December 1989 election in a landslide – ending thirty-two years of continuous National Party rule. Ahern commissioned an exit poll on election day that showed his party would have retained sufficient seats to govern in coalition with the Liberals if he had still been premier. His biographer Paul Reynolds says insufficient data exists to verify this claim.[131] It is nevertheless possible to speculate that Ahern's acute vulnerability to a leadership challenge during the Expo controversies may have fatally influenced the election outcome. After Goss's victory, it transpired that one of the Cooper government's last acts had been a Cabinet decision to classify money spent attending Expo as a ministerial expense. This directly contravened a 1987 Cabinet decision (made in the wake of ministerial expense scandals arising from the Fitzgerald Inquiry) to deny ministers, partners, and their guests free entry to the event.[132] At a subsequent National Party meeting in which Ahern unsuccessfully challenged for the role of Opposition leader, he called the expenses decision 'indefensible'.[133] He retired from politics the following year.

Atkinson's popularity was at its zenith during Expo. She was approached by senior members of the Liberal Party to run for a state seat in the 1989 state election, then by the federal president of the Liberal Party, John Elliott, to run for a federal seat in 1990; she turned both requests down.[134] In 1991, she lost a closely contested mayoral election to Labor's Jim Soorley (who had participated in community meetings critical of Expo) when preferences were directed away from her by Greens candidate (and Expo protester) Drew Hutton.[135]

The Goss government implemented key recommendations of the Fitzgerald Inquiry, such as the CJC (later the Crime and Misconduct Commission, later still the Crime and Corruption Commission), the EARC (which resulted in an overhaul of the zonal voting system), freedom of information legislation, a review of public assembly laws, and guidelines for reporting the pecuniary interests of parliamentarians. The government was not itself immune to controversy: in December 1990, EARC released a report into insupportable travel expenses from members of all parties. The scandal cost Cooper his leadership and threatened the careers of several Labor parliamentarians, including Cabinet ministers Terry Mackenroth and Ken McElligott.[136] Goss was under pressure to act on at least four other ministers over seemingly absurd parliamentary bowling expenses when Sir Llew Edwards re-entered the political arena 'in dramatic fashion', to confirm that he had ruled such activities 'parliamentary business' in 1980.[137] The crisis was averted, and Labor remained in government until 1996.

Other changes under Goss included equal opportunity and anti-discrimination legislation, the *Heritage Act*, the decriminalisation of homosexuality, a substantial arts policy, shopping and dining regulations approximate to those embraced by Expo attendees, and the state being declared debt free in 1994.[138] Despite perceived – and controversial – failures on issues such as decriminalising prostitution and abortion, and a suspected unwillingness to legislate Aboriginal land rights (considered a betrayal by action groups such as FAIRA), Goss's achievements (the cornerstone of which was implementing the Fitzgerald Inquiry recommendations to which Ahern had also agreed) were of sufficient magnitude for his biographer Jamie Walker to conclude that 'under his leadership, the state has come of age'.[139]

The South Bank Parklands

The former Expo site reopened to the public in June 1992 as the South Bank Parklands. It was opened by Premier Goss and promoted – somewhat audaciously – as a Labor government project.[140] The development honoured Expo's leisure ethos with an artificial beach, a canal, and eclectic dining options. It also echoed some old Coalition tendencies by providing few spaces in which protesters could assemble, and in the avoidance of pool fencing regulations at the site's signature fake beach.[141]

The redevelopment was enthusiastically received by much of mainstream Brisbane, but – as with Expo itself – less kindly by academics. Architectural theorist John Macarthur mused, 'It is so poorly designed and constructed ... we must judge whether South Bank is a new turn in the history of public spaces or a moment of hysteria as the concept of res publica teeters near collapse.'[142] Cultural insecurities were also prodded when Macarthur inquired whether the site design was 'evidence of some anxiety about why anyone would visit Brisbane except on route to the beach'.[143]

The South Bank canal was replaced by an arbour as part of a redesign by Denton Corker Marshall in 1997, the guiding premise of which was that there was nothing about the original redevelopment 'that a bobcat and a chainsaw couldn't fix'.[144] Goldston had some reservations about the outcome: 'I'm the last person to criticise a current manager because things change, people change ... I would have preferred to have kept the original design, but that might be just a little bit of excessive pride. The architects of Brisbane never liked our architect; he was a blow-in from Melbourne, worked for Christopher Skase putting resort-type architecture into the middle of the city. Well, I thought that resort park architecture was magnificent – and I thought we needed a "people's playground" sort of thing. It's easy for the rich to get resorts and what-have-you, but we needed something in Brisbane like that. And Des Brooks did that for us. But the other architects hated him – and when I, as his protector, disappeared, they changed the design.'[145]

Rebuffed developer Sir Frank Moore was not impressed with either outcome: 'I think what they've done with it is ghastly. Just ghastly. It's mediocre and second rate.'[146] The parklands continue to be modified, upgraded, and popular, with annual visitation rates exceeding ten million.[147] Like Expo, they offer a generally safe and harmonious gathering place. Unlike Expo, there is no entry fee. Families and tourists can freely avail themselves of an artificial beach, water parks, barbecues, concerts, special events, and numerous dining options.

Successive governments continue to shape the surrounding area into a cultural precinct of some repute. Controversies also continue, as with the Bligh Labor state government's decision to lease a section of the site to national broadcaster ABC for 120 years for $12 million in 2010.[148] In the grand tradition of Expo negotiations, the government was accused of conducting 'a deal done behind closed doors without any scrutiny of the approved development plan' by Liberal lord mayor Campbell Newman.[149] In 2012, Newman – who had entered state politics and become premier of Queensland following the 2011 election (which itself followed the 2008 merger of the Queensland Liberals and the Nationals) – announced that control of the South Bank Parklands would finally be restored to BCC.[150] Despite speculation the South Bank Corporation would be dissolved, precinct management was divided between the corporation and the BCC, with the state government retaining its retail, residential, and commercial interests.[151] In June 2017, the Palaszczuk Labor state government announced it would present its lease on a South Bank riverside restaurant block (unoccupied since the 2011 floods) to the South Bank Corporation so the space could be converted into parkland to mark the precinct's twenty-fifth anniversary.[152]

Ironically, a threat to South Bank's popularity has emerged in the form of a massive new development on the north bank of the Brisbane River that will consume close to twenty per cent of the CBD, including twelve hectares of prime riverfront land.[153] In November 2015, the Palaszczuk government concluded the tendering process begun by the Newman government to redevelop Queen's Wharf. The winning bidder, the Destination Brisbane Consortium, proposed to transform the area into a high-end casino, hotel, retail, and entertainment precinct, while redeveloping the existing Treasury Casino into a shopping centre or hotel.[154] A pedestrian bridge is expected to connect the site to South Bank.

South Bank Corporation Chief Executive Jeff Weigh purported to be confident that the precinct would weather any competition with assistance from the three-tower Southpoint in development at the top of Grey Street, and with South Bank's revamped cafe areas – though he suspected Queen's Wharf would 'change the fulcrum of the city of Brisbane', and represent 'the CBD moving across the river'.[155] Minister for State Development Anthony Lynham suggested the development would 'do what South Bank did for Brisbane 30 [sic] years ago'.[156] Certainly, there are echoes of the exposition's theme in State Development department claims that the new precinct will 'showcase' Brisbane 'to locals, interstate and international visitors'.[157] When asked if the new development would have 'Expo-like' transformative qualities upon Brisbane, Sir Llew Edwards diplomatically noted, 'It's a different piece of land in a different set of circumstances,' while theorising that its chances of success would increase with 'a sense of ownership by the people'.[158] It is difficult to imagine how such a sensation could be evoked in a space owned by a consortium of transnational corporations. The experience might more closely resemble a joyride in the glass elevator of the Hilton hotel.

World Expositions

When Brisbane was granted the right to host Expo, the future of world expositions had been in doubt, with only one more planned (Seville in 1992). The success of expositions in Brisbane and

Vancouver (1986) contributed to the concept's continuation. In the post–Gordon Gekko age, exposition themes returned to weightier matters than 'Leisure in the Age of Technology'. The change was driven by a 1994 BIE directive that expositions focus upon critical problems and environmental concerns.[159] For a time, the events appeared to have lost their appeal to some countries (the United States and Canada, for example, ceased to pay BIE membership from 2001 and 2012 respectively), but they remained popular in Europe and Asia; the 2010 Shanghai exposition broke records with seventy-three million visits, and Milan's 2015 exposition exceeded twenty-two million.[160] In May 2017, the nostalgia- and pomp-driven US president Donald Trump (who shares an uncanny array of leadership traits with Bjelke-Petersen) signed the *U.S. Wants to Compete for a World Expo Act*, which supports a return to the BIE fold and threatens to 'make expositions great again'.[161]

Meanwhile, world expositions' special-event rival and usurper the Olympic Games faces a plethora of issues, including 'rising costs and diminishing returns', corruption scandals, and a decline in liberal Western democracies capable of withstanding voter opposition to hosting the events.[162]

The continued success of the world exposition concept – intermittently presumed redundant from the late 1800s – is especially striking considering that many of the entertainments and technologies debuted at these events now compete with them for audience attention. Adam Nash, co-writer of the protest song 'Cyclone Hits Expo', considers expositions less relevant than ever: 'Everybody lives now in this giant fucking world expo with just this endless meaningless exchange where everything – including radicalism – is commodified and presented back.'[163]

Critics might well ask why a world wide web of expositions continues when there is a world wide web. A melding of the two was actually attempted in 1996, when an (unofficial) world exposition was held on the internet – participants were allocated pages within the website in place of pavilions. While a novel idea, it has not inspired subsequent attempts – possibly as it was effectively the internet with fewer options.[164]

Barbara Absolon attributes the enduring popularity of world expositions to the opportunities for shared moments: 'There's nothing like that personal experience. Millions of us go to the movies – whereas the cinemas were all supposed to be gone if you were listening to what they were saying back in the days of videotapes. So there's nothing like being there. Sporting events, concerts – now $180, $200 a ticket – you could go out and buy twenty CDs for that price, but people still want to be there for the moment.'[165]

Absolon hasn't attended a world exposition herself since Expo. Having spent so much time preparing and then executing the event, a number of its organisers admit to 'Expo fatigue'.[166] Many remain close, but prefer to keep their focus on the present. Sir Llew Edwards believes 'Expo has to be a great memory rather than a continuing event in some people's minds'.[167]

Many of Expo's organisers are also inclined against the prospect of another world exposition in Brisbane. After collaborating with Bill Hayden in the late 1990s on a (failed) Gold Coast Expo 2002 bid, Edwards estimates that the next Queensland world exposition is at least fifty years away from its Expo 88 predecessor: 'We were just lucky that Whitlam – who gets no credit for Expo – that Whitlam said in the '70s that we'll put in an application for Expo. It takes somebody like Whitlam, I think, to suddenly say we'll have another one.'[168]

If one were to transpire, Edwards suggests it take a completely different approach to Expo in order to gift a new set of legacies.

Legacy

Attempts to extract the legacy of Expo from the influence of other historical factors can become mired in intangibles and hypotheticals, but the event is typically credited with accelerating the liberalisation of shopping hours and eating and drinking habits in Brisbane. Prior to the event, weekend trading concluded at noon on Saturday, and drinking or consuming meals outdoors was almost an alien concept. A newfound interest in leaving the house seems to have been reflected in the rapid growth of cafe culture and the development of arts and events infrastructure. Goldston suspects that advertising campaigns warning of limited parking at Expo helped to acclimatise attendees to public transport: 'We terrified the living daylights out of people and forced them onto public transport and they loved it – again, it was a social experience.'[169] The rediscovery of the Brisbane River during Expo may also have played a part in the 1996 introduction of CityCats to bolster BCC's ageing ferry fleet. Historian Helen Gregory has observed that, post-Expo, buildings are rarely designed facing away from the Brisbane River as they used to be, and that the river's north and south banks are no longer divided along class lines: now, the wealthy own all of it.[170]

Marguerite Pepper believes that one of the great legacies of Expo was its effect on Brisbane's artistic community: 'Hundreds of outdoor performers on long contracts ... that left a real legacy of experienced artists with repertoire and a knowledge that it could be seen as an art form. It was an amazing experience for the tech crew – who came out of that time with enormous experience. For the cultural landscape of Brisbane, it was an awakening. If Expo hadn't been there, would the local art scene be as mature as it is? I don't think so.'[171]

Many of Expo's organisers, performers, and technicians continued to make significant contributions to Brisbane's artistic, business, and entertainment landscapes. Absolon recalls that after Expo there was a public hunger for entertainment, and 'People just weren't happy with the same old things that they'd been happy with before.'[172] She formed a production company with David Hamilton and John Watson that was swiftly inundated with requests for 'Expo-style' entertainment: 'People recognised what the difference was and they would call it that: "We don't know what we want but we want Expo-style entertainment" – and I guess that meant quality.'[173]

Absolon laughs when reminded that two of the most significant events in Brisbane's recent history occurred side by side: 'If only the Expo spirit lived on and corruption could have been something that happened twenty-five years ago.'[174]

Issues of corruption and impropriety continue to trouble Queensland governments of various political persuasions. Controversies during the Borbidge National–Liberal Coalition government (1996–98) included the revelation of a secret Memorandum of Agreement between that government and the Police Union, sustained attempts to reduce the power and credibility of the CJC, and violations of the Westminster convention.[175] Scandals during Peter Beattie's Labor premiership (1998–2007) included electoral rorting exposed by the Shepherdson Inquiry (which forced several resignations) and a Crime and Misconduct Commission investigation into ex–Beattie minister Gordon Nuttall that resulted in his conviction and jailing for corruptly receiving payments and secret business commissions.[176] Nevertheless, the circumstances that allowed systemic corruption to go unanswered for long stretches have been curtailed. In 2008, Chris Masters, whose *Four Corners* story 'The Moonlight State' precipitated the Fitzgerald Inquiry, observed:

> I hear from time to time that things are supposed to be as bad as ever. But when my colleagues and I search for the evidence, there – somewhat frustratingly – is little to find. It may be, as some think, that in this new era of open government the evidence, curiously, is easier to hide. It may be true that the smarties have found sneakier ways to disguise misbehaviour. What I know is that a couple of spivs from Fortitude Valley no longer control the Queensland Police. Homosexuals aren't routinely bashed. Honest police are much less likely to be punished for resisting corruption. And a dishonest police commissioner was sent to gaol – a terrific start.[177]

In some ways, that is what Expo was – a terrific start. Many of the changes attributed to it would have occurred in its absence, but it certainly expedited the process. Lady Edwards notes, 'A lot of people say Expo was the coming of age for Brisbane, but I think ... underneath ... it was like a volcano. People in Queensland wanted change – you know, there was a hunger for it ... and so Expo was just like lancing a boil a bit. Ghastly euphemism. Everyone went, "Yes, this is what we want."'[178]

The devisor of the campaign line 'We'll Show the World', Carol Lloyd, believes Expo also delivered a longed-for sense of worth: 'It certainly lifted Queenslanders' perception of themselves and the quality of their lifestyle; it somehow validated us as citizens of the world rather than Queenslanders first, then Australians, then participants of the world. We were as good as anybody else, and we shrugged off that whole cultural cringe thing that was still around; so many internationals, people from places that we aspired to visit, were telling us how good we had it here – and I think Queenslanders wanted to hear that stuff – and they'd worked hard to get it – and I think that acknowledgement lifted their spirits into another level.'[179]

The parochial concept of 'Queenslandness' is still deployed for rallying purposes ranging from State of Origin matches through to Labor's 2007 federal election campaign, which featured a photograph of Kevin Rudd with the headline 'Queenslander'.[180] That election saw Australia's political compass turning north for a time, with Queensland-based Prime Minister Kevin Rudd, Treasurer Wayne Swan (both key figures in the Goss government), and Governor-General Quentin Bryce (whose husband, Michael Bryce, contributed graphic and architectural designs to Expo).[181] That *their* state of origin was not reflexively and pejoratively remarked upon in connection with their careers was something of a triumph.

Academics and representatives of the southern press no longer seem consumed by the 'Queensland is different' concept, or with conflating the state and its controversial figures – today, it's more of a hobby.[182] Brisbane locals continue to periodically refer to their city disparagingly – or at least ironically – with nicknames such as

Bris Vegas, Bris-bland, or Brisneyland. Even dedicated Brisbane and Queensland promotions seem unclear on its adult form: Is it the River City? The Liveable City? The World City? Your Queensland? Tomorrow's Queensland? The Sunshine State? The Smart State? Of course, identity indecision is no more a legacy failing of Expo than relapses into corruption are the responsibility of the Fitzgerald Inquiry. These two extraordinary endeavours were, quite simply, important steps. A coming of age, if you will.

The magnitude of each event's lasting effects is evident in the shadows they still cast. Politicians insist the 2018 Commonwealth Games 'will bring lasting change and benefits to the Gold Coast – just as an earlier Commonwealth Games and Expo 88 had a huge social and economic impact on Brisbane'.[183] Even absurdly disparate occasions are squeezed into the Expo girdle, as when the G20 (the international government and central bank forum held in Brisbane in 2014) was expected to 'give Brisbane an Expo 88 boost'.[184]

The Newman Liberal–National Party state government (2012–15) evoked the spectre of Bjelke-Petersen when it embarked upon a series of actions that were perceived as a threat to civil liberties, environmental and heritage laws, independence of the judiciary, activists, artists, and special-interest groups, and when it was suspected of attempting to politicise the police force, obscure government accountability, and preference government allies during the tendering process. Alarm bells were sounded by the media and citizen journalists, inspiring a spate of 'Here we Joh again' comparisons, and compelling Tony Fitzgerald to express concern over 'troubling signs that the Liberal National Party's huge majority has re-enlivened old, bad habits'.[185] One commentator remarked, 'We need the Fitzgerald heritage to remain, as we thought it was, our birthright.'[186] When the government failed to secure a second term, another writer observed, 'The state learned the lessons of the Bjelke-Petersen era better, perhaps, than even many of the natives may have thought.'[187]

Politicians may not have been as studious as their electorate: in June 2017, Queensland Greens senator Larissa Waters accused the Labor Palaszczuk government of making a 'grubby deal' with 'their property developer mates' for the Queen's Wharf mega-casino, and of threatening her with a CCC [Crime and Corruption Commission] investigation when she sought to uncover the opaque details with a whistleblower campaign – a silencing gesture she claimed 'harks back to the days of Joh Bjelke-Petersen'.[188] In the same month, on a national front, Tony Fitzgerald lent his support to the idea of a Federal Independent Commission against corruption, stating:

> Politics today is a clash of interests, not ideas. The established
> parties, which receive large sums of public money to finance
> their campaigns, are controlled by professional, 'whatever
> it takes' politicians driven by self-interest and ideology and
> addicted to vested interest funding.[189]

The vast majority of federal politicians (and all Turnbull Coalition government members) declined to commit to seven simple Fitzgerald Principles based around honesty and accountability – an outcome that Fitzgerald believes 'puts the need for an effective anti-corruption commission beyond doubt'.[190]

For many, it is no doubt easier and more pleasant to remember Expo than the political upheaval that occurred alongside it and the associated reverberations. Expo's memorialising is surely aided by its physical legacy in the form of the South Bank Parklands, where people can gather as they did for those six months in 1988. The site would simply not exist without Expo, as much of the land would have been sold and developed in piecemeal fashion. The parklands continue to be encroached upon by commercial operations, but developers are unlikely to threaten popular public spaces such as the arbour or the prized fake beach. It is also unlikely that the surrounding precinct would be as well provisioned without public demand having focused the attention of successive state governments upon the area.

Ahern considers the South Bank Parklands a 'tremendous legacy of Expo', and one of the most successful examples of a world exposition redevelopment.[191] When asked if he feels a sense of satisfaction when driving past or coming across developments with which he has been associated, such as South Bank, Ahern demurs: 'You can do things of a negative nature on your own and be successful at it – but if you want to be constructive, you've got to have people working with you.'[192] When pressed, he concedes, 'When I said I don't think we can go with the full commercial proposal, I earned a lot of enemies in the National Party and in the land development business, but the city of Brisbane now today has got South Bank. You've asked me if you're driving past something and you say, "Gee this is nice. Did you have anything to do with it?" Yes. I did. Is it any good? Well, you tell me.'[193]

Sallyanne Atkinson considers South Bank a great cultural asset for Brisbane: 'The physicality of the site is extraordinary ... every weekend, there are people down there using it. I think it's affected the development of QUT [Queensland University of Technology] for the better – you know, the [Goodwill] bridge across – I think the Griffith University precinct down there is great. Institutions, governments, developers have been very aware of Expo as the jewel that must not be disturbed.'[194]

Long-term chairman of the Queensland Events Corporation Des Power believes the parklands play a critical role in the public's enduring love affair with Expo by virtue of their cultural and social value, and as a tangible remnant of the seismic event that begat them: 'Most events have an ephemeral quality about them. They're here today, they're gone tomorrow. Examples: the Goodwill Games. At the time, everybody shouted from the rooftops, "Fantastic!" Who remembers it? Nobody remembers it. It's gone. Did it leave anything? No. Not really. Commonwealth Games of 1982: it left a kangaroo that sits as a tourist attraction somewhere and a stadium with a use-by date that's long past. No real legacy from that. Expo? A very genuine rethink. A very genuine legacy. A tangible outcome. And that's why Expo will always be remembered – and with great fondness.'[195]

Bob Weatherall thinks the main benefits to Aboriginal people from Expo were the experience gained in protesting it, and the public solidarity signalled by the size of the marches: 'The numbers of people who joined in those marches – maybe 30,000 – it was just swelling; people were coming in off the footpath and joining. That was just amazing.'[196] Fewer than two months after Expo, the High Court of Australia found in *Mabo v Queensland (No 1)* that the Bjelke-Petersen government's attempt to retrospectively abolish native title rights (with the *Queensland Coast Islands Declaratory Act 1985*) was invalid under the *Racial Discrimination Act 1975*; this was a major step towards the recognition of native title confirmed in *Mabo v Queensland (No 2)*. For Weatherall and his peers, this was the real transformation of consequence in 1988: 'Things were changing,' he says, 'the atmosphere, politically; the legal system had been shaken and they had to start to investigate things and assess the laws in Australia.'[197]

A positive anti-Expo legacy identified in *The Big Party Syndrome* was 'a re-affirmation of community spirit and militant activism transcending social and institutional boundaries'.[198] The changing social landscape helped activists such as Ken Butler and Drew Hutton make a case for inner-city public housing that was implemented by the Goss government.[199] More than thirty years after Hutton and his peers squatted in a series of old West End houses to protect them from developers before Expo, he wryly observes another anti-Expo legacy: that they incidentally preserved the value of this belatedly appreciated architecture for wealthy owners.[200]

For some anti-Expo activists, the popularity of the South Bank Parklands and the surrounding precinct – and its status as a cultural asset – is of sufficient magnitude that they have reconciled themselves to the event through its legacy. *Cane Toad Times* editor Anne Jones is one such conflicted convert: 'The fact that having reclaimed all this inner-city land allowed them to expand what is a major cultural precinct on the South Bank of the city ... if you look around the world, it's pretty amazing what is there. It's now got GOMA [Gallery of Modern Art] at one end, the library, and the museum. The library and the art gallery have been expanded; you've got the cultural centre and all the other facilities that are there. It's really quite an important cultural precinct, and without Expo having happened it's unlikely that would have been there. The ABC is there now, the Conservatorium, Griffith University, the art college. It's a fairly important cultural asset for Queensland. The fact that it didn't happen in a very good way … that's the whole story of bloody Queensland, really.'[201]

Conclusion

Shine on Brisbane

NOT LONG BEFORE THE EXPO site was first fenced off, Sir Llew Edwards was strolling its perimeter when he was hailed by a couple taking their new puppy for a walk; they asked his permission to name it 'Llew'. Edwards demurred, suggesting they call it 'Expo' instead. Many years later, Lady Edwards received a call from a priest in South Brisbane who told her, 'Oh, we're very sad. We have a couple in here who've been bereaved and want to talk to Sir Llew ... Expo has passed away.' He spent around half an hour reminiscing with the grieving couple about both incarnations of Expo.[1]

Decades on from the event, Edwards is still approached by strangers seeking replacement exposition paraphernalia or the chance to reminisce. He is unable to grant wishes regarding lost season passes or uniforms, but he shares the nostalgia that fuels them: 'Expo 88 was the most wonderful part of my life ... the best and hardest part of my life.'[2]

Public affection for Expo has significantly outlasted the event itself. Peter Goldston recalls that for years after its conclusion, a single rose would appear outside the South Bank Corporation's offices; the accompanying note read, 'To my beloved Expo'.[3] In 2006, the lights of Expo's Night Companion fused and caught fire, partially destroying the structure. YouTube footage of the blaze attracted the comment 'It's like Brisbane's 9/11'.[4]

The twenty-fifth anniversary of Expo, in 2013, occasioned celebratory dinners, a 'family fun day' at the South Bank Parklands, the installation of a commemorative plaque at the site, and a major Museum of Brisbane exhibition (for which this writer provided the didactic text).[5] It joined a strong tradition of Expo commemorations, beginning with its first anniversary, and including its second, fifth, tenth, fifteenth, and twentieth (for which this writer produced audiovisual material for both the South Bank Corporation and Queensland Museum).[6] Expo protesters also hold retrospectives on occasion, although these are less celebratory in nature.[7]

Research academic Donna Lee Brien posits that world fairs 'occupy a special place in public memory globally, with a number of online collections of site and memorabilia imagery, event information and records of visitor memories', but that even 'within this memorialising context', the fervour with which Expo is feted is 'unusual'.[8] The event itself was not unusual. It shared myriad positive and negative traits with other world expositions, many of which hold superior claims in terms of visitor numbers, profitability, and global influence.

For all of its wonder, Expo didn't change the world – the world was changing anyway. International events the following year included the dismantling of apartheid in South Africa, the Soviet Union's exit from Afghanistan, the fall of the Berlin Wall, the collapse of European communism, the Tiananmen Square massacre, and Aung San Suu Kyi's house arrest in Burma. There were seismic shifts in pop culture: Nirvana released their first album; *The Simpsons* and *Seinfeld* made their television debuts; Nintendo launched Game Boy. In Brisbane, the National Party government fell, and the first Livid festival was promoted as an 'anti-Expo' event featuring 'artists that had been forced to leave the city to find an audience' during the Bjelke-Petersen years.[9] There was less appetite in the grunge-infused landscape of the 1990s for entrepreneurial adulation; many of the previous decade's business luminaries faced bankruptcy, investigations, and prison.

Expo didn't have an enduring national impact, either. It rarely rates a mention in the biographies of contemporary prime ministers and (non-Queensland) premiers, or in overviews of the era by interstate authors. Assessments of Australia's bicentennial celebrations typically exclude Expo or evaluate it as a separate regional event. These are entirely defensible choices, although they may surprise Expo devotees conditioned to thinking that 'we showed the world'.

In his book *The Eighties*, historian Frank Bongiorno paints a vivid picture of entrepreneur Alan Bond's 1983 America's Cup victory. Australian media provided saturation coverage, citing it as proof that 'we can still do anything when we try' and crediting it with instilling 'a pride that will mark the national consciousness, and will help to alter for the better the way in which the world sees Australia and Australians see themselves'.[10] Bongiorno writes that 'Many seemed convinced that the eyes of the world, and especially those of America, had turned to Australia', but that, in actuality, 'in the US, the event had been tucked away on a cable channel where few saw it; as so often before, Australians performed for "an imaginary grandstand"'.[11] A similarly illusory grandstand was constructed to seat 'the world' that Expo purported to 'show'. The construction team included powerful politicians, Expo's tireless and well-provisioned public relations team, a generally compliant national media, and (after some teething problems) local media coverage tantamount to boosterism. But while there may have been misconceptions about the show's demographics and signal range, its effect upon home viewers was no illusion.

There is a great chasm between the Expo experienced by visitors to Brisbane (however much they enjoyed it) and attendees who called the city home, between the exuberant local nostalgia felt for it and pallid recollections of Brisbane's 1982 Commonwealth Games, between the memorialising of this event and expositions globally. Traversing this space is not just a matter of 'You had to be there'. You had to live there.

Brisbane's very unsuitability as a platform from which to laud 'progress' in 1988 was a measure of the need for such an event, and goes some way towards explaining the enthusiasm with which it was received. In the years prior to Expo, Queensland's 'differences' combined to make its capital an improbable model of the sophistication and advancement implied by a world exposition. Its development had been stymied by two world wars punctuated by a depression, and successive city councils had struggled to provide basic infrastructure. Public entertainment and recreation avenues were limited, cultural activities were curtailed by puritanical censorship bodies, and education beyond junior level was deemed inessential, if not extravagant. Various state governments had normalised cronyistic and corrupt practices while eroding civic rights and manipulating the zonal voting system to subvert the wishes of the majority – a situation that reached its nadir during the nineteen-year premiership of Sir Joh Bjelke-Petersen.

Those who were oblivious to, or content with, the situation lived relatively peaceful lives, but those who exercised their democratic right to advocate for change – either from inside or outside the system – were bullied, ignored, discredited, or terrorised, while systemic corruption within the police force and sections of the government (and that government's perversion of the Westminster doctrine of separation of powers) allowed criminal elements to prosper. The situation in which the public was monitored and restricted while corrupt police sanctioned criminal behaviour was hardly conducive to social or recreational bliss. Activists and alternatives devised their own entertainment, and those with a penchant for illegal casinos and prostitutes were well catered for; but the people of mainstream Brisbane took turns in the Hilton's glass elevator.

How could Brisbane sustain a world exposition from 10 am to 10 pm every day for six months? How could it not? And where better than the land of the 'big things' to attract a big crowd for a big show? The state government also envisioned big outcomes, including economic stimulus, urban redevelopment, tourism, boosterism, cosmopolitanisation, and political aggrandisement. Such expectations – while wildly out of kilter with BIE ideals – incentivised its persistence in the face of formidable odds.

Bjelke-Petersen considered himself the father of Expo, and in many ways he was (although Maccormick, Moore, Hielscher, Schubert, and Edwards could lodge strong paternity suits). The event would not have been secured for Brisbane – and in all probability would not have been held in Australia – in the absence of some of Bjelke-Petersen's oft-censured traits: stubbornness, parochialism, democratic chicanery, and political cunning. Expo's prospects were further aided by his government's general disregard for accountability, its pro-business and development agenda, and its willingness to pursue that agenda to the point of hypocrisy by underwriting vast entrepreneurial risk.

The controversial premier's imprimatur also shackled the event with formidable obstacles. As both a National Party project and a Queensland event, Expo engendered local antipathy, national derision, international indifference, and opponents ranging from a prime minister through to the event's intended audience. Much of the opposition was valid: Australians could not be expected to relish being represented by a fount of national derision; Bjelke-Petersen's many and varied targets had been given little reason to believe the event was being staged in good faith; the Commonwealth and the states had good cause to resist a belligerent rival that kept threatening to secede.

Divinations of Expo's failure were as plentiful as the obstacles arrayed against it. And in the event's origins and early stages of execution – with controversies over lack of public consultation, the tendering process, resumptions, Bjelke-Petersen's intergovernmental baiting, Edwards's freely admitted autocratic managerial style, and the plethora of Coalition associates given plum positions and contracts – Expo was very much the 'Joh Show' its detractors feared. But something shifted along the way.

To gain the local, national, and international support so crucial to the event's success, Expo's organisers allied with or made concessions to many of the premier's former targets, including state and federal governments, unions, Aboriginal leaders, arts practitioners, entertainers, and heritage advocates. Edwards made adroit use of his political expertise to shield Expo from some of the state government's more controversial practices – while embracing and repurposing some of its other problematic traits (such as circumventing due process) in the interest of delivering the event. Expo was not a controversy- or cronyism-free entity; it was, after all, the 1980s, and Brisbane was beset by corruption. But Edwards's explicit warning to his colleagues against breaking the law (as opposed to merely 'brending' it) surely protected the event from many of the excesses exposed at the Fitzgerald Inquiry. Bjelke-Petersen's fall was the final and most emphatic step in Expo's shift from 'Joh Show' to 'people's party'.

It was entirely possible to love (or loathe) Expo in ignorance of or ambivalence towards the social and political dramas unfolding around it. At a basic level, Expo succeeded through the herculean efforts of its management and staff, who devised a vast and engaging cultural experience that was available for purchase in place of an entertainment black hole.

Expo provided an affordable, easily accessible, joyous, and safe environment in which visitors were exposed to an extraordinary array of cultural and educational experiences for an extended period. It appealed to people of all ages, many of whom were unaccustomed to travel – or even to leaving the house. People previously denied the right of assembly were encouraged to gather in the tens of thousands to explore, experience, and celebrate. They became accustomed to meeting strangers and having fun. Relationships were formed. National and international praise was proudly accepted. Confidence was boosted. The people of mainstream Brisbane learnt that a world-class event could be conceived, developed, staffed, and sustained in their home city. Many realised that they liked Brisbane and the people in it. Much of the local affection for Expo stems from this simple fact: Brisbane needed it. The event was more than a spectacular – it was a signal that the city could change.

Expo was seized upon by organisers, journalists, commentators, and large segments of the population as the city's long-prophesied, self-esteem-boosting, coming-of-age-inducing moment – unleashing a euphoric sense of optimism that extended beyond the exposition site and into the wider community. 'We'll show the world!' the tagline proclaimed, and the desire it tapped into was so compelling, its accuracy was somehow beside the point.

In the 2003 study 'Visitors' Long-Term Memories of World Expositions', David Anderson found that attendees had predominantly warm memories of Expo 88 (and of its predecessor, Vancouver's Expo 86), but that those memories had little to do with one of the central tenets of world expositions: education.[12] The content of pavilions was curiously absent from most recollections, which typically centred upon social encounters while queuing, eating a meal, or seeing a show.[13] It is nothing less than extraordinary that many of the memories fuelling a decades-old Brisbane–Expo love affair are of experiences supplementary to the organised event, and that could conceivably have taken place elsewhere. But there wasn't a great deal of 'elsewhere' to be had in 1980s Brisbane. Expo provided the wondrous atmosphere in which these ostensibly peripheral but ultimately crucial experiences could take place. And this is what the most commonly cherished memories of Expo 88 have at their core: people remember that they were happy.

Given the time and setting, the resources devoted to Expo (irrespective of the underlying motives attributed to the event) were phenomenal. For Barbara Absolon, the significance of such investment in a cultural endeavour is timeless: 'I think Expo – in a very basic way for people who may never have been to the theatre or opera or ballet or dance or anything like that ... who, when they read that stuff about culture, go, "What a load of baloney – we should be spending our money on education, hospitals and police" ... Expo is such a great example of the value of spending money on cultural exploits, because it just changed the psyche of hundreds of thousands of people. It lifted their expectations; it changed their lives in ways that they may not perceive – and they don't quite understand that, if the money is not put into things other than the basics of life, then life becomes basic.'[14]

Expo was indeed the catalyst for Brisbane's long-hoped-for, infamously stunted, frequently false-started 'coming of age' – but it had a little help. The 'big thing' Bjelke-Petersen tried to prevent – the Fitzgerald Inquiry – played a significant role in denying him his wish of attending Expo as premier, which spared the event considerable parochial grandstanding and intergovernmental scuffles, and removed what, for many, had been a barrier to enjoying Expo – for although the National Party was still in power, Ahern's leadership permitted a more inclusive tonal shift in public relations, managerial decisions, and programming outcomes.

In the midst of the contemporaneous Fitzgerald Inquiry revelations, Expo was charged with providing a bridge across 'the yawning gap between a folksy, bumbling and corrupt past, and a glorious future of urbanity, influence and open mindedness'.[15] That bridge was proven structurally unsound when – in the midst of a promised new era of governmental openness and accountability – the National Party was seen to be obfuscating Expo's financials, aiding an old ally during the World Expo Park controversy, and awarding the site redevelopment tender to another entrenched favourite in dubious circumstances. These scandals prompted one of Expo's biggest departures from the exposition norm: the popularity of the originating government sank in indirect proportion to the event's success. Instead of bathing in the reflected glory of the event it begat, the National Party withered in the exposing light of scandals it had inflicted upon itself. The great political event so successfully marketed as personal proved the old adage and became political once more.

A 'coming of age' implies, of necessity, the ending of another. National Party parliamentarians looked increasingly out of step with the times their party had inadvertently helped usher in. Expo's champions had promised change, and people had come to expect that of their government. The public outcry in relation to the site redevelopment showed that Brisbane had also been transformed, its mainstream population becoming the protesting hordes so deftly demonised by the former premier. In a post–Bjelke-Petersen world, their objections were heeded. Ahern withstood great pressure from his party and vested interests to write off the Expo debt, which enabled the event's significant physical legacy in the form of the South Bank Parklands.

In vastly different ways, Expo and the Fitzgerald Inquiry represented a necessary opening up of Brisbane. Both have their detractors, but each allowed people to entertain beliefs that they wanted to anyway: Brisbane had grown up, Queensland wasn't going to be corrupt anymore, the state would be less of a punchline. These seismic occasions extracted Brisbane from its sleepy backwater status and pointed it towards the modernity Expo purported to represent. Their continued relevance is evident in the frequency with which they are invoked in comparison with emerging controversies and events. These were the last grand acts of the National Party's thirty-two-year reign.

To the people of Brisbane, Expo 88 was a great deal more than a good party. Strangers don't leave roses out year after year for a good party. They don't mourn it along with their dearly departed pet. They don't devote hundreds of internet pages to it, or require counselling to recover from how good it was. Even extraordinary parties aren't memorialised every time the number of years since its passing ends in a five or a zero. Expo was far greater than the sum of its populist parts. It defied expectations from inception through to execution, and did so again in its aftermath.

As a calculated political ploy turned cultural phenomenon, Expo should have been a triumph for the National Party. It wasn't even a last hurrah. Ahern's relatively light public relations touch – dictated, in part, by his late entry into the Expo arena as Bjelke-Petersen's deposer – allowed the exposition to be a relatively apolitical event. This created a credit vacuum that the residents of Brisbane, long encouraged to feel ownership of Expo, were happy to fill. The more successful Expo became, the more tightly locals clutched it to their collective chest. The 'we' in 'Together we'll show the world' was well and truly claimed by the people of mainstream Brisbane. When that proprietorial situation was threatened by the site's redevelopment, the true change Expo had wrought – a change in expectation – forced a weakened National Party government to change its plans. Thirty years later, the public sense of ownership over this event – and the parklands many had united to protect – is so strong that its originating government is seldom thought of in connection with it. It is almost as though Expo seceded.

Appendix

Bicentennial Rap

It's one, nine, eighty-eight
And it's time for Oz to celebrate
Let's break, let's rap, let's get on down
And recreate old Sydney town
We're two hundred years on down the track
Having a party as we look back
Getting on down with a celebration
Of convicts, squatters and black decimation
Black decimation?
Seems to me
It's a party that's a pooper
For the Aborigine

Let's carry on with the celebration
And give a cheer for assimilation
And don't forget discrimination
Land rights, cell deaths and victimisation
Victimisation. Spell it with a 'V'
It's a party that's a pooper
For the Aborigine

It's a big bicentennial bash
And all the corporations are giving out cash
The Tall Ships T-shirts and Expo rights
And getting on down in a sacred site
Well it's one, nine, eighty-eight
And fair enough to celebrate
But let's remember when we have our fun
That this land was taken with a great big gun
We can't make up for the crimes of the past
By running our flag up a Tall Ship mast
Two hundred years is what we're cheering for
Remember forty thousand is a whole lot more.

Lyrics quoted with permission from Guy Hooper

Photo Credits

Acknowledgements

THIS PROJECT MAY HAVE BEEN possible – but would have been far less probable – without my 1987 Christmas present of an Expo 88 season pass, which allowed me to frequent 'the happiest place on earth' on weekends and during school holidays. For this – and for so much more – love and thanks to my mum and dad.

I savoured every minute of my time at Expo, but as I grew older I began to hear some disturbing things about its organising government. I wondered if it was possible to reconcile my love for this event with such information. The short answer is yes. The long answer is this book.

Thanks to my agent, Alex Adsett, for your advocacy and your outfits, to publisher extraordinaire Alexandra Payne for your interest, faith, and support, to editor Kevin O'Brien for your eagle eye and velvet glove, to project editor Vanessa Pellatt for your deft guidance and rad 1980s references, and to Christa Moffitt for your elegant cover. This book began as a PhD thesis, so I tip my hat to my supervisors, Professor Peter Spearritt and Dr Geoff Ginn, my examiners, and the Australian Postgraduate Awards Scholarship that enabled me to eat.

This work has benefited greatly from the generosity and candour of my interview subjects, all of whom were a genuine pleasure to meet: Barbara Absolon AM, Mike Ahern AO, Sallyanne Atkinson AO, Debra Beattie, Anni Davey, Lady Jane Edwards AM, Sir Llewellyn Edwards AC, Ross Given AM, Peter Goldston AO, David Hamilton, Sir Leo Hielscher, Drew Hutton, Anne Jones, Tony Kelly, Carol Lloyd, James Maccormick MBE, Danny May, Wayne McCamley, Bob Minnikin, David Monaghan, Sir Frank Moore, Mike Mullins OAM, Adam Nash, Marguerite Pepper, Des Power AM, Mary-Clare Power, Anthony Steel AM, Stephen Stockwell, John Watson, Bob Weatherall, and Ian Williams.

Thanks to those who smoothed the Expo path in various ways: Genevieve Atkinson, Tess Beck, Pascalle Burton, Antonella Casella, Andie Fox, Cameron Francis, Adam Hadley, Krissy Kneen, John McGregor, Tessa Mullen, Anthony Mullins, Kirstin Murray, Sharon Phillips, Bree Sergeant, Lance Sinclair, David Stavanger, Annie Te Whiu, Alexandra Tucker, Blair Ryan, Mary Ryan, and Avid Reader. Ian Powne didn't do anything but probably expects to see his name here. Thanks to Megan McGrath for sending an Outlook meeting request for my own book launch to me, Grace Lucas-Pennington, and Angela Renshaw within five minutes of ascertaining the date. Special props to Kristina Olsson and Katie Woods for going above and beyond the above and beyond.

I must also mention the journalists and academics who first chronicled this extraordinary place and time, and who made it so much easier for those of us who followed; my debt should be apparent from the extent of my referencing. I'm grateful to the relevant people and institutions for allowing quotations and images to be reproduced in this book.

Thanks to Carody Culver (who has read so many versions of this work that it borders on being inhumane) for her sartorial and emotional aplomb, and for being the classiest lady I've ever met.

And thank you to my dear friend Kathryn Kelly (who boycotted Expo as a much more politically engaged schoolgirl than I) for over twenty years of encouragement and support. Sorry you missed Expo, Kathryn. It was kind of a big deal.

Notes and References

Introduction   What If You Threw an Expo and Nobody Came?

1   Robert Haupt, 'Of All the Places to Unveil the 21st Century, They Chose Queensland', *Sydney Morning Herald*, 26 April 1988.

2   'Expo Millionaires Sad to See World's Fair Finish', *Sunday Mail* (Brisbane), 23 October 1988; 'New Base for Chuck', *Sunday Sun* (Brisbane), 23 October 1988. Sanders operated food outlets on Expo's boardwalk and in the USA Pavilion. His first exposition was in Chicago in 1933, and his twelfth was in Brisbane in 1988.

3   Queensland Government, *Queensland Past and Present: 100 Years of Statistics 1896–1996* (Brisbane: Government Statistician's Office, 1998), 69, 83.

4   Ken Brass, 'The Great Joh Show Gamble', *Weekend Australian Magazine*, 31 May–1 June 1986; Jennifer Craik, 'Expo 88: Fashions of Sight and Politics of Site', in eds Tony Bennett, Pat Buckridge, David Carter, and Colin Mercer, *Celebrating the Nation: A Critical Study of Australia's Bicentenary* (St Leonards: Allen & Unwin, 1992), 146.

5   'Expo Millionaires Sad to See World's Fair Finish'.

6   BESBRA, *World Expo 88 Report* (Brisbane: BESBRA, 1988), section A7; Australian Bureau of Statistics, 'Population Size and Growth', accessed 15 July 2015, http://www.abs.gov.au/ausstats/abs@.nsf/0/24E36F628AD35006CA2577 3700169C5C?opendocument. Australia's population in 1988 was 16,532,000. In its report, BESBRA gives the final Expo attendance figure (including staff, VIPs and repeat visitors) as 18,560,447.

7   Shane Rodgers, 'What a Party', *Courier-Mail* (Brisbane), 31 October 1988.

8   Steve Bishop, *The Most Dangerous Detective: The Outrageous Glen Patrick Hallahan and the Rat Pack*, 2nd edition (Brisbane: Steve Bishop, 2015), 127. Police attending the raid included Rat Pack member Tony Murphy. The football match was part of a controversial 1971 South Africa rugby tour that prompted anti-apartheid protests around the country.

9   Louise Noble, 'South Bank Dreaming', *Architecture Australia* (September/October 2001), accessed 4 November 2013, http://architectureau.com/articles/south-bank-dreaming.
10   Craik, 'Expo 88', 148.
11   Sir Edward Williams, *Report of the Commissioner-General of Expo 88 on the Australian Government's Involvement in Expo 88* (Canberra: Department of Sport, Recreation and Tourism, 1989), 1.
12   Rachel Sanderson, 'Celebration, Commemoration and Consumption: World Expo 88 and the Australian Bicentenary' (working paper, 2007).
13   Lisa Munro, 'Investigating World's Fairs: An Historiography', *Studies in Latin American Popular Culture* 28 (2010), 82.
14   I am particularly indebted to Peter Carroll for his work on the origin and intergovernmental relations of Expo, to Carroll and Kerry Donohue for their study of Expo's accounting practices, and to Jennifer Craik for her analysis of Expo's financial arrangements and visitation profile.

1   On the Origin of the Expo Species

1   Paul Greenhalgh, *Ephemeral Vistas: The Expositions Universelles, Great Exhibitions and World's Fairs, 1851–1939* (Manchester: Manchester University Press, 1988), 1.
2   Lisa Munro, 'Investigating World's Fairs: An Historiography', *Studies in Latin American Popular Culture* 28 (2010), 80.
3   Tony Bennett, *The Birth of the Museum: History, Theory, Politics* (London: Routledge, 1995), 66, 73.
4   Ibid., 20, 21–6.
5   Ibid., 6, 54–5, 72, 87. Bennett notes the first world exposition was a 'transitional form' of public assembly, with classes effectively separated by varying prices of admission on designated days.
6   Corinne A. Kratz and Ivan Karp, 'Museum Frictions: Public Cultures/Global Transformations', in eds Ivan Karp, Corinne A. Kratz, Lynn Szwaja, and Tomás Ybarra-Frausto, *Museum Frictions: Public Cultures/Global Transformations* (Durham and London: Duke University Press, 2006), 3; Bennett, *Birth of the Museum*, 1–4, 67.
7   Bennett, *Birth of the Museum*, 1–4.
8   Ibid., 39, 78.
9   Michel Foucault, trans. Jay Miskowiev, 'Of Other Spaces', *Diacritics: A Review of Contemporary Criticism*, 16, 1 (Spring 1986), 26. See also Bennett, *Birth of the Museum*, 1–4.
10   Bennett, *Birth of the Museum*, 6, 67.
11   Ibid., 80–1.
12   Judith McKay, *Showing Off: Queensland at World Expositions 1862–1988* (Rockhampton: Central Queensland University Press, 2004), 18–19. Queensland's display featured various timbers and examples of colonial furniture. Australia eschewed industrial displays at early expositions, favouring agriculture, Aboriginal culture, flora, and fauna. Organisers also emphasised the white colonial inhabitants' similarity to the British. See Linda Young, 'How Like England We Can Be', in eds Kate Darian-Smith, Richard Gillespie, Caroline Jordan, and

Elizabeth Willis, *Seize the Day: Exhibitions, Australia and the World* (Clayton: Monash University ePress, 2008), 06.1.

13 Philip T. Smith, 'London 1851: The Great Exhibition of the Works of Industry of All Nations', in ed. John E. Findling, *Historical Dictionary of World's Fairs and Expositions, 1851–1988* (New York: Greenwood Press, 1990), 7.

14 Jeffrey A. Auerbach, *The Great Exhibition of 1851: A Nation on Display* (New Haven and London: Yale University Press, 1999), 54–88.

15 Simon Heffer, *High Minds: The Victorians and the Birth of Modern Britain* (London: Windmill Books, 2014), 306.

16 Carl Malamud, *A World's Fair for the Global Village* (Cambridge: MIT Press, 1997), 15.

17 Greenhalgh, *Ephemeral Vistas*, 18–24; Burton Benedict, with contributions by Marjorie M. Dobkin et al., *The Anthropology of World's Fairs: San Francisco's Panama Pacific International Exposition of 1915* (Berkeley: Lowie Museum of Anthropology; London: Scolar Press, 1983), 2. See also Kate Darian-Smith, 'Seize the Day', in Darian-Smith et al., *Seize the Day*, 01.7. To emphasise the cultural and educational value of expositions (and distinguish them from retail districts), direct sales of display items was prohibited. The ban did not extend to exposition memorabilia, and could be circumvented in myriad ways.

18 Arthur Chandler, 'Paris 1867: Exposition Universelle', in Findling, *Historical Dictionary*, 35, 40. Emperor Napoleon III was the first president and last emperor of France.

19 Findling, *Historical Dictionary*, vii–x, 376–81, 395–402. Some of these events were too small and specialised to be included in many world exposition listings.

20 Barry Dyster, 'Sydney 1879: Colonial City, Global City', in eds Peter Proudfoot, Roslyn Maguire, and Robert Freestone, *Colonial City, Global City: Sydney's International Exhibition 1879* (Darlinghurst: Crossing Press, 2000), 8–12.

21 Robert Freestone, 'Space, Society and Urban Reform', in Proudfoot, Maguire, and Freestone, *Colonial City, Global City*, 31–3. This attendance figure was half Australia's population at the time. The exposition contributed to a permanent art gallery in Sydney, supported technical museums that preceded the Powerhouse Museum, and drew attention to the potential of Sydney Harbour as a site for hallmark events.

22 Joanne Scott and Ross Laurie, 'Within Her Own Boundaries', in Darian-Smith et al., *Seize the Day*, 06.17. The quotation is from the *Brisbane Courier*.

23 Ibid., 06.2, 06.10. There was some cause for this swelling of local pride. Scott and Laurie report 34,000 visits to the exposition (the non-Aboriginal population was roughly 27,000 at the time).

24 Greenhalgh, *Ephemeral Vistas*, 15.

25 D. Clive Hardy, 'New Orleans 1884–1885: The World's Industrial and Cotton Centennial Exposition', in Findling, *Historical Dictionary*, 88.

26 Richmond F. Brown, 'Guatemala City 1897: Exposicion Centroamericana', in Findling, *Historical Dictionary*, 145.

27 David Glassberg, 'Philadelphia 1926: Sequi-Centennial International Exposition', in Findling, *Historical Dictionary*, 246.

28   Robert W. Brown, 'Paris 1900: Exposition Universelle', in Findling, *Historical Dictionary*, 156, 161. The event went on to attract over fifty million visitors.

29   Robert W. Rydell, 'New Directions for Scholarship about World Expos', in Darian-Smith et al., *Seize the Day*, 21.5.

30   Wray Vamplew, 'Adelaide 1887–1888: Jubilee International Exhibition', in Findling, *Historical Dictionary*, 98–9.

31   Joy H. Hall, 'Paris 1889: Exposition Universelle', in Findling, *Historical Dictionary*, 110–11.

32   Raymond Starr, 'San Diego 1915–1916: The Panama California Exposition', in Findling, *Historical Dictionary*, 229.

33   R. Reid Badger, 'Chicago 1893: World's Columbian Exposition', in Findling, *Historical Dictionary*, 122, 130.

34   Erik Larson, *The Devil in the White City: Murder, Magic, and Madness at the Fair that Changed America* (New York: Vintage Books, 2003), 385. Holmes's labyrinthine hotel was purpose built for murder: it contained soundproof rooms, doors that could not be opened from inside, gas-lines for asphyxiation, incineration devices, and lime and acid pits. He confessed to twenty-seven murders, though it has been estimated that the true figure exceeds 200.

35   Benedict, *Anthropology of World's Fairs*, 1–11.

36   Munro, 'Investigating World's Fairs', 81.

37   John Allwood, *The Great Exhibitions* (London: Studio Vista, 1977), 55.

38   Munro, 'Investigating World's Fairs', 88; Robert W. Rydell, John E. Findling, and Kimberly D. Pelle, *Fair America: World's Fairs in the United States* (Washington: Smithsonian Institution Press, 2000), 37.

39   Russell Duncan, 'Atlanta 1895: Cotton States and International Exposition', in Findling, *Historical Dictionary*, 139–40. The speech provided the foundation for the Atlanta compromise (in which Southern African Americans were to waive civil rights in exchange for free vocational education).

40   Badger, 'Chicago 1893', in Findling, *Historical Dictionary*, 129. Palmer was a well -known businesswoman, philanthropist, and socialite.

41   Ibid.

42   McKay, *Showing Off*, 35; Penelope Edmonds, 'We Think that This Subject of the Native Races Should Be Thoroughly Gone Into at the Forthcoming Exhibition', in Darian-Smith et al., *Seize the Day*, 04.1–17. See also Elizabeth Willis, 'The Productions of Aboriginal States', in Darian-Smith et al., *Seize the Day*, 02.1–15. Willis suggests curators may have made genuine attempts to show 'the industry, skill, and adaptability of the Aboriginal people whom they knew', and that this seems less kind through the lens of 'the post-Darwin codification of ideas about a hierarchy of races'.

43   Rydell, Findling, and Pelle, *Fair America*, 54.

44   Ibid., 65, 75.

45   Ibid., 29.

46   'President McKinley Favors Reciprocity', *New York Times*, 6 September 1901. Reprinted in Robert W. Rydell, *All the World's a Fair* (Chicago: University of Chicago Press, 1984), 4.

47   Rydell, Findling, and Pelle, *Fair America*, 51–2.

48 R. Reid Badger, 'Buffalo 1901: Pan-American Exposition', in Findling, *Historical Dictionary*, 165.
49 Yvonne M. Condon, 'St Louis 1904: Louisiana Purchase International Exposition', in Findling, *Historical Dictionary*, 179–80.
50 Rydell, Findling, and Pelle, *Fair America*, 53.
51 John E. Findling, 'World's Fairs and the Olympic Games', *World's Fair* 10, 4 (1990), 13–15.
52 Ibid.
53 Allwood, *Great Exhibitions*, 75–7.
54 Ibid., 129.
55 Badger, 'Chicago 1893', 130.
56 Burton Benedict, 'San Francisco 1915: Panama Pacific International Exposition', in Findling, *Historical Dictionary*, 223.
57 Alfred Heller, *World's Fairs and the End of Progress: An Insider's View* (Corte Madera: World's Fair Inc., 1999), 97.
58 Rydell, Findling, and Pelle, *Fair America*, 1; Badger, 'Chicago 1893', 126.
59 Rydell, Findling, and Pelle, *Fair America*, 84.
60 Ibid., 82–94.
61 Ibid., 87–94, 105. See also Heller, *World's Fairs*, 86. Other shenanigans included naked girls playing ping-pong on donkeys in San Francisco's 1939–40 exposition, and topless dancing girls pretending to seduce astronauts at the Seattle exposition in 1962.
62 Rydell, Findling, and Pelle, *Fair America*, 56.
63 Findling, *Historical Dictionary*, 59, 68–70, 112, 129, 224, 272.
64 Benedict, 'San Francisco 1915', 224. The pavilion was toured by Henry Ford and Thomas Edison.
65 Bureau International des Expositions, 'Our History', accessed 12 January 2015, http://www.bie-paris.org/site/en/bie/our-history. The BIE was formed at the Paris Convention of 1928 and commenced operating in 1931.
66 Ibid. The present-day exposition terminology is 'Registered' for large and 'Recognised' for smaller events.
67 Peter Carroll, 'The Intergovernmental Relations of Expo '88' (PhD thesis, UQ, 1994), 104.
68 Rydell, Findling, and Pelle, *Fair America*, 99, 132–3.
69 Robert W. Rydell, *World of Fairs: The Century-of-Progress Expositions* (Chicago: University of Chicago Press, 1993), 215.
70 Michael Mullen, 'New York 1939–1940: New York World's Fair', in Findling, *Historical Dictionary*, 297; Daniel T. Lawrence AIA, 'New York 1964–1965: New York World's Fair', in Findling, *Historical Dictionary*, 324.
71 Benedict, *Anthropology of World's Fairs*, 25.
72 Mullen, 'New York 1939–1940', 293, 299.
73 Arthur Chandler, 'Paris 1937: Exposition Internationale des Arts et Techniques dans la Vie Moderne', in Findling, *Historical Dictionary*, 288–9.
74 Allwood, *Great Exhibitions*, 48; Mullen, 'New York 1939–1940', 299.
75 Mullen, 'New York 1939–1940', 299.
76 Allwood, *Great Exhibitions*, 149–50.

77   Ibid., 153, 156.
78   Rydell, 'New Directions', 21.5, 21.7. Prior to his Midway fame, Bloom managed
     the boxer 'Gentle Jim'. Another career launched at a world exposition was that
     of Thomas Cook (the founder of what was to become a global travel company).
     Some of Cook's first organised tours were to the Crystal Palace.
79   Darian-Smith, 'Seize the Day', 01.1.
80   Graeme Davison, 'Welcoming the World: The 1956 Olympic Games and the
     Re-Presentation of Melbourne', *Australian Historical Studies* 27, 109 (1997),
     67–73. Sceptics worried the city 'would be the laughing stock of the world', and
     social anxiety prompted a Keep Calm for the Games campaign.
81   Ibid., 75.
82   Robert W. Rydell, 'Brussels 1958: Exposition Universelle et Internationale de
     Bruxelles (Expo '58)', in Findling, *Historical Dictionary*, 311–13. The exposition
     was first proposed in 1947 and intended for 1955 but was delayed owing to
     financial and political complications arising from the Korean War.
83   Rydell, *World of Fairs*, 200.
84   Ibid., 207.
85   Paul Ashdown, 'Seattle 1962: Seattle World's Fair (Century 21 Exposition)', in
     Findling, *Historical Dictionary*, 319–21.
86   Rydell, Findling, and Pelle, *Fair America*, 132–3.
87   Lawrence, 'New York 1964–1965', 323, 324.
88   Heller, *World's Fairs*, 97.
89   Lawrence, 'New York 1964–1965', 327.
90   Rydell, Findling, and Pelle, *Fair America*, 107.
91   Ibid., 129.
92   Carolyn Barnes and Simon Jackson, 'A Significant Mirror of Progress', in Darian-
     Smith et al., *Seize the Day*, 20.1, 20.6–16. The writers attribute this shift to
     Australia's 'economic disentanglement from Britain' and subsequent pivot towards
     Asian markets expected to look favourably upon an advanced and independent
     trading partner. The pavilion featured Featherston 'sound chairs' and hostess
     uniforms designed by Zara Holt (wife of Prime Minister Harold Holt).
93   Allwood, *Great Exhibitions*, 176.
94   Martin Manning, 'Osaka 1970: Japan World Exposition (Expo '70)', in Findling,
     Historical Dictionary, 341.
95   Ibid., 345.
96   Ibid.
97   Heller, *World's Fairs*, 95.
98   Ashdown, 'Seattle 1962', 319–21; Rydell, Findling, and Pelle, *Fair America*, 102.
99   Allwood, *Great Exhibitions*, 160.
100 Jane Jacobs, *The Death and Life of Great American Cities* (New York: Random
     House, 1961), 24–5.
101 Ibid., 25.
102 Roberta Brandes Gratz, *The Battle for Gotham: New York in the Shadow of
     Robert Moses and Jane Jacobs* (New York: Nation Books, 2010), xxii, 121–8.
     Le Corbusier's other design contributions were quite elegant.
103 Jacobs, *Death and Life*, 439.

104   Renate Howe, David Nichols, and Graeme Davison, *Trendyville: The Battle for Australia's Inner Cities* (Clayton: Monash University Publishing, 2014), 2–3.

105   Ibid., 3, 29, 45, 182.

106   Ibid., 3, 5, 31, 135, 182–4.

107   Peter M. Warner, 'Montreal 1967: Expo 67: Universal and International Exhibition of 1967', in Findling, *Historical Dictionary*, 334, 339.

108   D. Clive Hardy, 'New Orleans 1984: Louisiana World Exposition', in Findling, *Historical Dictionary*, 358.

109   Rydell, Findling, and Pelle, *Fair America*, 129.

110   Robert A. Baade and Victor A. Matheson, 'Going for the Gold: The Economics of the Olympics', *Journal of Economic Perspectives* 30, 2 (Spring 2016), 212, 214. The Los Angeles Games were the first to finish in profit since 1932 but were advantaged by being permitted to repurpose existing facilities. The event was not scandal- or boycott-free, but it marked the beginning of a more optimistic period for the Games, cemented with the 1992 Barcelona Olympics (the first to be unaffected by boycotts since 1972). See also Jeremy Venook, 'The Olympics Haven't Always Been an Economic Disaster', *Atlantic*, 4 August 2016, accessed 24 August 2016, http://www.theatlantic.com/business/archive/2016/08/the-olympics-havent-always-been-an-economic-disaster/494534/.

111   Davison, 'Welcoming the World', 64.

112   Ibid.

113   Ibid.

114   Carroll, 'Intergovernmental Relations', 104–5.

115   Peter Carroll, 'The Origins of Expo 88', *Australian Journal of Public Administration* 48, 1 (March 1989), 42–3.

116   Ibid., 44.

117   John Young, 'Civil Government Boundaries', *Queensland Historical Atlas*, 2010, accessed 12 October 2015, http://www.qhatlas.com.au/content/civil-government-boundaries. Several European explorers 'discovered' Australia in the 1600s and 1700s, but James Cook claimed it for Great Britain in 1770. Matthew Flinders explored the Moreton Bay area in 1799, as did John Oxley in 1823 (at the behest of Sir Thomas Brisbane). A settlement was established in Redcliffe in 1824 but moved to Brisbane the next year to gain better access to water. The convict station was closed in 1839 and free settlement began in 1842.

118   Helen Gregory, 'Brisbane River', *Queensland Historical Atlas*, 2010, accessed 12 October 2015, http://www.qhatlas.com.au/content/brisbane-river.

119   Ibid.

120   Young, 'Civil Government Boundaries'.

121   John R. Cole, *Shaping a City: Greater Brisbane 1925–1985* (Queensland: William Brooks, 1984), 148.

122   See Geoff Ginn and Michael Westaway, 'Fortress Queensland 1942–45', *Queensland Historical Atlas*, 2010, accessed 12 October 2015, http://www.qhatlas.com.au/fortress-queensland-1942-45. General Douglas MacArthur was based in Brisbane between 1942 and 1944. During this time, Brisbane and Townsville provided bases for thousands of American troops. In addition to being a significant psychological drain, the war placed considerable strain

on infrastructure. Airstrips, roads, railways, and ports were all commandeered for military purposes. Brisbane rooftops held anti-aircraft guns, and the streets were filled with air-raid shelters. Multiple Japanese air raids were conducted across Queensland between 1942 and 1943, and a Japanese submarine sank the Australian Hospital Ship (AHS) *Centaur* off North Stradbroke Island, with a loss of 268 lives. Northern Queenslanders were also unsettled by rumours that the Curtin government had determined everything north of the 'Brisbane Line' was indefensible and should be abandoned in the event of a Japanese invasion.

123 Cole, *Shaping a City*, 196.
124 Ibid., 220, 387–9.
125 Ibid., 338.
126 Gregory, 'Brisbane River'.

2 We Need to Talk about Queensland

1 Hugh Lunn, *Joh: The Life and Political Adventures of Johannes Bjelke-Petersen* (Melbourne: Sun Books, 1979), xi.

2 Imelda Miller, 'Sugar Slaves', *Queensland Historical Atlas*, 2010, accessed 12 October 2015, http://www.qhatlas.com.au/content/sugar-slaves. Miller writes that from 1863 to 1904, approximately 62,000 South Sea Islanders were 'forced, coerced, deceived or persuaded' to travel to Queensland, where they built the sugar industry in extreme conditions causing a high death rate, for six pounds a year (white workers received thirty pounds). This practice was formalised with the *Pacific Labourers Act 1880*. It ceased under the White Australia Policy, resulting in deportation and hardship for many.

3 Sir Leo Hielscher (under treasurer and BESBRA board member), interview with the author, April 2013.

4 Joanne Holliman, *Sir Leo Hielscher: Queensland Made* (St Lucia: University of Queensland Press, 2014), 35–95; Cameron Hazlehurst, *Gordon Chalk: A Political Life* (Toowoomba: Darling Downs Institute Press, 1987), 261–8. Modernisation efforts included restructuring the public service as a meritocracy, developing the mining industry and associated infrastructure in tandem with significant increases in royalties, reconstructing state building societies, courting overseas investment, and successfully appealing for a fairer share of federal funding. Less orthodox undertakings involved using State Government Insurance Organisation funds to circumvent Loan Council restrictions, and appealing to the World Bank for development funding when denied at a federal level.

5 Holliman, *Sir Leo Hielscher*, 40.

6 Lunn, *Joh*, 216.

7 Rae Wear, *Johannes Bjelke-Petersen: The Lord's Premier* (St Lucia: University of Queensland Press, 2002), 154. Zonal manipulations denied Gordon Chalk the opportunity to become premier after the 1974 election; his party was nine seats behind the Nationals – despite winning 31.1 per cent of the primary vote against 27.9 per cent for the Nationals. Labor was reduced to eleven seats.

8 Lunn, *Joh*, 13–30.

9 Hugh Lunn, *Behind the Banana Curtain* (St Lucia: University of Queensland Press, 1980), 122.

10   Rosemary Kyburz, interview by Lindsay Marshall, *Decades of Division*, National
     Library of Australia, 21 August 2010, TRC 6150/7, accessed 12 October 2013,
     http://nla.gov.au/nla.obj-219196863/listen.

11   Peter Charlton, *State of Mind: Why Queensland Is Different* (North Ryde: Methuen
     Haynes, 1987), 25; Ian Townsend, 'I Am the Egg Man: Katter', News ABC, 1 July
     2004, accessed 18 October 2014, http://www.abc.net.au/news/2004-06-30/i-am
     -the-egg-man-katter/2002186; William Hatherell, *The Third Metropolis: Imagining
     Brisbane through Art and Literature 1940–1970* (St Lucia: University of Queensland
     Press, 2007), 34. Hatherell reports that Bjelke-Petersen sought to intervene in the
     cohabitation arrangements of two (unmarried) members of ABBA – presumably on
     the basis of conservative ideas about sex outside of marriage.

12   Hatherell, *Third Metropolis*, 13, 34–8. The cultural invasion also brought social
     friction. Rivalries between US and Australian soldiers led to a skirmish dubbed the
     'Battle of Brisbane' in 1942, resulting in hundreds of injuries.

13   Andrew Stafford, *Pig City* (St Lucia: University of Queensland Press, 2004).

14   Hatherell, *Third Metropolis*, 19, 110–14. The QCC was funded by sales of Golden
     Casket tickets and Scratch-Its. See also John Macarthur, Donald Watson, and
     Robert Riddel, 'Civic Visions for Brisbane', in eds John Macarthur, Deborah
     Van Der Plaat, Janina Gosseye, and Andrew Wilson, *Hot Modernism: Queensland
     Architecture 1945–75* (London: Artifice, 2015), 232–3. Architect Robin Gibson
     won a competition to build the QAG in 1973. Chalk secretly conspired with
     Gibson after this win to extend the art gallery commission into the QCC
     (including a library, museum, and performing arts complex) with flood-prone
     South Brisbane land resumed from willing businesses after the 1974 floods, in the
     expectation the centre would form part of the 1974 Liberal election policy. His
     party failed to achieve senior Coalition status at this election, but the government
     retained the plan.

15   Hatherell, *Third Metropolis*, 19.

16   Peter Anderson, *Ephemeral Traces: Brisbane's Artist-Run Scene in the 1980s*,
     catalogue essay (St Lucia: University of Queensland Art Museum, 2016), 2–15.
     See also *Return to Sender*, University of Queensland Art Museum, accessed 20
     June 2016, http://www.artmuseum.uq.edu.au/return-to-sender-publication.

17   Anne Jones (an editor of *The Cane Toad Times*), interview with the author,
     December 2012.

18   Ibid.

19   Tony Kelly (former QCOSS director, and contributor to the Expo 88 study *The
     Big Party Syndrome*), interview with the author, February 2013.

20   Barbara Absolon (Entertainment deputy director and Walkways producer for
     Expo 88), interview with the author, December 2012. See also Joanne Scott and
     Ross Laurie, 'Queensland in Miniature: The Brisbane Exhibition', *Queensland
     Historical Atlas*, 2010, accessed 12 October 2015, http://www.qhatlas.com.au/
     content/queensland-miniature-brisbane-exhibition. The annual agricultural show
     popularly referred to as the Ekka offered displays, a marketplace, entertainment,
     and a rural-focused celebration of 'the Queensland way of life'.

21   Matthew Condon, *All Fall Down* (St Lucia: University of Queensland Press,
     2015), 8, 46–7. Grundy's Entertainment Centre formed part of Paradise Centre,

which was controversially developed on Gold Coast City Council land by white shoe developer and Hinze associate Eddie Kornhauser. Tourism entrepreneur and fellow white shoe wearer Keith Williams established Sea World and Hamilton Island Resort. The tender for Conrad Jupiters casino was awarded to Jennings Industries Ltd – a company founded by the father of National Party member for Southport Doug Jennings.

22 Hatherell, *Third Metropolis*, 32–5. The Chermside centre was opened just a year after the first fully enclosed complex (the Southdale Center) opened in the United States.

23 John R. Cole, *Shaping a City: Greater Brisbane 1925–1985* (Queensland: William Brooks, 1984), 239.

24 Ibid., 256–61. Jones was also responsible for redeveloping King George Square, improving the George Street Botanic Gardens, developing the Roma Street Forum and the Botanic Gardens at Mt Coot-tha (with Glasshouse dome and Planetarium), and purchasing considerable riverside land from the city through to Indooroopilly for conversion into public parkland.

25 Ibid., 222.

26 Renate Howe, David Nichols, and Graeme Davison, *Trendyville: The Battle for Australia's Inner Cities* (Clayton: Monash University Publishing, 2014), 112–15. Anti-freeway coordinator Betty Hounslow recalls Special Branch officers informing her – while laughing about it – that a neo-Nazi was travelling to Brisbane to kill her.

27 Hatherell, *Third Metropolis*, 32–5.

28 Lunn, *Joh*, 57; Wear, *Johannes Bjelke-Petersen*, 92. Bjelke-Petersen was represented in court over the matter by Walter Campbell QC, who became governor of Queensland.

29 Deane Wells, *The Deep North* (Fitzroy: Globe Press, 1979), 130.

30 Lunn, *Joh*, 58–9.

31 Wells, *Deep North*, 130; Charlton, *State of Mind*, 166. Some members of the Opposition also accepted shares.

32 Wear, *Johannes Bjelke-Petersen*, 51–3.

33 Lunn, *Joh*, 65–6.

34 Charlton, *State of Mind*, 82.

35 Chris Salisbury, 'Queensland: The Slogan State', *Queensland Historical Atlas*, 2010, accessed 12 October 2015, http://www.qhatlas.com.au/queensland-slogan-state; Lunn, *Joh*, 90.

36 Lunn, *Joh*, 90.

37 David Monaghan (journalist), email to the author, 18 December 2012.

38 John Wallace, 'Reporting the Joh Show: The Queensland Media', in eds Margaret Bridson Cribb and P.J. Boyce, *Politics in Queensland: 1977 and Beyond* (St Lucia: University of Queensland Press, 1980), 205–6.

39 Colin A. Hughes, *The Government of Queensland* (St Lucia: University of Queensland Press, 1980), 307–9.

40 Wear, *Johannes Bjelke-Petersen*, 214.

41 Lunn, *Joh*, 80–91; Wear, *Johannes Bjelke-Petersen*, 218.

42 Steve Bishop, *The Most Dangerous Detective: The Outrageous Glen Patrick Hallahan and the Rat Pack*, 2nd edition (Brisbane: Steve Bishop, 2015), 7.

43 Gerald Fitzgerald, *Commission of Inquiry into Possible Illegal Activities and Associated Police Misconduct* (Brisbane: Crime and Misconduct Commission, 1989), 32–3. See also Bishop, *Most Dangerous Detective*, 69–73. Improper government and police relations originated along sectarian lines during the Catholic-dominated Labor Party's period in office prior to 1957, with the Catholic-dominated police force controlling police corruption. Police tolerated hotels operating outside legal hours, bookies, and prostitution in return for 'donations'. These were collected by police around the state on behalf of the government and channelled to favoured electoral campaigns. After the Gair split, the Protestant-dominated Nicklin government knowingly appointed a corrupt police commissioner, Protestant Frank Bischof, over a widely respected Catholic rival. When the new government did not continue these graft-collecting activities, Bischof resumed them with himself as the primary beneficiary.

44 Matthew Condon, *Three Crooked Kings* (St Lucia: University of Queensland Press, 2013).

45 Ray W. Whitrod, *Before I Sleep: Memoirs of a Modern Police Commissioner* (St Lucia: University of Queensland Press, 2001), 153–4.

46 Phil Dickie, *The Road to Fitzgerald* (St Lucia: University of Queensland Press, 1988), 7.

47 Ibid.; Bishop, *Most Dangerous Detective*, 150, 151, 153, 159, 167–8, 180.

48 Bishop, *Most Dangerous Detective*, 92–122.

49 Dickie, *Road to Fitzgerald*, 7; Evan Whitton, *Can of Worms II*, 2nd edition (Broadway: The Fairfax Library, 1987), 12, 71–4.

50 Des Power (former chairman of Queensland Events Corporation and executive producer of *Today Tonight*), interview with the author, March 2013. Power's other roles include being foreign correspondent for the ABC and a reporter and executive producer of *This Day Tonight*. He also produced video footage for the Queensland Pavilion of Expo, and a documentary that played during the ABA travelling exhibition.

51 Charlton, *State of Mind*, 40.

52 Sir Frank Moore (former chairman of QTTC, director of Dreamworld and Jupiters Casino, developer, and member of the National Party's management committee), interview with the author, July 2013.

53 Sir Leo Hielscher, interview by Brian Head and Chris Salisbury, *Queensland Speaks*, Centre for the Government of Queensland, 2011, accessed 14 October 2013, http://www.queenslandspeaks.com.au/leo-hielscher.

54 Holliman, *Sir Leo Hielscher*, 125.

55 Wells, *Deep North*, 29–31.

56 Ibid., 31.

57 Sir Llew Edwards (former Queensland Liberal Party leader, deputy premier, and chairman of Expo 88), interview with the author, October 2012.

58 Evan Whitton, *The Hillbilly Dictator: Australia's Police State* (Crows Nest: ABC, 1989), 18.

59 Whitton, *Can of Worms II*, 20.

60 Whitrod, *Before I Sleep*, 142, 166.

61 Ibid., 141.

62   Ibid., 141–2.
63   Des Sturgess, *The Tangled Web* (Brisbane: Bedside Books, 2001), 13, 47, 49, 57–62, 77. Sturgess has also been a defence barrister and Queen's Counsel.
64   Ibid., 57–63.
65   Whitrod, *Before I Sleep*, 139.
66   Power, interview with the author. Moore appeared as Constable Dave on the children's television show *Wombat*, and alongside the puppet Agro. Power also exposed the Milan Brych controversy. See also Whitton, *Hillbilly Dictator*, 75, 96–8; Condon, *All Fall Down*, 140–6, 314–15.
67   Ibid.
68   Kelly, interview with the author.
69   Ibid. Kelly received the call from a senior figure at the school of medicine at UQ, who said, 'If you continue that campaign against [Minister for Health] Llew Edwards I will ensure that you will never work again in Queensland'.
70   Wells, *Deep North*, 31.
71   Wear, *Johannes Bjelke-Petersen*, 197. Sinclair, a teacher, was also transferred from his Maryborough home to Ipswich.
72   Charlton, *State of Mind*, 69, 67, 74; Lunn, *Joh*, 153.
73   Wells, *Deep North*, 46.
74   Hazlehurst, *Gordon Chalk*, 225.
75   Charlton, *State of Mind*, 122.
76   Raymond Evans, 'Springbok Tour Confrontation', in eds Raymond Evans and Carole Ferrier, *Radical Brisbane: An Unruly History* (Carlton North: The Vulgar Press, 2004), 280–3.
77   Condon, *Three Crooked Kings*, 245; Charlton, *State of Mind*, 125. Bjelke-Petersen also offered the police assistance with a claim before the industrial court, financially unsustainable superannuation, and early retirement.
78   Whitrod, *Before I Sleep*, 178.
79   Ross Fitzgerald, *A History of Queensland: From 1915 to the 1980s* (St Lucia: University of Queensland Press, 1984), 571–2. The costly raid included 'forty government officers, two black trackers, light aircraft, a helicopter, a navy patrol vessel and a customs launch'.
80   Dickie, *Road to Fitzgerald*, vii; Charlton, *State of Mind*, 125; Whitrod, *Before I Sleep*, 187; Wear, *Johannes Bjelke-Petersen*, 202–3. It is believed that Lewis contrived to meet Bjelke-Petersen while at this rural posting.
81   Kelly, interview with the author.
82   Fitzgerald, *History of Queensland*, 571–2. Only one officer was brought to trial. (He was acquitted.)
83   Dickie, *Road to Fitzgerald*, vii.
84   Fitzgerald, *History of Queensland*, 571–2.
85   Whitrod, *Before I Sleep*, 192.
86   Wells, *Deep North*, 40.
87   Sturgess, *Tangled Web*, 88, 91, 94–5. The report made recommendations designed to prevent fabrication of evidence (such as tape-recording interviews, and early logging of activities) and requested action be taken to reduce corruption temptations, such as replacing police at watch houses and in the Licensing Commission with prison

officers, and appointing only seasoned officers to the licensing branch (which involved undercover work at casinos and brothels) on strictly limited rotations.

88   Ibid., 88–97. Sturgess met with Minister for Police Ron Camm and Sir Robert Sparkes to urge them to reconsider such inaction, but he knew from Sparkes's expression that 'I'd wasted my time'. Terry Lewis was present at both meetings.

89   Ibid., 122–34.

90   Whitton, *Can of Worms II*, 41; Whitton, *Hillbilly Dictator*, 27–8, 47, 55, 95.

91   Bishop, *Most Dangerous Detective*, 217–25.

92   Ibid., 226–80.

93   Ibid., 349–50. Williams was also chairman of the 1982 Commonwealth Games Committee and of Australia's National Crimes Commission, and a member of the United Nations Narcotics Control Board. Bishop believes Prime Minister Fraser, Deputy Prime Minister Doug Anthony, and Commonwealth Police Commissioner Sir Colin Woods 'stand condemned' for failing to ensure a proper investigation into damning allegations of corruption in the police force.

94   Roger Scott, Peter Coaldrake, Brian Head, and Paul Reynolds, 'Queensland', in ed. Brian Galligan, *Australian State Politics* (Melbourne: Longman Cheshire, 1986), 60.

95   Edwards, interview with the author.

96   Charlton, *State of Mind*, 39.

97   Wear, *Johannes Bjelke-Petersen*, 158. The company was Brisbane Wharves and Wool Dumping, a suspected donor to the Bjelke-Petersen Foundation.

98   Charlton, *State of Mind*, 64–7.

99   Edwards, interview with the author.

100 Hielscher, interview with the author.

101 Rosemary Kyburz, interview by Robin Sullivan, *Queensland Speaks*, Centre for the Government of Queensland, 7 September 2010, accessed 14 October 2014, http://www.queenslandspeaks.com.au/rosemary-kyburz.

102 Mike Ahern (former premier of Queensland), interview with the author, December 2012.

103 Wear, *Johannes Bjelke-Petersen*, 132–3.

104 Ahern, interview with the author.

105 Charlton, *State of Mind*, 181–3.

106 Wear, *Johannes Bjelke-Petersen*, 145–6.

107 Peter Coaldrake, *Working the System: Government in Queensland 1983–1989* (St Lucia: University of Queensland Press, 1989); Hazlehurst, *Gordon Chalk*, 254.

108 Ahern, interview with the author.

109 Wear, *Johannes Bjelke-Petersen*, 59. Such appointments included Peter Delamothe and Wally Rae (each served as agent-general for Queensland in London), Ron Camm (chairman of the Queensland Sugar Board), Bill Lamond (chairman of the Queensland Small Business Corporation), Max Hodges (chairman of the Brisbane Port Authority), and Vicki Kippin and Bob Moore (departmental liaison officers).

110 Scott et al., 'Queensland', 60.

111 Rae Wear, 'Johannes Bjelke-Petersen: Straddling a Barbed Wire Fence', *Queensland Historical Atlas*, 2010, accessed 12 October 2015, http://www.qhatlas.com.au/content/johannes-bjelke-petersen-straddling-barbed-wire-fence.

112 Carol Gistitin, 'Iwasaki Project', *Queensland Historical Atlas*, 2010, accessed 12 October 2015, http://www.qhatlas.com.au/content/iwasaki-project. Two men charged with the bombing were found not guilty after a witness appeared to have collaborated with police.

113 Wear, *Johannes Bjelke-Petersen*, 188–9.

114 Charlton, *State of Mind*, 158–62.

115 Wear, *Johannes Bjelke-Petersen*, 102–3.

116 Ibid., 104.

117 Edwards, interview with the author.

118 Charlton, *State of Mind*, 163.

119 Ahern, interview with the author.

120 Ibid.

121 Fitzgerald, *History of Queensland*, 563–4, 572–5; Terry O'Gorman, 'The Political Impact of the Games on Queensland: II', in *The 1982 Commonwealth Games: A Retrospect* (St Lucia: Australian Studies Centre, Humanities and Social Sciences, UQ, 1984), 44. Such restrictions inspired the formation of the Queensland Council for Civil Liberties in 1966.

122 Fitzgerald, *History of Queensland*, 572–9; Hughes, *Government of Queensland*, 304–5.

123 Fitzgerald, *History of Queensland*, 574–9, 588; Wells, *Deep North*, 36; Lunn, *Joh*, 217–18.

124 Lunn, *Joh*, 217–18. See also page 3. Lunn notes that many of Bjelke-Petersen's speeches contained anti-communist rhetoric, and that the premier declared, 'I have always found Communism is the best thing to campaign on'.

125 Adam Nash (co-writer of the protest song 'Cyclone Hits Expo'), interview with the author, February 2012.

126 Sallyanne Atkinson (former lord mayor of Brisbane), interview with the author, December 2012.

127 Jeff Rickertt, 'Right to March Movement', in Evans and Ferrier, *Radical Brisbane*, 296; Allan Gardiner, 'Punks and Police', in Evans and Ferrier, *Radical Brisbane*, 303; Whitton, *Hillbilly Dictator*, 59, 60; Fitzgerald, *History of Queensland*, 574–9, 588. Bjelke-Petersen also inappropriately used the Special Branch to compile 'dirt' files on his rivals.

128 Nash, interview with the author.

129 Ibid.

130 Power, interview with the author.

131 Wells, *Deep North*, 12–15, 48. Wells also observes ideological irregularities in Bjelke-Petersen's dealings with the police force, marvelling that 'the National Party, which would be horrified if a major resource was nationalised, sits back quietly when the Premier appropriates it himself'.

132 Charlton, *State of Mind*, 64, 88; Hazlehurst, *Gordon Chalk*, 268. The Whitlam government offered economic assistance to Queensland through measures such as a forty per cent rise in special-purpose payments for new programs, and the alleviation of healthcare costs through the Medibank scheme.

133 Hughes, *Government of Queensland*, 290.

134 Fitzgerald, *History of Queensland*, 509–52.

135 Charlton, *State of Mind*, 139–45.

136 Ibid., 141–6.

137 Hughes, *Government of Queensland*, 292.

138 Wear, *Johannes Bjelke-Petersen*, 180–1.

139 Lunn, *Joh*, 182–92; Wells, *Deep North*, 26–7, 41.

140 Lunn, *Joh*, 191–3.

141 Margaret Bridson Cribb and Dennis J. Murphy, 'Winners and Losers in Queensland Politics', in Cribb and Boyce, *Politics in Queensland*, 8.

142 Lunn, *Joh*, 212–14, 231. Bjelke-Petersen went so far as to make a (failed) bid to the Privy Council to have the Queen declared Queen of Queensland – a move designed to force a referendum in Australia should Whitlam declare it a republic.

143 Ross Fitzgerald, Lyndon Megarrity, and David Symons, *Made in Queensland: A New History* (St Lucia: University of Queensland Press, 2009), 171; Mungo MacCallum, *Mungo on the Zoo Plane* (St Lucia: University of Queensland Press, 1979), 163.

144 'Castrovalva', *Doctor Who*, Writ. Christopher H. Bidmead, Dir. Fiona Cumming (series 19, episode 1 of 4; originally aired 4 January 1982), YouTube, accessed 4 July 2017, https://www.youtube.com/watch?v=S-pdrmKEjmg.

145 Thompson and Butel, *The World of Joh*, 13.

146 Dennis Murphy, 'Queensland's Image and Australian Nationalism', *Australian Quarterly* 50, 2 (June 1978), 82–5.

147 Debra Beattie (director of the protest film *Expo Schmexpo*), interview with the author, February 2013.

148 Kelly, interview with the author.

149 Charlton, *State of Mind*, 39.

3   The Getting of Expo

1 Sallyanne Atkinson, interview by Peter Spearritt, Danielle Miller, and Kathryn Talbot, *Queensland Speaks*, Centre for the Government of Queensland, 22 February 2012, accessed 14 October 2014, http://www.queenslandspeaks.com.au/sallyanne-atkinson.

2 James Maccormick (early instigator of Expo 88), interview with the author, November 2012.

3 James Maccormick, private documents.

4 Ibid.

5 'Brisbane Expo: $150 Million Plan for 1988', *Courier-Mail* (Brisbane), 10 March 1977.

6 John R. Cole, *Shaping a City: Greater Brisbane 1925–1985* (Queensland: William Brooks, 1984), 350–3.

7 'Brisbane Expo'.

8 Maccormick, private documents. Wilbur Smith and Associates predicted a high number of 'total visitor days' (eighty-eight per cent) from local residents based on the (correct) assumption that they would be more likely to visit the exposition numerous times than those impeded by distance.

9 Brisbane Chamber of Commerce, 'Brisbane Expo 88', *Brisbane Chamber of Commerce: The Voice of Business* 90 (May 1978), 1.

10   Ibid.; Bruce Juddery, 'The Man Who Brought Expo to Brisbane', *Sunday Mail Magazine* (Brisbane), 1 May 1988; Maccormick, private documents.

11   Peter Carroll, 'The Origins of Expo 88', *Australian Journal of Public Administration* 48, 1 (March 1989), 44.

12   Bruce Juddery, 'The Man Who Won Expo for Qld', *Canberra Times*, *Sunday Magazine*, 30 April 1988.

13   Maccormick, private documents.

14   Sir Llew Edwards (former Queensland Liberal Party leader, deputy premier, and chairman of Expo 88), interview with the author, October 2012. Edwards praises the Whitlam government for introducing Medibank, and Labor premier Hanlon for introducing a free public health system for Queensland in the 1930s, noting, 'I don't think Hanlon gets near enough credit for what he did in Queensland in those days.'

15   Ibid.

16   Terry White, interview by Lindsay Marshall and Malcolm McMillan, *Decades of Division*, National Library of Australia, 14 July 2011, TRC 6150/18, accessed 10 October 2013, http://nla.gov.au/nla.oh-vn5581674.

17   Susan Terrencia Yarrow, 'Split, Intervention, Renewal: The ALP in Queensland 1957–1989', (Masters thesis, UQ, 2014): 46–52, 58.

18   Rosemary Kyburz (24 April 1979), *Queensland Parliamentary Debates*, 4169–72.

19   Rosemary Kyburz, interview by Lindsay Marshall, *Decades of Division*, National Library of Australia, 21 August 2010, TRC 6150/7, accessed 12 October 2013, http://nla.gov.au/nla.obj-219196863/listen; Ross Fitzgerald, *A History of Queensland: From 1915 to the 1980s* (St Lucia: University of Queensland Press, 1984), 582.

20   Kyburz, interview by Marshall.

21   Tom Thompson and Elizabeth Butel, eds, *The World of Joh* (Sydney: Unwin Paperbacks, 1983), 26.

22   Carroll, 'Origins of Expo 88', 44.

23   Peter Carroll, 'The Intergovernmental Relations of Expo '88' (PhD thesis, UQ, 1994), 112.

24   Juddery, 'The Man Who Brought Expo to Brisbane'.

25   Sir Frank Moore (former chairman of QTTC, director of Dreamworld and Jupiters Casino, developer, and member of the National Party's management committee), interview with the author, July 2013.

26   Juddery, 'The Man Who Brought Expo to Brisbane'.

27   Moore, interview with the author.

28   BCC, 'Shine on Brisbane' (28 December 1981, television commercial), YouTube, accessed 1 July 2015, http://www.youtube.com/watch?v=cKFdgtPXRzw.

29   BTQ Channel Seven, 'Love You Brisbane' (7 January 1982, television commercial), YouTube, accessed 1 July 2015, http://www.youtube.com/watch?v=cgwbHz19VbY.

30   John M. Garnsey, 'Queensland and Brisbane as a Focus for Advertising Strategies and the Games', in *The 1982 Commonwealth Games: A Retrospect* (St Lucia: Australian Studies Centre, Humanities and Social Sciences, UQ, 1984), 19, 21. The Love You Brisbane campaign launched just ten days after the Shine on Brisbane campaign (which debuted on 28 December 1981), though it had been

in planning for two months. Garnsey notes that such content was a big departure from typical television promos 'crowing about how good they are' and that the Games 'provided a perfect focal point to allow us to tap in to a strong sense of community belonging, pride and achievement'. The campaign also contributed to the best year in BTQ Seven's history – especially in Brisbane, 'with the Channel now having a unique positioning in the minds and hearts of local viewers'.

31 Ibid., 22.
32 Carroll, 'Intergovernmental Relations', 111.
33 Ibid., 131–4.
34 Ibid., 135.
35 Edwards, interview with the author.
36 Sallyanne Atkinson (former lord mayor of Brisbane), interview with the author, December 2012.
37 Carroll, 'Intergovernmental Relations', 136.
38 Sir Leo Hielscher (Queensland under treasurer during Expo 88), interview with the author, April 2013.
39 Carroll, 'Origins of Expo 88', 46.
40 Edwards, interview with the author.
41 Carroll, 'Intergovernmental Relations', 134, 143–5.
42 Rosemary Kyburz (25 April 1981), *Queensland Parliamentary Debates*, 1792–3.
43 Carroll, 'Origins of Expo 88', 46.
44 Maccormick, interview with the author.
45 Ibid.
46 Rosemary Kyburz (20 October 1981), *Queensland Parliamentary Debates*, 2857–8.
47 Carroll, 'Origins of Expo 88', 47.
48 Maccormick, private documents.
49 Carroll, 'Origins of Expo 88', 47.
50 Carroll, 'Intergovernmental Relations', 179, 183.
51 Ibid., 182–4.
52 Ibid., 177, 180.
53 Ibid., 177.
54 Edwards, interview with the author.
55 Steve Bishop, 'The Man Who Dreamed Up Expo', *Sunday Sun* (Brisbane), 1 May 1988.
56 Angus Innes, 'The Political Impact of the Games on Queensland', in *1982 Commonwealth Games*, 39.
57 Sallyanne Atkinson, *Sallyanne Atkinson's Brisbane Guide* (St Lucia: University of Queensland Press, 1985), 24; Sallyanne Atkinson, *No Job for a Woman* (St Lucia: University of Queensland Press, 2016), 170; Joseph M. Siracusa, *Sallyanne: Portrait of a Lord Mayor* (Milton: Jacaranda Press, 1987), 29.
58 Atkinson, *Sallyanne Atkinson's Brisbane Guide*, 2.
59 Bishop, 'The Man Who Dreamed Up Expo'.
60 Barbara Absolon (Entertainment deputy director and Walkways producer for Expo 88), interview with the author, December 2012. Absolon laughs at the 1980s optimism regarding leisure time: 'I think we're all living proof of what went wrong. It's extraordinary, isn't it? What happened?'

61   Carroll, 'Origins of Expo 88', 48.

62   Carroll, 'Intergovernmental Relations', 188.

63   Moore, interview with the author. The proposal could have been lodged at the next BIE meeting, but the Queensland Government intimated it was not prepared to wait another six months.

64   Carroll, 'Origins of Expo 88', 48.

65   Carroll, 'Intergovernmental Relations', 193.

66   Jennifer Craik, 'Expo 88: Fashions of Sight and Politics of Site', in eds Tony Bennett, Pat Buckridge, David Carter, and Colin Mercer, *Celebrating the Nation: A Critical Study of Australia's Bicentenary* (St Leonards: Allen & Unwin, 1992), 145.

67   Carroll, 'Intergovernmental Relations', 205.

68   Moore, interview with the author.

69   Bob Minnikin (general manager of Expo 88), interview with the author, January 2013.

70   Carroll, 'Intergovernmental Relations', 207.

71   Minnikin, interview with the author.

72   Bob Minnikin, 'Entrepreneurship and Governments in Major Events', in eds John Wanna, John Forster, and Peter Graham, *Entrepreneurial Management in the Public Sector* (South Melbourne: MacMillan Education Australia, 1996), 180. These plans were rendered redundant with the dissolution of the Coalition.

73   Carroll, 'Intergovernmental Relations', 207.

74   'Taking a Vital Step for City's Future', *Daily Sun* (Brisbane), 31 May 1983.

75   'Brisbane Captures Expo 88', *Courier-Mail* (Brisbane), 16 June 1983.

76   Ibid.

77   Marion Smith, 'A Vision of Expo 88', *Courier-Mail* (Brisbane), 1 June 1983.

78   'Brisbane Gets Expo 88 Approval', *Daily Sun* (Brisbane), 6 June 1983.

79   Rae Wear, *Johannes Bjelke-Petersen: The Lord's Premier* (St Lucia: University of Queensland Press, 2002), 163.

80   Ibid., 156–8. The premier broke protocol by refusing to accept Liberal attorney -general Sam Doumany's recommendation for a new chief justice, Judge James Douglas, following allegations Don Lane had acquired proof that Douglas had voted for Labor in 1972. Terry Lewis allegedly helped persuade Bjelke-Petersen to champion Justice Dormer Andrews – already the beneficiary of an 'unusual' promotion from the District Court to the Supreme Court. Walter Campbell was appointed chief justice by way of a compromise, and Andrews was elevated – against the express wishes of all Liberal Cabinet ministers noted on the Executive Council minute for his appointment – to become senior puisne judge. Governor Sir James Ramsay signed the minute regardless. When Campbell eventually left to become state governor, Andrews was appointed in his place.

81   Paul Reynolds, *Lock, Stock & Barrel: A Political Biography of Mike Ahern* (St Lucia: University of Queensland Press, 2002), 63–5. In discussions between Peter Beattie and Terry White, Labor agreed to form a temporary coalition to wrest power from the National Party – provided the malamander was subsequently adjusted in the Liberal Party's favour at the expense of the National Party.

82   Kyburz, interview by Marshall.

83   White, interview by Marshall and McMillan.

84 Wear, *Johannes Bjelke-Petersen*, 164–5.

85 Alan Metcalfe, *In Their Own Right: The Rise to Power of Joh's Nationals* (St Lucia: University of Queensland Press, 1984), 150.

86 Edwards, interview with the author.

87 Jamie Walker, *Goss: A Political Biography* (St Lucia: University of Queensland Press, 1995), 66. Kyburz said she preferred to have lost to Labor than to the Nationals.

88 Edwards, interview by Roger Scott and Ann Scott, *Queensland Speaks*, Centre for the Government of Queensland, 22 September 2009, accessed 20 October 2013, http://www.queenslandspeaks.com.au/llew-edwards.

89 Bishop, 'The Man Who Dreamed Up Expo'.

90 Jim Fouras (30 November 1983), *Queensland Parliamentary Debates*, 340–2.

91 Ibid.

4 'Brending' the Rules

1 Bob Minnikin, 'Entrepreneurship and Governments in Major Events', in eds John Wanna, John Forster, and Peter Graham, *Entrepreneurial Management in the Public Sector* (South Melbourne: MacMillan Education Australia, 1996), 180.

2 Sir Llew Edwards, interview by Roger Scott and Ann Scott, *Queensland Speaks*, Centre for the Government of Queensland, 22 September 2009, accessed 20 October 2013, http://www.queenslandspeaks.com.au/llew-edwards. See also Bob Minnikin (general manager of Expo 88), interview with the author, January 2013. Minnikin said former Coordinator-General Sir Sydney Schubert has speculated such actions could still be authorised under the Coordinator-General's Act if required. Minnikin observes, 'It's amazing the powers that are still there that don't get used all the time.'

3 Peter Carroll, 'The Intergovernmental Relations of Expo '88' (PhD thesis, UQ, 1994), 234, 268; Ian Gill, 'Making Peace with the Past', *World's Fair* 8, 2 (Spring 1988), 4–5. Brown gave verbal approval for Bob Rogers of California to provide the special effects for the Rainbow Serpent Theatre before a government committee voted 4 to 2 against the submission (in favour of an Australian contender). Brown misrepresented those numbers as 2 to 2 – discounting two public servants who he said were not entitled to vote.

4 'Govt Refuses Qld $12m Expo Grant', *Townsville Bulletin*, 1 March 1986.

5 Geoff Sterling and Lane Calcutt, '$14 Mil. Expo Offer "Final": Lousy Deal Says an Angry Joh', *Telegraph* (Brisbane), 28 February 1986.

6 John R. Cole, *Shaping a City: Greater Brisbane 1925–1985* (Queensland: William Brooks, 1984), 355–72; Minnikin, 'Entrepreneurship and Governments', 179–80; Bob Minnikin, 'World Expo 88', *Urban Policy and Research* 5, 2 (1987), 179.

7 Sir Edward Williams, *Report of the Commissioner-General of Expo 88 on the Australian Government's Involvement in Expo 88* (Canberra: Department of Sport, Recreation and Tourism, 1989), 3–5. The representatives were the deputy prime minister of Australia, the federal minister for Expo, the premier of Queensland, the deputy premier of Queensland, and the lord mayor of Brisbane.

8 BESBRA, *World Expo 88 Report* (Brisbane: BESBRA, 1988), section A4, D.

9 Steve Bishop, *The Most Dangerous Detective: The Outrageous Glen Patrick Hallahan and the Rat Pack*, 2nd edition (Brisbane: Steve Bishop, 2015), 217–25; Minnikin,

interview with the author. Minnikin notes that Williams was close friends with both Bjelke-Petersen and Fraser.

10   BESBRA, *World Expo 88 Report*, section A4.

11   Williams, *Report*, 20; Tom Veivers, *Commissioner-General's Executive Report* (Canberra: Australian Pavilion, 1988), 6.

12   Minnikin, interview with the author.

13   Veivers, *Commissioner-General's Executive Report*, 5, 7, 15. See also Len Stephan (17 October 1989), *Queensland Parliamentary Debates*, 1499; and Jamie Walker, *Goss: A Political Biography* (St Lucia: University of Queensland Press, 1995), 77. While an MLA, Veivers was known as a member of SHIT (Special Hinze Investigations Team), dedicated to exposing that minister's improper dealings. Veivers' position was critiqued by National Party MLA Len Stephan as a 'jobs for the boys' appointment.

14   Lady Jane Edwards (née Brumfield, Communications director for Expo 88), interview with the author, October 2012.

15   John Watson (River Stage producer for Expo 88), interview with the author, January 2013. See also Sir Joh Bjelke-Petersen (28 November 1985), *Queensland Parliamentary Debates*, 2943–4. The BLF was a militant union with a strong environmental heritage record (including a successful campaign to prevent the 1960s urban-renewal-inspired plan to raze and redevelop Sydney's Rocks district) but was also linked with corrupt activities to the extent that the Hawke government deregistered it in 1986. Bjelke-Petersen taunted Victoria and NSW over the BLF, alleging they feared to host an exposition with the Victorian probe into the organisation.

16   Watson, interview with the author.

17   Williams, *Report*, 23.

18   Ibid., 12, 25.

19   Damaso de Lario, 'Report by Dr Damaso de Lario, President of the Steering Committee of the College of Commissioners-General at Expo to the Executive Committee of the BIE', appendix 1, in Williams, *Report*, 5–10.

20   Sir Llew Edwards (former Queensland Liberal Pary leader, deputy premier, and chairman of Expo 88), interview with the author, October 2012.

21   Cole, *Shaping a City*, 289, 307–9, 332–5.

22   Carroll, 'Intergovernmental Relations', 385.

23   Peter Carroll, 'Organising for Expo', *Australian Journal of Public Administration* 50, 1 (March 1991), 80–1. The original BCC representative was town clerk Tony Philbrick.

24   Carroll, 'Intergovernmental Relations', 388.

25   Sallyanne Atkinson, interview by Peter Spearritt, Danielle Miller, and Kathryn Talbot, *Queensland Speaks*, Centre for the Government of Queensland, 22 February 2012, accessed 14 October 2013, http://www.queenslandspeaks.com.au/sallyanne-atkinson.

26   Jane Edwards, interview with the author.

27   Atkinson, interview by Spearritt, Miller, and Talbot.

28   Sallyanne Atkinson (former lord mayor of Brisbane), interview with the author, December 2012.

29   Edwards, interview by Scott and Scott. See also Barbara Absolon (Entertainment deputy director and Walkways producer for Expo 88), interview with the author, December 2012.
30   Peter Goldston (Site Development director for Expo 88, and founding general manager of the South Bank Corporation), interview with the author, November 2012.
31   Jane Edwards, interview with the author.
32   Ross Given (Operations director for Expo 88), interview with the author, April 2015.
33   Ibid.
34   Absolon, interview with the author. After retelling the story of Birch's early instruction to 'keep working' while he travelled overseas, Absolon laughs, shrugs and says, 'Doing what?'
35   Ibid.
36   Ibid.
37   Ibid.
38   BESBRA, *World Expo 88 Report*, section D4.
39   Jane Edwards, interview with the author.
40   Absolon, interview with the author.
41   Ibid; Andrew Stewart, 'Where's Our Expo Enthusiasm?', *Chronicle* (Toowoomba), 2 February 1985.
42   Absolon, interview with the author.
43   Andrew Stewart, 'Local Apathy Haunts Expo Officials', *Morning Bulletin* (Rockhampton), 2 February 1985; Stewart, 'Where's Our Expo Enthusiasm?'.
44   Joanne Watson, 'Always Will Be', in eds Raymond Evans and Carole Ferrier, *Radical Brisbane: An Unruly History* (Carlton North: The Vulgar Press, 2004), 309. Responsibility for Musgrave Park was returned to BCC after a fiery and protracted debate. In 1998, the Musgrave Park Aboriginal Corporation formally acquired a portion of the park.
45   'World Expo Looks Good for Brisbane', *Daily Sun* (Brisbane), 31 May 1983; 'Govt Acts on Site', *Courier-Mail* (Brisbane), 1 June 1983.
46   'Govt Acts on Site', *Courier-Mail* (Brisbane), 1 June 1983.
47   Edwards, Interview by Scott and Scott. One can only imagine Bjelke-Petersen's reaction, had he been alive to hear his former deputy observe that there 'was a bit of communism in it'.
48   Philip Hammond, 'Not All Quiet on the South Bank', *Courier-Mail* (Brisbane), 14 July 1983.
49   Jim Fouras (31 October 1984), *Queensland Parliamentary Debates*, 2011.
50   Tony Bennett, 'The Shaping of Things to Come: Expo 88', *Cultural Studies* 5, 1 (1991), 46–7.
51   Tony Fry and Anne-Marie Willis, 'Expo 88: Backwoods into the Future', *Cultural Studies* 2, 1 (1988), 129.
52   Jennifer Craik, 'Expo 88: Fashions of Sight and Politics of Site', in eds Tony Bennett, Pat Buckridge, David Carter, and Colin Mercer, *Celebrating the Nation: A Critical Study of Australia's Bicentenary* (St Leonards: Allen & Unwin, 1992), 108.
53   Ibid., 146.

54 Ibid.; Ken Brass, 'The Great Joh Show Gamble', *Weekend Australian Magazine*, 31 May–1 June 1986.

55 Nic Van Oudtshoorn, 'Accounting for World Expo 88', *Australian Accountant* 58, 7 (August 1988), 12.

56 Sir Leo Hielscher (Queensland under treasurer during Expo 88), interview with the author, April 2013.

57 Van Oudtshoorn, 'Accounting for World Expo 88', 13; 'Expo Will Apply for Private Bank Loans for Amount', *Courier-Mail* (Brisbane), 1 May 1986.

58 Hielscher, interview with the author.

59 Ibid.

60 Minnikin, 'Entrepreneurship and Governments', 179–80; Minnikin, 'World Expo 88'.

61 Glenn Schloss, 'Expo Benefited Property Owners – Minnikin', *Courier-Mail* (Brisbane), 26 August 1983.

62 Philip Day, *The Big Party Syndrome: A Study of the Impact of Special Events and Inner Urban Change in Brisbane* (St Lucia: Department of Social Work, UQ, 1988), iii, iv, 1, 21. This study was funded by Senator the Hon. Margaret Reynolds, Commonwealth Minister for Local Government, as part of the Australian Government's Local Government Development Program under the auspices of UQ's Department of Social Work. Kelly says his main contribution was lending the project UQ's imprimatur, and that Day deserves much of the credit for the report.

63 'Pensioner Blames Expo for Being "Forced on the Street"', *Courier-Mail* (Brisbane), 9 March 1988.

64 'Enduring Renters Asked to Move On', *Courier-Mail* (Brisbane), 9 March 1988.

65 Ibid.

66 Gill, 'Making Peace with the Past', 2.

67 Drew Hutton (Expo 88 protester and co-founder of the Queensland Greens), interview with the author, May 2007. Hutton says he was first told about Expo in 1983 by future Labor Brisbane lord mayor Tim Quinn.

68 Ibid.

69 Day, *Big Party Syndrome*, 20.

70 Henry Palaszczuk (24 March 1988), *Queensland Parliamentary Debates*, 5583–4.

71 David Monaghan, email to the author, December 2012.

72 Ibid.

73 Debra Beattie, *Expo Schmexpo*, u-matic tape (independent production directed by Debra Beattie, 1985). Excerpts from this film have been quoted with permission from Debra Beattie.

74 Ibid.

75 Ibid.

76 Adam Nash (co-writer of the protest song 'Cyclone Hits Expo'), interview with the author, February 2013. The song was co-written by Adam Nash with John Rogers for their band Choo Dikka Dikka early in 1988. Lyrics have been quoted with permission from Adam Nash.

77 Ibid.

78 John Jiggens, Anne Jones, Damien Ladwich, Matt Mawson, and Roberty Whyte, eds, *Cane Toad Times Warts and All: Best of Collection 1977–1990* (Brisbane:

Cane Toad Times Collectives, 2001), 35; *Cane Toad Times* 10 (Autumn 1988), 28; *Cane Toad Times* 11 (Spring 1988), 37; Stephen Stockwell (*Cane Toad Times* contributor), interview with the author, February 2013. The group also produced 'Tony Fitzgerald fan club: official member' T-shirts. Stockwell recalls an amusingly clandestine T-shirt sale during the Fitzgerald Inquiry: 'I did at one stage deliver a carton of Tony Fitzgerald fan club T-shirts. We got a call from the Inquiry itself and they wanted all the staff to have one – so one night about ten o'clock I walked up this back alley and up the back stairs in some place in town [deep voice]: "I've got the T-shirts" [laughs]. They give me the money. I walked out – the bagman.' When editor Anne Jones is reminded that the magazine operated during two of the most important events in Brisbane's modern history, she laughs and says, 'and there we were – selling T-shirts'.

79 Anne Jones (an editor of satirical magazine *The Cane Toad Times*), interview with the author, December 2012.

80 Gay Alcorn, 'Trust Angered by Expo Ads on Restoration', *Courier-Mail* (Brisbane), 10 July 1987. Gibson, perhaps best known for his design of QCC, had little patience with restoration skirmishes relating to his work on the then 112-year-old Ship Inn hotel, stating, 'I don't know why people don't shut up and wait until the thing is finished.' 'Govt Keeps Wraps on Details of Its Expo Display', *Courier-Mail* (Brisbane), 3 December 1986.

81 Steve Rous, 'Expo Our Biggest Event: Bjelke', *Daily Sun* (Brisbane), 2 May 1984; 'Expo a Mixture of New and Old', *Sunday Sun* (Brisbane), 17 June 1984.

82 Stewart, 'Where's Our Expo Enthusiasm?'.

83 Goldston, interview with the author. Goldston says preserving Collins Place 'wrecked the planning of the site'. The dwelling served as the Spaghetti House during Expo. It reopened as Little Big House in 2017 as part of Southpoint.

84 Llew Edwards, interview with the author. See also Jim Fouras (31 October 1984), *Queensland Parliamentary Debates*, 2011. Fouras says that Bloss offered to lease the property to BESBRA free of cost during Expo rather than have it resumed. When this offer was rejected, she asked to be given first option to buy the property back at market value after the event (which was denied under the *Expo '88 Act*). Fouras considered this 'legal robbery' on the part of the state government.

85 BESBRA, *World Expo 88: Closing Financial Report 1988* (Brisbane: BESBRA, 1989), 4; Pamela Sweetapple, 'Expo '88 Plagued by Money Worries', *West Australian* (Perth), 14–15 November 1985.

86 'Expo Seals Off Major Southside Streets', *Courier-Mail* (Brisbane), 28 June 1985.

87 BESBRA, *World Expo 88 Report*, section B2; Llew Edwards, interview with the author. Edwards says that Bligh bore greater responsibility for the site.

88 BESBRA, *World Expo 88 Report*, section B; Goldston, interview with the author. Goldston championed the design change from flat sails to tent-like structures.

89 BESBRA, *World Expo 88 Report*, section B.

90 Ibid.

91 Tom Burns (22 March 1988), *Queensland Parliamentary Debates*, 5392–5.

92 Ibid.

93 Ibid.

94 Minnikin, interview with the author.
95 Llew Edwards, interview with the author.
96 Ibid. Edwards singles out Thiess Watkins's project director Bob Roche for particular praise.
97 Goldston, interview with the author. The business was sold by Thiess to a business half-owned by Kerry Packer.
98 Evan Whitton, *The Hillbilly Dictator: Australia's Police State*, rev. ed. (Crows Nest: ABC Books, 1993), 207; Jim Fouras (4 September 1986), *Queensland Parliamentary Debates*, 929–930; Bill Gunn (6 September 1989), *Queensland Parliamentary Debates*, 422–3; Matthew Condon, *All Fall Down* (St Lucia: University of Queensland Press, 2015), 453–6.
99 Goldston, interview with the author.
100 Jane Edwards, interview with the author.
101 Given, interview with the author.
102 Carroll, 'Organising for Expo', 76–8.
103 'Marketing Contractor Released from Expo 88', *Courier-Mail* (Brisbane), 6 September 1985. This took place shortly after the resignation of two marketing executives.
104 Carroll, 'Organising for Expo', 78.
105 Jane Edwards, interview with the author.
106 Llew Edwards, interview with the author; 'The Short Circuit to Success', *Bulletin*, 9 February 1988, 54.
107 Llew Edwards, interview with the author.
108 Minnikin, 'Entrepreneurship and Governments', 180.
109 Goldston, interview with the author.
110 Edwards, interview by Scott and Scott.
111 Ibid.
112 Raymond Evans, *A History of Queensland* (Cambridge: Cambridge University Press, 2007), 239–40; Peter Charlton, *State of Mind: Why Queensland Is Different* (North Ryde: Methuen Haynes, 1987), 227–9.
113 Evans, *History of Queensland*, 239–40; Bernie Neville, 'Joh's Attacks on Electricity Workers', *Green Left Weekly*, 4 May 2005, accessed 12 October 2015, https://www.greenleft.org.au/node/32610; Charlton, *State of Mind*, 227–9; Rae Wear, *Johannes Bjelke-Petersen: The Lord's Premier* (St Lucia: University of Queensland Press, 2002), 139–40.
114 Minnikin, interview with the author; Rous, 'Expo Our Biggest Event', *Daily Sun* (Brisbane), 2 May 1984.
115 Minnikin, interview with the author.
116 Shane Rodgers, 'It's All Work on Site that Never Sleeps', *Courier-Mail* (Brisbane), 30 October 1987.
117 Neville Warburton (28 October 1987), *Queensland Parliamentary Debates*, 3641.
118 Minnikin, interview with the author.
119 Ibid.
120 Ross Fitzgerald, 'Censorship in Queensland', *Australian Journal of Politics and History* 30, 3 (1984), 350–6.
121 Williams, *Report*, appendix 7, 2.

122 David Hamilton (Piazza producer for Expo 88), interview with the author, January 2013.
123 Anthony Steel, *Painful in Daily Doses: An Anecdotal Memoir* (Kent Town: Wakefield Press, 2009), 282.
124 Mary-Clare Power (Amphitheatre producer for Expo 88), interview with the author, January 2013; Watson, interview with the author; Hamilton, interview with the author.
125 Watson, interview with the author.
126 Absolon, interview with the author.
127 Ric Birch, *Master of the Ceremonies: An Eventful Life* (Crows Nest: Allen & Unwin, 2004), 123–33.
128 Minnikin, interview with the author.
129 Hamilton, interview with the author.
130 Absolon, interview with the author; Mary-Clare Power, interview with the author; Anthony Steel (Consultant Producer, World Expo on Stage), interview with the author, December 2012; Marguerite Pepper (Consultant Producer, World Expo on Stage), interview with the author, January 2013.
131 Mike Mullins (Parades producer for Expo 88), interview with the author, January 2013.
132 Ibid.
133 BESBRA, *World Expo 88 Report*, section D2.
134 Ibid.; Mary-Clare Power, interview with the author.
135 Mary-Clare Power, interview with the author.
136 Danny May (production coordinator for Expo 88), interview with the author, February 2013. May left the division owing to internal conflict, but he stayed connected with the exposition when contracted to design the exclusive Expo Ball – a black-tie affair for which the Piazza was transformed into a gossamer castle.
137 Absolon, interview with the author.
138 May, interview with the author.
139 Absolon, interview with the author.
140 May, interview with the author.
141 Hamilton, interview with the author.
142 Ibid.
143 Ibid.
144 Absolon, interview with the author.
145 May, interview with the author.
146 Mullins, interview with the author.
147 Ibid.
148 Mary-Clare Power, interview with the author.
149 Watson, interview with the author.
150 Ibid. Watson requested that the name of the caller be withheld out of consideration for their family.
151 Tony Bennett, 'Introduction', in Bennett et al., *Celebrating the Nation*, xv. Bennett is quoting a response to 1888 celebrations that appeared in *The Bulletin*.
152 Kevin Carmody, 'The Bitter Cake', *Social Alternatives* 7, 1 (March 1988), 3.

153 Julie Go-Sam, 'Talking to Robert Weatherall on the Bicentenary and Expo', *Social Alternatives* 7, 1 (March 1988), 27–8. FAIRA and a coalition of community councils conducted state-wide and national campaigns to expose the treatment of Aboriginal people by Australian governments.

154 Bob Weatherall (executive officer of FAIRA), interview with the author, July 2017.

155 Shane Rodgers, 'Aboriginal Flag to Fly in Support of Expo', *Courier-Mail* (Brisbane), 13 May 1988; Shane Rodgers, 'Aborigines Threaten to Disrupt Expo', *Courier-Mail* (Brisbane), 7 November 1987.

156 Rodgers, 'Aborigines Threaten to Disrupt Expo'.

157 'Racism Fears at Brisbane's World Expo', *Cairns Post*, 16 November 1987. Queensland Council for Civil Liberties president Matthew Foley (later a state Labor parliamentarian) claimed the racist overtones of such activities could draw comparisons with the 1936 Berlin Olympics under Hitler.

158 Neville Warburton (12 November 1987), *Queensland Parliamentary Debates*, 4078–9.

159 'Racism Fears at Brisbane's World Expo'.

160 'Aborigine Warns of Expo "Bloodbath"', *Sunshine Coast Daily* (Maroochydore), 3 March 1988.

161 Go-Sam, 'Talking to Robert Weatherall', 27–8.

162 'Dreamtime Expo Magic', *Daily Sun* (Brisbane), 8 August 1987; Gill, 'Making Peace with the Past', 6.

163 'Dreamtime May Attract 15,000 a Day', *Courier-Mail* (Brisbane), 12 January 1988.

164 Oodgeroo Noonuccal, Expo Compile 1A, u-matic tape (TVO Brisbane, 1988).

165 Weatherall, interview with the author.

166 Minnikin, interview with the author. In Weatherall's interview with this author, he agreed that Bob Katter (and his father) had generally done the right thing by Aboriginal people, and that he was 'the full bottle'.

167 Gill, 'Making Peace with the Past', 6; Bob Katter (18 November 1987), *Queensland Parliamentary Debates*, 4424.

168 Mullins, interview with the author.

169 Watson, interview with the author.

170 Hamilton, interview with the author.

171 Anni Davey (Circus Oz performer), interview with the author, April 2016. Davey recalls arriving in Brisbane prior to the first show with other members of the company in a graffiti-covered Valiant. They received a still-typical 'Queensland welcome' when their car was pulled over and searched by the police. Circus Oz also participated in a benefit performance at Musgrave Park for people who were boycotting Expo. The cast and crew wheeled their equipment (including a stunt cannon) from the Expo site to the park.

172 Guy Hooper, 'Bicentennial Rap' (1988). The complete rap can be seen in an archival recording from an outdoor performance at Maningrida in 1988: '1988 – Maningrida, Australia, Outdoor Rig – 14 July', Circus Oz: Living Archive, accessed 9 May 2016, http://archive.circusoz.com/clips/view/44.

173 David Hamilton, email to the author, May 2016. Circus Oz unfortunately had another booking and was unavailable.

174 Sterling and Calcutt, '$14 Mil. Expo Offer "Final"'; Don Peterson, 'Canberra Will Refuse Plea to "Bail Out" State', *Courier-Mail* (Brisbane), 28 February 1986; Williams, *Report*, 14.

175 Joh Bjelke-Petersen (28 November 1985), *Queensland Parliamentary Debates*, 2943; 'Olympic Bid "Threat": Joh', *Sunday Mail* (Brisbane), 2 March 1986; Marianne Bilkey, 'Expo Chief to Blast Hawke over Funding', *Daily Sun* (Brisbane), 1 March 1986; Peterson, 'Canberra Will Refuse Plea'. See also Roger Scott, Peter Coaldrake, Brian Head, and Paul Reynolds, 'Queensland', in ed. Brian Galligan, *Australian State Politics* (Melbourne: Longman Cheshire, 1986), 67. Bjelke-Petersen's hatred of this higher authority was such that he typically referred to it as 'Canberra' instead of acknowledging it as 'the Australian Government'.

176 Ian Gill, 'Sir Joh and the Expo', *World's Fair* 8, 1 (Winter 1988), 4; David Landers, 'States Say a Definite No to Expo', *Sunday Mail* (Brisbane), 26 April 1987; Kris Houghton, 'Premiers "Politicise" Expo 88', *Australian*, 22 December 1986; Steve Rous, 'Expo a Waste for Us: SA, WA Premiers', *Courier-Mail* (Brisbane), 23 December 1986.

177 Houghton, 'Premiers "Politicise" Expo 88'.

178 Llew Edwards, interview with the author. Edwards recalls visiting 'all the various premiers' every few months during the first two years of Expo preparations. He also remembers a particularly overt dismissal involving Brian Burke. Edwards had secured an appointment and flown to Perth to see the premier. 'When I got there, he said, "I don't need to see him. He can leave his literature here."'

179 Brass, 'The Great Joh Show Gamble'.

180 Ibid.

181 Stewart, 'Where's Our Expo Enthusiasm?'.

182 'All States Asked to Back Expo', *Courier-Mail* (Brisbane), 13 March 1987. Kirk's comments were made at an 'Invest in Brisbane' seminar held for Sydney business people.

183 Landers, 'States Say a Definite No to Expo'; Llew Edwards, interview with the author.

184 Shane Rodgers, 'ALP Push Wins States for Expo', *Courier-Mail* (Brisbane), 5 October 1987. Warburton was also acting in his capacity as chairman of the Queensland Bicentennial Sport and Recreation Committee.

185 Charlton, *State of Mind*, 212.

186 Des Sturgess, *The Tangled Web* (Brisbane: Bedside Books, 2001), 135–48.

187 Ibid., 142, 143.

188 Paul Reynolds, *Lock, Stock & Barrel: A Political Biography of Mike Ahern* (St Lucia: University of Queensland Press, 2002), 91.

189 Charlton, *State of Mind*, 174.

190 Wear, *Johannes Bjelke-Petersen*, 107.

191 Ibid., 76–7.

192 Charlton, *State of Mind*, 174; Wear, *Johannes Bjelke-Petersen*, 161; Frank Bongiorno, *The Eighties: The Decade that Transformed Australia* (Collingwood: Black Inc., 2015), 10–11, 51. Rothwells was established when the Coalition awarded entrepreneur Laurie Connell (a Queensland Liberal Party supporter) the

first money marketer's licence issued by the Queensland Treasury. Bongiorno says Rothwells 'was a bank in name only, more a racket designed to finance Connell's expensive taste in thoroughbreds and other forms of extravagance'.

193 Wear, *Johannes Bjelke-Petersen*, 118.
194 Whitton, *Hillbilly Dictator*, 201.
195 Des Power (former chairman of Queensland Events Corporation and executive producer of *Today Tonight*), interview with the author, March 2013.
196 Charlton, *State of Mind*, 179–80.
197 Wear, *Johannes Bjelke-Petersen*, 103.
198 Charlton, *State of Mind*, 179.
199 Mike O'Connor, 'Des Power Bows Out as Events Boss', *Courier-Mail* (Brisbane), 27 May 2009, accessed 10 October 2014, http://www.couriermail.com.au/news/des-power-bows-out-as-events-boss/story-e6frerex-1225716620937.
200 Wear, *Johannes Bjelke-Petersen*, 103.
201 Ibid., 199; Des Power, interview with the author. Power recalls that Maybury 'got around in a green Rolls-Royce'. Power had to work with him when contracted to do post-production work on video footage for the Queensland Pavilion.
202 Wear, *Johannes Bjelke-Petersen*, 190–1.
203 Ibid., 192.
204 Scott et al., 'Queensland', 61.
205 Rosemary Whip, John Western, and David John Gow, 'Election Issues', in eds Rosemary Whip and Colin A. Hughes, *Political Crossroads: The 1989 Queensland Election* (St Lucia: University of Queensland Press, 1991), 72; Mark Bahnisch, *Queensland: Everything You Ever Wanted to Know, but Were Afraid to Ask* (Sydney: NewSouth Publishing, 2015), 72.
206 'The Moonlight State', *Four Corners*, ABC, 1987, accessed 8 July 2015, http://www.abc.net.au/4corners/stories/2011/08/08/3288495.htm.
207 Gill, 'Sir Joh and the Expo', 2; Wear, *Johannes Bjelke-Petersen*, 113; Evan Whitton, *Can of Worms II*, 2nd edition (Broadway: The Fairfax Library, 1987), 75.
208 Evan Whitton, 'Preface', in *Can of Worms: A Citizen's Reference Book to Crime and the Administration of Justice*, 3rd edition (Broadway: The Fairfax Library, 1987).
209 Ibid., 35, 37.
210 Tony Kelly (former QCOSS director and contributor to the Expo 88 study *The Big Party Syndrome*), interview with the author, February 2013. Kelly recalls a number of Bjelke-Petersen government 'apologists' at the university when he was a senior lecturer: 'There was quite a network of these wombats out at UQ that were supporting them'. See also Ross Fitzgerald, *A History of Queensland: From 1915 to the 1980s* (St Lucia: University of Queensland Press, 1984), 579. Fitzgerald details a number of UQ academics who mobilised against the Bjelke-Petersen government. Fitzgerald himself played a role in holding Queensland political parties to account when he had the temerity to produce historical records of their activities. His book caused such consternation that Bjelke-Petersen ordered it pulped. Under threat of serious legal action from embarrassed conservatives and their allies, Fitzgerald and the University of Queensland Press issued a 'somewhat sanitised' version of the book. Fitzgerald's *History of the Queensland Labor Party* (co-written with Harold Thornton) caused a similar uproar among the left. See

also 'A Book Better Dead than Read?', *Sydney Morning Herald*, 18 January 1989; Ross Fitzgerald, *My Name Is Ross: An Alcoholic's Journey* (Sydney: NewSouth, 2010), 116–17.

211 Wear, *Johannes Bjelke-Petersen*, 192–3. The National Party's claims were aided by its monopoly on development-related portfolios, including (since 1983) Treasury.

212 Charlton, *State of Mind*, 64, 154, 155, 223, 224, 226, 244. The state government also sought to introduce a flat tax, which would benefit the wealthy and cost more to the poor.

213 Peter Coaldrake, *Working the System: Government in Queensland 1983–1989* (St Lucia: University of Queensland Press, 1989), 10.

214 Charlton, *State of Mind*, 6.

215 Ibid., 2.

216 Bongiorno, *The Eighties*, 180; Charlton, *State of Mind*, 187.

217 Charlton, *State of Mind*, 184.

218 Paul Davey, *Joh for PM: The Inside Story of an Extraordinary Political Drama* (Sydney: NewSouth Publishing, 2015), 45–56.

219 Charlton, *State of Mind*, 8.

220 Ibid., 232.

221 'It's Time the State Leaders Got Behind Expo', *Sunday Sun* (Brisbane), 5 April 1987.

222 William Kahrl, 'The Surprising Success of World Expo 88', *World's Fair* 8, 3 (Summer 1988), 13–20; Mark Hairsine, 'Patriotic Platypus a Fair-Dinkum Yankee!', *Telegraph* (Brisbane), 4 December 1986; 'Expo Survives Series of Body Blows', *Sunday Sun* (Brisbane), 15 June 1986; Malcolm Farr, 'Rocky Road to Expo 88', *Daily Sun* (Brisbane), 14 August 1986; Steve Bishop, '$100 Expo Tickets: What You'll Get for the Big Outlay!', *Sunday Sun* (Brisbane), 9 November 1986; 'Expo Symbol Boomerangs', *Daily Sun* (Brisbane), 3 May 1984. National Aboriginal Conference Queensland chairman Steve Mam said he had received numerous complaints from Aboriginals about the Expo symbol incorrectly representing their culture. Bjelke-Petersen countered that Mam and his fellow complainants should be supporting things that were 'good for Queensland' rather than 'trying to drag the State down'.

223 Bishop, '$100 Expo Tickets'.

224 'Expo Survives Series of Body Blows'.

225 Ibid.

226 Ibid.

227 Goldston, interview with the author.

228 Anne Fussell, 'Price Great for Expo 88', *Daily Sun* (Brisbane), 19 November 1986.

229 Carol Lloyd (joint creative director for the Expo 88 advertising account), interview with the author, December 2012.

230 Ibid. See also Walker, *Goss*, 28, 41–2. Goss's 'performance' took place in 1974. He had been admitted as a solicitor of the Supreme Court of Queensland the previous year.

231 Lloyd, interview with the author.

232 Ibid.

233 Absolon, interview with the author.

234 Harry Gordon, 'Expo Exposed', *Time*, 13 April 1987, 32–6.

235 Ibid., 34.

236 *7:30 Report*, ABC, 31 March 1987. Reproduced by permission of the Australian Broadcasting Corporation © 1987. Other ex-employees mentioned were Pam Hankey (Protocol manager), David Park (International Participation), Val McKenzie (Communications director), and Paul Lynch (Media Liaison manager).

237 Ibid.

238 Ibid.

239 Goldston, interview with the author.

240 Absolon, interview with the author.

241 *7:30 Report*, ABC, 2 April 1987. Reproduced by permission of the Australian Broadcasting Corporation © 1987. Truscott also worked on *Paint Your Wagon* and *The Great Gatsby*.

242 Ibid., 31 March 1987. Reproduced by permission of the Australian Broadcasting Corporation © 1987.

243 Ibid., 30 March 1987. Reproduced by permission of the Australian Broadcasting Corporation © 1987.

244 Goldston, interview with the author.

245 *7:30 Report*, ABC, 2 April 1987. Reproduced by permission of the Australian Broadcasting Corporation © 1987.

246 The Night Companion didn't assume its 'Stefan Tower' moniker until purchased by Stefan Ackerie after Expo.

247 Hamilton, interview with the author.

248 Absolon, interview with the author. Absolon says Sir Llew Edwards also emphasised the need for the grounds to look impeccable, and for even the cleaners to wear spotless uniforms and carry attractive rubbish containers: 'That whole spirit of everything looking fantastic all the time … you never saw the sort of stuff that grates us all.' She says Truscott's influence could also be felt in small 'fix-its': 'Some of the Walkways entertainers were so popular that people were standing in the garden beds … so rather than "Keep Off the Garden" signs, we got our set design group to make up signs which said, "Gnomes Live Here, Please Stay Off Our Garden" – so there were ways of attending to potential problems without it being the big stick approach, and I think that was one of the things that the Entertainment Division potentially taught the more serious divisions.'

249 Llew Edwards, interview with the author.

250 Goldston, interview with the author. The advertising balloons remained regardless.

251 Richard Owen, 'Rolling Thundercloud Rips Expo's Sails', *Daily Sun* (Brisbane), 12 November 1987; Minnikin, interview with the author. Minnikin reveals the damage 'almost boiled to a Germany versus Switzerland, because it was German engineers that designed it, and Zurich were our insurer. Zurich said Germany didn't know what it was doing, Germany said Zurich was just being evil.'

252 Minnikin, interview with the author.

253 Ibid. The signage was considerably reduced. BP also received naming rights to the waterski events.

254 Goldston, interview with the author.

255 Ibid.

256 Minnikin, interview with the author.

257 Mary-Clare Power, interview with the author.

258 Absolon, interview with the author.

259 Hielscher, interview with the author.

260 Brass, 'The Great Joh Show Gamble'.

261 Hielscher, interview with the author.

262 Ibid; 'Expo Will Apply for Private Bank Loans for Amount', *Courier-Mail* (Brisbane), 1 May 1986.

263 Carroll, 'Intergovernmental Relations', 107–11.

264 Hielscher, interview with the author.

265 'Media Lashed over Expo Stories', *Daily Sun* (Brisbane), 12 June 1987. Fraser may also have been spurred into diplomatic action by the comments attributed to him by the *7:30 Report*.

5   We'll Show the World

1 Lady Jane Edwards (née Brumfield, Communications director for Expo 88), interview with the author, October 2012.

2 'Sir Llew Survives the 14-Month Itch', *Courier-Mail* (Brisbane), 30 October 1987.

3 Jennifer Craik, 'Expo 88: Fashions of Sight and Politics of Site', in eds Tony Bennett, Pat Buckridge, David Carter, and Colin Mercer, *Celebrating the Nation: A Critical Study of Australia's Bicentenary* (St Leonards: Allen & Unwin, 1992), 102–3.

4 'Sir Llew Survives'; Robert S. Anderson and Eleanor Wachtel, 'Vancouver 1986: Expo 86 – The 1986 World Exposition', in ed. John E. Findling, *Historical Dictionary of World's Fairs and Expositions, 1851–1988* (New York: Greenwood Press, 1990), 288–9.

5 Alfred Heller, *World's Fairs and the End of Progress: An Insider's View* (Corte Madera: World's Fair Inc., 1999), 143, 144.

6 'Sir Llew Survives'.

7 Sir Llew Edwards (former Queensland Liberal Party leader, deputy premier, and chairman of Expo 88), interview with the author, October 2012.

8 BESBRA, *World Expo 88 Report* (Brisbane: BESBRA, 1988), section D1, D6.

9 Ibid.

10 Paul Syvret, 'The Business Side of Expo', *Australian Business*, 4 May 1988, 56–7; 'Big Business Backing Expo', *Daily Sun* (Brisbane), 28 February 1986.

11 Syvret, 'Business Side of Expo', 56–7; Ronnie Gibson, '$10m Seals Expo TV Rights', *Daily Sun* (Brisbane), 3 August 1985; Jamie Walker, *Goss: A Political Biography* (St Lucia: University of Queensland Press, 1995), 139.

12 Bob Minnikin (general manager of Expo 88), interview with the author, January 2013.

13 Ian Gill, 'Sir Joh and the Expo', *World's Fair* 8, 1 (Winter 1988), 7; 'Expo Link', *Chronicle* (Toowoomba), 23 July 1987; Syvret, 'Business Side of Expo', 56–7; Gibson, '$10m Seals Expo TV Rights'.

14 Peter Goldston (Site Development director for Expo 88, and founding general manager of the South Bank Corporation), interview with the author, November 2012.

15 Carol Lloyd (joint creative director for the Expo 88 advertising account), interview with the author, December 2012.
16 Llew Edwards, interview with the author.
17 Lloyd, interview with the author.
18 Ibid.
19 Phil Dickie, *The Road to Fitzgerald* (St Lucia: University of Queensland Press, 1988), 120.
20 Ibid., 124–5.
21 'The Moonlight State', *Four Corners*, ABC, 1987, accessed 8 July 2015, http://www.abc.net.au/4corners/stories/2011/08/08/3288495.htm.
22 Des Sturgess, *The Tangled Web* (Brisbane: Bedside Books, 2001), 150.
23 Dickie, *Road to Fitzgerald*, 150–1.
24 *Queensland Times* (Ipswich), 27 April 1987; Bob Hart, 'River Spectacle as Expo Lifts the Lid', *Sunday Mail* (Brisbane), 1 May 1988.
25 'Expo Tickets Launched with Flair', *Courier-Mail* (Brisbane), 1 May 1987.
26 'The Moonlight State'; Evan Whitton, *Can of Worms II*, 2nd edition (Broadway: The Fairfax Library, 1987), 37, 38.
27 Whitton, *Can of Worms II*, 77.
28 Ibid., 38.
29 Ibid., 77.
30 Ibid., 38.
31 Sturgess, *Tangled Web*, 151, 152.
32 Peter Charlton, *State of Mind: Why Queensland Is Different* (North Ryde: Methuen Haynes, 1987), 250–6; Joanne Holliman, *Sir Leo Hielscher: Queensland Made* (St Lucia: University of Queensland Press, 2014), 146.
33 Paul Davey, *Joh for PM: The Inside Story of an Extraordinary Political Drama* (Sydney: NewSouth Publishing, 2015), 128.
34 Charlton, *State of Mind*, 250–6; Holliman, *Sir Leo Hielscher*, 146.
35 Bob Hawke, *The Hawke Memoirs* (Port Melbourne: William Heinemann Australia, 1994), 185, 387.
36 Ibid., 387, 388, 392. Hawke says the schism within the Coalition was an incentive for an early election, but that other issues included equal access to television services and the Senate's refusal to pass legislation for the Australia Card Bill.
37 Charlton, *State of Mind*, 250–9.
38 Whitton, *Can of Worms II*, 77.
39 'Sir Llew Buoyed by Ticket Sales', *Courier-Mail* (Brisbane), 28 July 1987.
40 Ibid.
41 Whitton, *Can of Worms II*, 38–9.
42 Ibid., 78–83.
43 Ibid.
44 Ibid., 78.
45 Goldston, interview with the author.
46 Wayne McCamley (general manager of Von Roll in Queensland), interview with the author, 23 May 2013. McCamley was no stranger to monorail systems, having been responsible for the first one to be introduced to Australia, at Sea World

in 1986. Von Roll also had permission to install a ski/gondola lift that would transport attendees from the Treasury building in the Brisbane CBD across the Brisbane River and into the Expo site, but the plans were deemed commercially unviable with early visitor estimates at 7.5 million. 'Hindsight,' says McCamley, 'is a wonderful thing.'

47   Peter Coaldrake, 'The Campaign', in eds Rosemary Whip and Colin A. Hughes, *Political Crossroads: The 1989 Queensland Election* (St Lucia: University of Queensland Press, 1991), 86.
48   Paul Reynolds, *Lock, Stock & Barrel: A Political Biography of Mike Ahern* (St Lucia: University of Queensland Press, 2002), 94.
49   Ibid.
50   'Cain Jumps Aboard Expo Wagon', *Telegraph* (Brisbane), 22 October 1987.
51   Goldston, interview with the author.
52   Martin Warneminde, 'The Dictator and the Gold Mine', *Bulletin*, 9 February 1988, 52.
53   Shane Brady, 'Expo Handover Rebuffs Critics', *Daily Sun* (Brisbane), 2 November 1987.
54   Coaldrake, 'Campaign', 86; Rae Wear, *Johannes Bjelke-Petersen: The Lord's Premier* (St Lucia: University of Queensland Press, 2002), 86–7.
55   Whitton, *Can of Worms II*, 85.
56   Ibid.
57   Reynolds, *Lock, Stock & Barrel*, 95–6.
58   Ibid.
59   Sallyanne Atkinson (former lord mayor of Brisbane), interview with the author, December 2012.
60   Reynolds, *Lock, Stock & Barrel*, 96.
61   Ibid.
62   Matthew Condon, *All Fall Down* (St Lucia: University of Queensland Press, 2015), 372.
63   Margaret Bridson Cribb, 'The National Party', in Whip and Hughes, *Political Crossroads*, 115.
64   Reynolds, *Lock, Stock & Barrel*, 97.
65   Whitton, *Can of Worms II*, 85.
66   'Beyond Bethany', *Four Corners*, ABC, 3 March 2008, program transcript, accessed 8 October 2014, http://www.abc.net.au/4corners/content/2008/s2178617.htm.
67   Tony Koch, 'Legacy of Beattie's Cowshed Dance with Joh', 27 April 2005, accessed 12 October 2015, http://www.tony-koch.com/index.php?page=detail&id=302.
68   Mike Ahern (former premier of Queensland), interview with the author, December 2012.
69   Ibid.
70   Ian Gill, 'Making Peace with the Past', *World's Fair* 8, 2 (Spring 1988), 2–3.
71   Walker, *Goss*, 106–7. Factional infighting at this time raised the prospect of another federal intervention.
72   Sir Leo Hielscher (under treasurer and BESBRA board member), interview with the author, April 2013.

73 Ahern, interview with the author.

74 John R. Cole, *Shaping a City: Greater Brisbane 1925–1985* (Queensland: William Brooks, 1984), 298.

75 Denver Beanland, *Brisbane: Australia's New World City* (Salisbury: Boolarong Press, 2016), 111.

76 BESBRA, *World Expo 88 Report*, section D5. These figures comprise approximately 500,000 season passes (and the expectation they would be used for multiple visits), 500,000 three-day passes, and day and evening ticket sales.

77 Jane Cadzow, 'Expo City A-Flutter, but with a Touch of the Butterflies', *Australian*, 28 April 1988.

6   Brisbane Comes of Age – Again

1 Alfred Heller, *World's Fairs and the End of Progress: An Insider's View* (Corte Madera: World's Fair Inc., 1999), 148. Heller is presumably referring to the Queensland Police Force.

2 Mary-Clare Power (Amphitheatre producer for Expo 88), interview with the author, January 2013.

3 Expo Compile 4, u-matic tape (TVO Brisbane, 1988); BESBRA, *World Expo 88 Report* (Brisbane: BESBRA, 1988), section B4. The public entrance points were the Melbourne Street Gate (adjacent to the South Brisbane railway station and QPAC), the Vulture Street Gate (adjacent to the Vulture Street railway station and Expo House), the Ferry Gate (on the riverfront adjacent to the Boardwalk), and the Merivale Street Gate (otherwise known as the Amusement Park Gate, opposite the Expo coach terminal).

4 Jane Cadzow, 'Brazen Brissie Joins the Big League', *Weekend Australian*, 30 April– 1 May 1988.

5 'At Last, We Are All Set', *Sun* (Brisbane), 29 April 1988.

6 Ibid.; 'You Bewdy!', *Sunday Mail* (Brisbane), 1 May 1988.

7 Office of Commissioner-General, Expo 88, *Opening Ceremony Speeches, National Day Speeches, Closing Ceremony Speeches* (Brisbane: Office of Commissioner-General, Expo 88, 1988), 5–6.

8 Ibid., 7–8.

9 Ibid., 9–10. Excerpt from Hawke's speech licensed from the Commonwealth of Australia under a Creative Commons Attribution 4.0 International Licence.

10 Sir Llew Edwards (former Queensland Liberal Party leader, deputy premier, and chairman of Expo 88), interview with the author, October 2012.

11 Ibid.

12 Martin Warneminde, 'The Dictator and the Gold Mine', *Bulletin*, 9 February 1988, 52; 'River Spectacle as Expo Lifts the Lid', *Sunday Mail* (Brisbane), 1 May 1988; 'Joh, Fraser Not Thanked', *Courier-Mail* (Brisbane), 2 May 1988. Edwards reportedly dropped a reference to Bjelke-Petersen in his speech. Neither Bjelke-Petersen nor Fraser were thanked in the speeches.

13 'Miffed Sir Joh Denied a Stage Seat at Expo Bash', *Courier-Mail* (Brisbane), 11 April 1988; 'Day by Day with Des Partridge', *Courier-Mail* (Brisbane), 2 May 1988; Edwards, interview with the author; Tony Koch, 'Legacy of Beattie's Cowshed Dance with Joh', 27 April 2005, accessed 12 October 2015,

http://www.tony-koch.com/index.php?page=detail&id=302. Bjelke-Petersen also found himself in close proximity to Peter Beattie at Expo – shortly after Beattie had played himself in a TV dramatisation of Bjelke-Petersen's downfall, *Dance with the Devil* (the manuscript for which was edited by Koch and Des Power). The former premier quipped, 'We'll have to stop meeting like this, Peter.'

14 Edwards, interview with the author.
15 Sallyanne Atkinson (former lord mayor of Brisbane), interview with the author, December 2012.
16 Peter Goldston (Site Development director for Expo 88, and founding general manager of the South Bank Corporation), interview with the author, November 2012.
17 Ibid.
18 Office of Commissioner-General, Expo 88, *Opening Ceremony Speeches* (Brisbane: Office of Commissioner-General, Expo 88, 1988), 11–12. This speech contains public sector information licensed under the Open Government Licence v3.0 from The National Archives, United Kingdom.
19 BESBRA, *World Expo 88 Report*, section A7. The biggest attendance day at Expo 88 was 29 October, with 182,762. The smallest was 23 August, with 46,578.
20 Goldston, interview with the author.
21 Barbara Absolon (Entertainment deputy director and Walkways producer for Expo 88), interview with the author, December 2012.
22 Steve Bishop, 'We Showed 'Em', *Sunday Sun* (Brisbane), 1 May 1988.
23 'The Spirit of Expo', *Australian*, 29 April 1988.
24 Cadzow, 'Brazen Brissie Joins the Big League'.
25 'The Spirit of Expo'.
26 'Police Praise Aborigines over Protest', *Sunday Mail* (Brisbane), 1 May 1988; 'Angry Blacks Blast Persecution', *Sunday Sun* (Brisbane), 1 May 1988.
27 'Angry Blacks Blast Persecution'.
28 'Police Praise Aborigines over Protest'.
29 Jane Doughty and Roslyn Murray, 'Aborigines Interrupt Queen's Church Visit', *Courier-Mail* (Brisbane), 2 May 1988.
30 Lindy Rowett and Doug Button, 'Aborigines Storm Hotel', *Courier-Mail* (Brisbane), 3 May 1988.
31 Ibid.
32 Adrian McGregor, 'The Games v. Land Rights as a Media Event', in *The 1982 Commonwealth Games: A Retrospect* (St Lucia: Australian Studies Centre, Humanities and Social Sciences, UQ, 1984), 9–12. Aboriginal activists borrowed the protest slogan 'The Whole World Is Watching' to great effect during the games. McGregor estimated that protest coverage in *The Courier-Mail* alone would fill the whole news section of that paper, and recalls that a survey found forty per cent of foreign games reporters had filed stories about land rights.
33 Rowett and Button, 'Aborigines Storm Hotel'.
34 Matt Robbins and Tracy Maurer, 'Ahern Signals Crackdown', *Australian*, 4 May 1988; Peter Gleeson, 'Ahern Vows to Get Tough: Expo Demo Anger', *Sun* (Brisbane), 3 May 1988.

35 Robbins and Maurer, 'Ahern Signals Crackdown'. See also Jamie Walker, *Goss: A Political Biography* (St Lucia: University of Queensland Press, 1995), 31–40, 56, 110. As an architect of the ALS, Goss was held to a higher standard than many politicians. The ALS was established under the auspices of the Brisbane Aboriginal Tribal Council, of which Oodgeroo Noonuccal (then known as Kath Walker) was a principal founder. Staff included radical activist Dennis Walker (Oodgeroo's son), Sam Watson (father of the poet Samuel Wagan Watson), Aboriginal elder Don Davidson, Steve Mam (who later sat on the National Aboriginal Conference and the Council for Aboriginal Reconciliation), Lindsay Morrison (also a member of The Go-Betweens), and Roisin Hirschfeld (who married Goss). Goss was also instrumental in founding the Labor Lawyers Association and the Caxton Street Legal Centre.

36 Shane Rodgers, 'Aboriginal Flag to Fly in Support of Expo', *Courier-Mail* (Brisbane), 13 May 1988.

37 'Flag Will Not Fly at Site', *Courier-Mail* (Brisbane), 3 June 1988.

38 Peter Spearritt, 'Celebration of a Nation: The Triumph of Spectacle', *Australian Historical Studies* 23, 91 (October 1988), 3, 12, 15, 19.

39 Peter Cochrane and David Goodman, 'The Great Australian Journey: Cultural Logic and Nationalism in the Postmodern Era', *Australian Historical Studies* 23, 91 (October 1988), 25, 27, 31, 33–9.

40 Ibid.

41 Ian Gill, 'Making Peace with the Past', *World's Fair* 8, 2 (Spring 1988), 4; Rachel Sanderson, 'Celebration, Commemoration and Consumption: World Expo 88 and the Australian Bicentenary', working paper (2007).

42 Oodgeroo Noonuccal and Kabul Oodgeroo, *The Rainbow Serpent* (Canberra: AGPS, 1988).

43 Sanderson, 'Celebration'; Shane Brady, 'Take a Step Back in Time', *Sun* (Brisbane), 2 May 1988.

44 'You Bewdy!'. The newspaper reported, 'The Queen was puzzled for a moment [by Bluey], but then she smiled.'

45 Rachel Sanderson, 'Queensland Shows the World: Regionalism and Modernity at Brisbane's World Expo 88', *Journal of Australian Studies* 79 (2003), 65; BESBRA, *World Expo 88: The Official Souvenir Program* (Sydney: Australian Consolidated Press, 1988), 57. Sanderson remarks upon the incongruity of the pavilion's showpiece people-mover technology being supplied by another country.

46 BESBRA, *Expo 88 Souvenir Program*, 57. This was a contravention of BIE rules designed to curb participants' inclinations to treat expositions as trade fairs (though this is not an unusual occurrence).

47 Alec McHoul, 'Not Going to Expo: A Theory of Impositions', *Meanjin* 48, 2 (1989), 222. *Under Wraps* was a Street Arts production.

48 Philip Day, *The Big Party Syndrome: A Study of the Impact of Special Events and Inner Urban Change in Brisbane* (St Lucia: Department of Social Work, UQ, 1988), 155.

49 Joanne Watson, 'Always Will Be', in eds Raymond Evans and Carole Ferrier, *Radical Brisbane: An Unruly History* (Carlton North: The Vulgar Press, 2004), 312–15; 'Aborigines Offer Brisbane an Expo Sideshow', *Courier-Mail* (Brisbane), 28 April 1988. Committee members of the United Indigenous Cultural Survival

Gathering included Bob Weatherall, Shortie O'Neill, Lyall Munro Jnr, and Ross Watson.

50 Bob Weatherall (executive officer of FAIRA), interview with the author, July 2017.

51 Don Petersen, 'Hello Loneliness!', *Courier-Mail* (Brisbane), 28 October 1988.

52 Absolon, interview with the author.

53 Anne Jones (an editor of *The Cane Toad Times*), interview with the author, December 2012.

54 Ibid.

55 '738,000 Visitors Already for Expo', *Sun* (Brisbane), 9 May 1988.

56 'City Stays Up Late', *Courier-Mail* (Brisbane), 25 May 1988.

57 William Kahrl, 'The Surprising Success of World Expo 88', *World's Fair* 8, 3 (Summer 1988), 14.

58 'City Stays Up Late'.

59 Ronnie Gibson, 'All Work, No Play, but Expo Hosts All Smiles', *Sunday Mail* (Brisbane), 5 June 1988.

60 Don Petersen, 'Expo: The Losers and the Winners', *Courier-Mail* (Brisbane), 14 June 1988.

61 Power, interview with the author.

62 Ibid.

63 David Hamilton (Piazza producer for Expo 88), interview with the author, January 2013. This area was basically a 'green room' for performers between gigs.

64 Absolon, interview with the author.

65 Hamilton, interview with the author.

66 Ibid.

67 'Record Low Turnover of Staff for World Expositions', *Sun* (Brisbane), 16 September 1988.

68 Peter Charlton, 'Expo Reveals the Secrets of Its Striking Success', *Courier-Mail* (Brisbane), 13 October 1988.

69 Murray Massey, 'Expo Management Style Revolutionary', *Australian Financial Review, Supplement,* 8 September 1988.

70 Edwards, interview with the author.

71 Jane Doughty, 'Expo: It's a Place Where the World Comes to You', *Courier-Mail* (Brisbane), 13 June 1988; 'Workers at Expo Find Fate Aids Love', *Courier-Mail* (Brisbane), 27 October 1988.

72 Doughty, 'Expo'.

73 Brady, 'Take a Step Back in Time'. While the writer makes mention of Russia, it was more correctly known as the USSR.

74 Heller, *World's Fairs*, 150. The novelty of a 'passport' for collecting pavilion stamps had proven popular at earlier expositions, such as Expo 67 in Montreal.

75 Jennifer Craik, 'The Expo Experience: The Politics of Expositions', *Australian-Canadian Studies* 7, 1–2 (1989), 102, 103.

76 Tony Bennett, 'The Shaping of Things to Come: Expo 88', *Cultural Studies* 5, 1 (1991), 35–42.

77 Ibid.

78 Ibid. Bennett noted that countries at the 'cutting edge of modernity' (Europe, North America, Japan, Australia) used video and display technologies and were

followed by those 'displaying artefacts as if in a nineteenth-century museum' (USSR, China), then those relying solely on live performance (Fiji, Tonga).

79 Susan Hope, 'Team Who Put the Show on the Road', *Australian*, 19 April 1988.

80 Susan Hope, 'Magic behind Expo Scenes', *Australian*, 19 April 1988.

81 BESBRA, *World Expo 88: Media Handbook* (Brisbane: BESBRA, 1988), 54–7. See also Power, interview with the author. Power says the Entertainment Division preferred programming with 'big sheets of paper divided into the week, 10 am to 10 pm, half-hour slots' to wrestling with 1980s computer technology.

82 '60 Screens for Visitors: Data System to Highlight Expo Features', *Sunday Sun* (Brisbane), 12 July 1987.

83 Hope, 'Magic behind Expo Scenes'.

84 Kahrl, 'Surprising Success', 13.

85 Jones, interview with the author.

86 Edwards, interview with the author.

87 Ibid. See also Ian Gill, 'Battler for World Expo 88', *World's Fair* 8, 1 (Winter 1988), 8. Edwards accepted no fee as chairman for the first year in a bid to 'allay fears of patronage', after which his annual salary became $61,000.

88 John Watson (River Stage producer for Expo 88), interview with the author, January 2013. Watson adds that he was approached by various agents and offered kickbacks to program their performers at the event. (Needless to say, he turned them down.)

89 Ibid.

90 Edwards, interview with the author.

91 Mike Ahern (former premier of Queensland), interview with the author, December 2012.

92 Ibid.

93 Mike Mullins (Parades producer for Expo 88), interview with the author, January 2013.

94 Alan Moir, 'Queues for Expo 88 and the Fitzgerald Inquiry', John Oxley Library, State Library of Queensland, 3190 Alan Moir Cartoons.

95 Atkinson, interview with the author.

96 Kahrl, 'Surprising Success', 14–18.

97 Atkinson, interview with the author; Joanne Holliman, *Sir Leo Hielscher: Queensland Made* (St Lucia: University of Queensland Press, 2014), 147–9; Sir Leo Hielscher, interview by Brian Head and Chris Salisbury, *Queensland Speaks*, Centre for the Government of Queensland, 2011, accessed 14 October 2013, http://www.queenslandspeaks.com.au/leo-hielscher.

98 'Royals Galore in 88', *Daily Sun* (Brisbane), 9 May 1987; BESBRA, *World Expo 88 Report*, section C5.

99 Edwards, interview with the author. This may have been in relation to fallout from Iran–Contra, or the nuclear disarmament summits held with Gorbachev.

100 Ibid.; 'Hopes High for Reagan, Gorbachev to Visit Expo', *Australian*, 18 March 1988.

101 Holliman, *Sir Leo Hielscher*, 146–9; Hielscher, interview by Head and Salisbury.

102 Ahern, interview with the author.

103 Doug Hall, 'The Dictators Dinner?', *Courier-Mail*, QWeekend (Brisbane), 12 November 2011.

104 Ibid.

105 'Expo Signs the Stars to Rock the River', *Courier-Mail* (Brisbane), 16 January 1988; Kay Dibben, 'Chance to Meet the Aliens', *Sunday Sun* (Brisbane), 11 September 1988; 'Tony Jets in for LA – and Fun', *Courier-Mail* (Brisbane), 2 May 1988; 'Aboriginal Group at NT's Day', *Sunday Sun* (Brisbane), 25 September 1988; 'King Meets Queen', *Sunday Sun* (Brisbane), 1 May 1988; Ric Birch, *Master of the Ceremonies: An Eventful Life* (Crows Nest: Allen & Unwin, 2004), 93; 'Catch Max, the Computer Megastar', *Courier-Mail, Magazine* (Brisbane), 19 September 1988. Computer megastar Max Headroom video clips were played as filler before and after River Stage shows.

106 Crowded House, Expo Compile 55, u-matic tape (TVO Brisbane, 1988).

107 Ian Williams (Walkways coordinator for Expo 88), interview with the author, January 2016.

108 Ibid.

109 Kay Dibben, 'Let's Keep the Spirit of Expo: Sir Llew', *Sunday Sun, Magazine* (Brisbane), 31 July 1988; Anthony Walsh and James Hall, *World Expo 88: Brisbane – Australia* (Bathurst: Robert Brown & Associates, 1988), 103.

110 Williams, interview with the author.

111 Hamilton, interview with the author.

112 Anthony Steel (Consultant Producer, World Expo on Stage), interview with the author, December 2012; Marguerite Pepper (Consultant Producer, World Expo on Stage), interview with the author, January 2013; Brett Cochrane, *That's Entertainment: World Expo 88* (Brisbane: Brett Cochrane, 1988), 175. Steel was the first general manager of the Adelaide Festival Centre and had been artistic director of the Adelaide Festival five times. He was often ably assisted by Pepper. Their Expo program included a twenty-production festival of Australian theatre, an International Theatresports, and the World Drum Festival.

113 Pepper, interview with the author.

114 Mullins, interview with the author.

115 Absolon, interview with the author.

116 Cochrane, *That's Entertainment*, 188; Anthony Steel, *Painful in Daily Doses: An Anecdotal Memoir* (Kent Town: Wakefield Press, 2009), 286–8.

117 Steel, interview with the author; Cochrane, *That's Entertainment*, 188. *Cosmic Odyssey Nippon* was a surreal spectacle featuring Japanese performance artist Goro Namerikawa amid opera singers, sound and visual technicians, kendama players, and 'bio-artists'.

118 Steel, *Painful in Daily Doses*, 288.

119 Shane Rodgers, 'Fun Park Winds Down Its Staffing Numbers', *Courier-Mail* (Brisbane), 6 May 1988; Shane Rodgers, 'Fun Park Entry Free in Effort to Boost Numbers', *Courier-Mail* (Brisbane), 10 August 1988.

120 Petersen, 'Expo'.

121 Ibid.

122 'Strippers Bare Their Wares in Mall Demo', *Courier-Mail* (Brisbane), 24 June 1988. As 10 pm was still considered late in Brisbane, presumably many of these complaints related to business losses suffered during Expo's operation hours – including at strip-clubs.

123 'North Hit as Tourists Rush Expo', *Townsville Bulletin*, 15 June 1988.

124 Peter Grimshaw, 'NSW Hit as Expo Attracts Tourists', *Daily Telegraph* (Sydney), 1 August 1988; 'Brisbane's Expo Joy Becomes NT's Woe', *Weekend Australian Magazine*, 6–7 August 1988; 'Expo Hits Coast Business by up to 30 Per Cent', *Gold Coast Bulletin*, 11 June 1988; 'North Hit as Tourists Rush Expo'.

125 'NSW Hit as Expo Attracts Tourists'.

126 Kahrl, 'Surprising Success', 18.

127 'Airline Bookings Take Off', *Courier-Mail* (Brisbane), 10 June 1988; 'Expo Brings $54 Million to Brisbane's Hotels, Motels', *Courier-Mail* (Brisbane), 27 September 1988.

128 Robert Hadler and Paul Lynch, 'Expo Binge Gives Qld Huge Bite of Retail Sales', *Australian*, 22 July 1988.

129 'Today Is Expo Halfway Mark', *Courier-Mail* (Brisbane), 30 July 1988.

130 Power, interview with the author.

131 Goldston, interview with the author; Craik, 'Expo Experience', 102, 103.

132 'Cunning Cons Mark Final Days', *Courier-Mail* (Brisbane), 9 March 1988; 'Expo Geared Up for Final People Blitz', *Courier-Mail* (Brisbane), 9 September 1988. The paper also reported a 3.5-hour wait for the religiously themed (in defiance of BIE protocols against using expositions to preach religion) Pavilion of Promise.

133 Absolon, interview with the author.

134 Kahrl, 'Surprising Success', 18.

135 Heller, *World's Fairs*, 149; Tony Fry and Anne-Marie Willis, 'Expo 88: Backwoods into the Future', *Cultural Studies* 2, 1 (1988), 129.

136 Goldston, interview with the author.

137 'Sobering Prices Leave the Pubs with No Beer', *Sunday Sun* (Brisbane), 1 May 1988; Shane Rodgers, 'Site Security Increased to Halt Vandals', *Courier-Mail* (Brisbane), 21 May 1988; Matthew Franklin, 'Expo Fines Boost City Coffers by Extra $1 Million', *Courier-Mail* (Brisbane), 18 November 1988. The Council's Finance Committee Chairman, Alderman Graham Quirk (later Lord Mayor of Brisbane), said 64,858 tickets had been issued; Shane Rodgers, 'Woman, 61, Dies after Meal at Expo Site', *Courier-Mail* (Brisbane), 14 June 1988; 'Expo Inquest Decision Due', *Sunday Mail* (Brisbane), 23 April 1988; 'Expo as Mystery Killer', *Sunday Mail* (Brisbane), 8 January 1989; Lindy Rowett, 'Four Workers Hurt in Expo Ride Fire', *Courier-Mail* (Brisbane), 14 June 1988; 'Expo's Laser "Needle" Ablaze', *Courier-Mail* (Brisbane), 8 July 1988; 'Expo Monorail Stops', *Courier-Mail* (Brisbane), 20 August 1988; 'Govt Urged to Set Up Probe on Killings', *Courier-Mail* (Brisbane), 17 May 1988; 'Balancing Slab Fell on Worker at Expo Site, Inquest Told', *Courier-Mail* (Brisbane), 21 June 1989; 'Fines Follow Fatal Accident', *Townsville Bulletin*, 5 December 1989; Jane Doughty, 'Sir Llew Hits Rights Group', *Courier-Mail* (Brisbane), 17 October 1988. The Amnesty International dossiers included information on each government's alleged violations of human rights, including torture and killing. News coverage of unfortunate events after the conclusion of Expo included two men killed during the dismantling of the sunsails, and another killed during the dismantling of a monorail station. See also Birch, *Master of the Ceremonies*, 127, 131–2. Birch chronicles several other mishaps over the course of Expo 88, including all of the Aquacade swimming girls getting ear infections.

138 Office of Commissioner-General, *Ceremony Speeches*, 115–18.
139 Dot Whittington, 'Greed, Truancy Blamed on Expo', *Sun* (Brisbane), 7 December 1988.
140 Watson, interview with the author.
141 Ibid.; Hamilton, interview with the author.
142 Watson, interview with the author. See also Tom Burns (12 April 1989), *Queensland Parliamentary Debates*, 4491–2. Burns alleged that suspected paedophiles had managed to work at Expo for a time.
143 Williams, interview with the author.
144 Absolon, interview with the author.
145 Day, *Big Party Syndrome*, 155.
146 Steve Bishop, 'We're the Envy of Expo World', *Sunday Sun* (Brisbane), 29 May 1988.
147 Bob Hart, 'Here's What YOU Think about Expo', *Sunday Mail* (Brisbane), 15 May 1988.
148 'Record Is Dig at the Knockers', *Sunday Sun* (Brisbane), 2 October 1988.
149 John Wright, 'PM Snubbed Qld Pavilion at Expo: Spokesman', *Sunday Mail* (Brisbane), 19 June 1988.
150 'Hawke "Snub" Still Upsets Fair Officials', *Courier-Mail* (Brisbane), 21 June 1988.
151 Tom Veivers, *Commissioner-General's Executive Report* (Canberra: Australian Pavilion, 1988), 16.
152 Ibid., 6, 15.
153 Damaso de Lario, 'Report by Dr Damaso de Lario', in Sir Edward Williams, *Report of the Commissioner-General of Expo 88 on the Australian Government's Involvement in Expo 88* (Canberra: Department of Sport, Recreation and Tourism, 1989), 4–10.
154 'Good Expo Guide', *Sunday Mail* (Brisbane), 8 May 1988.
155 'Expo Didn't Let the States Down', *Cairns Post*, 11 November 1988.
156 'Visit Inspires Sydney Expo Push in 2000', *Courier-Mail* (Brisbane), 14 July 1988.
157 Keith De Lacy (1 September 1988), *Queensland Parliamentary Debates*, 432.
158 *World Expo 88: The Official Souvenir Program* (Sydney: Australian Consolidated Press, 1988), 5; Walsh and Hall, *World Expo 88*, 7–11.
159 Goldston, interview with the author.
160 Shane Rodgers, 'Dear Diary, Today I Made Speech 5200', *Courier-Mail* (Brisbane), 21 October 1988. These figures are likely to have been supplied by Expo 88's Communications Division.
161 Ibid.
162 'Entertaining Protest', *Sun* (Brisbane), 8 December 1988.
163 BESBRA, *World Expo 88: Closing Financial Report 1988* (Brisbane: BESBRA, 1989), 2.
164 Sir Frank Moore (former chairman of QTTC, director of Dreamworld and Jupiters Casino, developer, and member of the National Party's management committee), interview with the author, July 2013. Moore was also a key instigator in other bicentennial enterprises, such as the Australian Stockman's Hall of Fame and Barrier Reef Marine World.
165 'Why Were Some Honoured and Some Not?', *Sun* (Brisbane), 27 January 1989; 'Expo Honours Omissions an Insult to All', *Sun* (Brisbane), 3 February 1989;

Peter Gleeson, 'Gunn Fuels Expo Honours Row', *Sun* (Brisbane), 3 February 1989; 'Edwards Leads Expo Honours Scoop', *Courier-Mail* (Brisbane), 26 January 1989; Birch, *Master of the Ceremonies*, 138. Sir Llew Edwards was made a companion of the Order of Australia; Lady Edwards, Ross Given, and Barbara Absolon became members of the Order of Australia; Peter Goldston became an officer of the Order of Australia; and medals of the Order of Australia were given to Merchandising Manager Marilyn Elliot, volunteer coordinators Frances Look and Marie Rogers, Project Director Bob Roche, Site Maintenance Manager Brian Purcell, and Technology Director Ken Pope. Deputy Premier Bill Gunn said he was 'amazed' Minnikin and Williams had been omitted. Former director Richard John (also omitted) said Williams's diplomacy had been essential to 'hosing down' difficulties between internationals and BESBRA when some nations had threatened to 'pack up and leave'. Birch expressed bewilderment that he had been overlooked in favour of his deputy, Absolon. He, Finance Director Tony Philips, and Marketing Director Graham Currie were all overlooked, which Birch attributed to Sir Llew Edwards being 'a bit cavalier towards the interstate and international people who'd assisted the Queenslanders in their hour of need'. The nominations were made in secret.

166 Sir Leo Hielscher (under treasurer and BESBRA board member), interview with the author, April 2013.

167 Ahern, interview with the author.

168 Ibid. This advice was given during a personal tour that Thatcher gave Ahern of her residence at 10 Downing Street (Thatcher had invited him during her Expo visit). She said it was the press secretary's responsibility to look at the newspapers.

169 'Expo Reason to Celebrate', *Queensland Times* (Ipswich), 6 June 1988.

170 Kay Dibben, 'Sir Llew Says Crowd Doesn't Whinge', *Sunday Sun* (Brisbane), 24 July 1988. This article is an angry response to an *Australian Financial Review* article by David Clark headlined 'Don't Open the Expo Envelope: It's a Guaranteed Disappointment'.

171 Goldston, interview with the author.

172 Petersen, 'Hello Loneliness!'. Less glowing reminiscences included 'obnoxious pedi-cab drivers, sky-high rents and homelessness in West End' and 'Expo stopped the flying foxes from eating our paw-paws this season. They normally fly straight over South Brisbane but not this year'.

173 Ibid.

174 Ibid.

175 Ibid.

176 John Leonard Cotterell and Ian F. Jobling, *Brisbane Youth and World Expo 88: A Report on Leisure Patterns of Brisbane Young People* (St Lucia: UQ, 1989), 19, 36–8.

177 'Party Has Been Way to Escape', *Sunday Sun* (Brisbane), 25 September 1988.

178 Steve Bishop, 'The Great Expomania Puzzle', *Sunday Sun* (Brisbane), 6 November 1988.

179 Kahrl, 'Surprising Success', 13–20.

180 Birch, *Master of the Ceremonies*, 128.

181 Bishop, 'Great Expomania Puzzle'.

182 'After the Party's Over', *Sunday Mail Magazine* (Brisbane), 16 October 1988.

183 Goldston, interview with the author.

184 Peter Osborne, 'Thriving Expo Surges Past Attendance Forecasts', *Australian Financial Review, Supplement*, 8 September 1988.

185 BESBRA Communications Division, 'News Release: World Expo 88 – The Vital Statistics', 31 October 1988, 2.

186 Ibid., 3–4; BESBRA, *World Expo 88 Report*, section C5. An average of 19,000 meals were sold each hour on site.

187 BESBRA Communications Division, 'News Release', 4.

188 Massey, 'Expo Management Style Revolutionary'.

189 Andrew Stewart, 'Expo Widens Horizon of Things to Do in Brisbane', *Australian Financial Review*, 20 October 1988. Stewart was Brisbane-born.

190 Ibid.

191 Tracy Maurer, '$100m Debt Now the Carnival Is Over', *Australian*, 31 October 1988.

192 Shane Rodgers, 'Mayor Regrets Speaker Snub', *Courier-Mail* (Brisbane), 20 October 1988. See also Shane Rodgers, 'Labor Man Champions Mayor', *Courier-Mail* (Brisbane), 21 October 1988. Peter Beattie deemed this slight to the Lord Mayor a 'petty and silly' way to finish Expo. Reportedly, Atkinson was also initially excluded from the Expo opening ceremony speeches; she was added after making her objections clear.

193 'The Carnival Is Over', *Courier-Mail* (Brisbane), 27 October 1988; Paul Wicks, 'Mayor Has the Final Say After All', *Courier-Mail* (Brisbane), 27 October 1988.

194 Cindy Wockner, 'Seekers Star Protest', *Courier-Mail* (Brisbane), 31 October 1988.

195 Neale Maynard, 'Visitors Riled by Llew's VIP Snub: Expo Exit Party Shuts Out Public', *Sun* (Brisbane), 24 October 1988. The gates were also shut to the public early in a bid to protect the site from last-minute souveniring.

196 Ibid.

197 Ibid.

198 Maurer, '$100m Debt'; 'Visitors Sad but Staff Celebrate', *Courier-Mail* (Brisbane), 31 October 1988.

199 Hielscher, interview with the author.

200 Office of Commissioner-General, *Ceremony Speeches*, 411–18.

201 Ibid., 411–14.

202 Ibid., 420–1. Excerpt from Hawke's speech licensed from the Commonwealth of Australia under a Creative Commons Attribution 4.0 International Licence.

203 Ibid., 417.

204 Ibid., 418.

205 Maurer, '$100m Debt'.

206 Maynard, 'Visitors Riled'.

207 Jane Doughty, 'Emotional Finale to Six Months of Work, Sweat, Laughs and Tears', *Courier-Mail* (Brisbane), 31 October 1988.

7 After Party

1 Anthony Steel (Consultant Producer, World Expo on Stage), interview with the author, December 2012.

2   Marguerite Pepper (Consultant Producer, World Expo on Stage), interview with the author, January 2013.

3   Morray Hogan, 'Long Queues Won't Stretch Expo Authority's Profit', *Weekend Australian Magazine*, 30–31 July 1988.

4   Bob Hart, 'The Party's Just Begun', *Sunday Mail Colour Magazine* (Brisbane), 3 July 1988.

5   Susan Hocking, 'How to Keep that Expo Spirit Going', *Sunday Mail* (Brisbane), 30 October 1988.

6   Helen Meredith, 'Queensland Looks for Life after Expo', *Australian*, 18 October 1988.

7   Janelle Miles, 'Party Addicts Face Life without Their Daily Fix', *Townsville Bulletin*, 9 November 1988.

8   Jason Gagliardi and Nicki Byrne, '"Expo Anonymous" to Assist People after World Fair Ends', *Courier-Mail* (Brisbane), 24 October 1988.

9   'Staff Debriefing Needed after Expo: Psychologist', *Courier-Mail* (Brisbane), 14 September 1988.

10   Mike Ahern (former premier of Queensland), interview with the author, December 2012.

11   Shane Rodgers, 'Thanks for the Memories!', *Courier-Mail, Weekend* (Brisbane), 29 April 1989.

12   Ibid; BESBRA, *World Expo 88 Report* (Brisbane: BESBRA, 1988), section A7.

13   Lady Jane Edwards (née Brumfield, Communications director for Expo 88), interview with the author, October 2012.

14   Paul Lynch, 'A Million Beers Later, Expo 88 Hangover Sets In', *Weekend Australian Magazine*, 22–23 October 1988.

15   'Sir Llew Wants an "Expo Mall"', *Courier-Mail* (Brisbane), 14 August 1988.

16   Susan Hope, 'Expo Sparks Science Centre Plan', *Australian*, 2 August 1988; '"Big-Event" Body Urged', *Courier-Mail* (Brisbane), 28 July 1988. Both ideas were suggested by Expo Marketing director Graham Currie.

17   Tony Bennett, 'The Shaping of Things to Come: Expo 88', *Cultural Studies* 5, 1 (1991), 41–2.

18   Ibid., 46–7.

19   Ric Birch, *Master of the Ceremonies: An Eventful Life* (Crows Nest: Allen & Unwin, 2004), 135–6. Birch says the bid 'took a lot of heat' as it involved a casino. He also says Frank Zappa heard about it and wanted to have similar zones in key world cities, but with all the buildings painted blue; Zappa's theory was that other businesses would want to be part of it and paint their buildings blue too – resulting in a blue city.

20   Ian Grayson, 'Row over $1.15m Statue', *Sun* (Brisbane), 18 November 1988; 'Magic on a Massive Scale', *Sunday Mail* (Brisbane), 24 April 1989.

21   'Taxman Blocks Charity at Expo', *Courier-Mail* (Brisbane), 26 October 1988.

22   Emma Sykes, 'Expo-sing What's Left from '88', 612 ABC Brisbane, 29 April 2013, accessed 8 February 2016, http://www.abc.net.au/local/stories/2013/04/29/3747609.htm.

23   John McGregor, 'Where Has It Gone to Now?', Celebrate 88!, accessed 2 July 2015, http://www.celebrate88.com/wherehasitgonetonow.html. This page is

part of a comprehensive Expo fan website, Celebrate 88! (previously known as Foundation Expo 88), founded and maintained by John McGregor, who worked at the Japan Pavilion during the exposition.

24   'Public Thank Saviours', *Sunday Sun* (Brisbane), 5 March 1989.

25   Cameron Atfield, 'Skyneedle "Should Never Have Left South Bank": Stefan', *Brisbane Times*, 22 August 2015, accessed 20 October 2015, http://www. brisbanetimes.com.au/queensland/skyneedle-should-never-have-left-south-bank -stefan-20150819-gj34to.html. The designer no longer wishes his name to be associated with the sculpture.

26   Stefan Ackerie, Expo Compile 105, u-matic tape (TVO Brisbane, 1988).

27   Cameron Atfield, 'World Expo Skyneedle to Get New Life in Pradella Development', *Brisbane Times*, 19 August 2015, accessed 20 October 2015, http://www.brisbanetimes.com.au/queensland/world-expo-skyneedle-to-get-new -life-in-pradella-development-20150819-gj2j2s.html; Atfield, 'Skyneedle'. Prior to the arrangement with Pradella, Ackerie said he sought to return the sculpture to the South Bank Parklands at no cost, but negotiations with the South Bank Corporation (of which he was a board member) were unsuccessful.

28   Steve Rous, 'Use Monorail after Expo for Uni Commuters: MLA', *Courier-Mail* (Brisbane), 3 March 1986; Peter Goldston, email to the author, November 2012; Wayne McCamley (general manager of Von Roll in Queensland – responsible for the monorail), interview with the author, May 2013. McCamley says it would not have been practical to turn the monorail into high-frequency public transport, as it was not designed for it.

29   'Fair's Landmarks Bound to Be Spread around the World', *Courier-Mail* (Brisbane), 31 October 1988; McGregor, 'Where Has It Gone to Now?'.

30   Sir Llew Edwards (former Queensland Liberal Party leader, deputy premier, and chairman of Expo 88), interview with the author, October 2012.

31   'First See the Show, Now Picture It All on Record', *Courier-Mail* (Brisbane), 10 October 1988. Much of the material held at the Queensland State Archives was embargoed for thirty or more years.

32   Bob Minnikin (general manager of Expo 88), interview with the author, January 2013. See also John R. Cole, *Shaping a City: Greater Brisbane 1925–1985* (Queensland: William Brooks, 1984), 374–6. After the success of the 1982 Commonwealth Games, Lord Mayor Harvey bid to host the 1987 World University Games and the 1992 Olympic Games. Two facilities were to be built at Boondall to accommodate this: an indoor sports stadium that could serve as an entertainment centre (completed in 1986), and an outdoor stadium. The second stage did not proceed when Brisbane failed in its Olympic bid.

33   Henry Palaszczuk (4 October 1984), *Queensland Parliamentary Debates*, 1082.

34   Tom Burns (4 August 1987), *Queensland Parliamentary Debates*, 1695.

35   Terry Mackenroth (28 October 1987), *Queensland Parliamentary Debates*, 3640.

36   Queensland Government, *The Expo '88 Act 1984*, No. 9 of 1984.

37   Peter Carroll, 'The Intergovernmental Relations of Expo '88' (PhD thesis, UQ, 1994), 382.

38   Ibid., 391.

39   Ibid., 453.

40   Sallyanne Atkinson (former lord mayor of Brisbane), interview with the author, December 2012.

41   'Row Brews over Expo Interest Bill', *Sunday Sun* (Brisbane), 19 February 1989; Carroll, 'Intergovernmental Relations', 409–10.

42   Sallyanne Atkinson, interview by Peter Spearritt, Danielle Miller, and Kathryn Talbot, *Queensland Speaks*, Centre for the Government of Queensland, 22 February 2012, accessed 14 October 2014, http://www.queenslandspeaks.com.au/sallyanne-atkinson.

43   Atkinson, interview with the author.

44   Cole, *Shaping a City*, 220; Joseph M. Siracusa, *Sallyanne: Portrait of a Lord Mayor* (Milton: Jacaranda Press, 1987), 37; Hugh Lunn, *Joh: The Life and Political Adventures of Johannes Bjelke-Petersen* (Melbourne: Sun Books, 1979), 223; 'Judy Goes In to Bat for Expo', *Daily Sun* (Brisbane), 14 August 1987. Chappell became an Expo ambassador. His wife, Judy, became an Expo volunteer team leader.

45   Atkinson, interview by Spearritt, Miller, and Talbot.

46   'Row Brews'; Carroll, 'Intergovernmental Relations', 409–10.

47   Shane Rodgers, '$130m Expo Sponsorship World Record', *Courier-Mail* (Brisbane), 9 January 1988.

48   Carroll, 'Intergovernmental Relations', 436–40. The proposal was worth $16 million less than some rival tenders.

49   Rodgers, '$130m Expo Sponsorship'.

50   Peter Goldston (Site Development director for Expo 88, and founding general manager of the South Bank Corporation), interview with the author, November 2012.

51   Len Ardill (27 October 1988), *Queensland Parliamentary Debates*, 2089.

52   Denver Beanland (12 April 1988), *Queensland Parliamentary Debates*, 5656. The Toowong railway station and Roma Street transit centre were Frank Moore developments; neither found favour with architects.

53   Eric Shaw (8 March 1988), *Queensland Parliamentary Debates*, 4866.

54   Ibid., 4863–4.

55   Sir Frank Moore (former chairman of QTTC, director of Dreamworld and Jupiters Casino, developer, and member of the National Party's management committee), interview with the author, July 2013.

56   Carroll, 'Intergovernmental Relations', 451.

57   Llew Edwards, interview with the author.

58   Carroll, 'Intergovernmental Relations', 442.

59   'Sanders Entertainment Ventures Manages the American Village', *Sunday Mail* (Brisbane), 5 June 1988.

60   Carroll, 'Intergovernmental Relations', 444.

61   Ahern, interview with the author.

62   Ibid.

63   Hart, 'Party's Just Begun'.

64   Goldston, interview with the author.

65   Mike Ahern (20 April 1989), *Queensland Parliamentary Debates*, 5027.

66   'No Left-Over Expo Blot on Brisbane, Says Llew', *Courier-Mail* (Brisbane), 29 July 1988.

67   Ahern, interview with the author.
68   Atkinson, interview with Spearritt, Miller, and Talbot.
69   Ahern, interview with the author.
70   Llew Edwards, interview with the author.
71   Don Petersen, 'Hello Loneliness!', *Courier-Mail* (Brisbane), 29 October 1988.
72   Harry Gordon, editorial, *Courier-Mail* (Brisbane), 19 June 1988.
73   Don Petersen, 'Post-Expo Concerns Remain Still', *Courier-Mail* (Brisbane),
     16 August 1988.
74   Goldston, interview with the author.
75   'Row Brews'.
76   'ALP Claims $200m Expo Debt Bungle', *Sunday Mail* (Brisbane), 19 February
     1989.
77   BESBRA, *World Expo 88: Closing Financial Report 1988* (Brisbane: BESBRA,
     1989), 1.
78   Lisa Green, 'Picking Up the Pieces after the Party', *Sun* (Brisbane), 28 December
     1988.
79   Peter Morley and Shane Rodgers, 'Expo Will Announce $653,000 Profit from
     $480m Investment', *Courier-Mail* (Brisbane), 30 March 1989.
80   'Public Expo Tab Huge', *Courier-Mail* (Brisbane), 1 October 1988.
81   John Stubbs, '$120m Expo Loss! Secret Study's Shock Finding', *Sunday Sun*
     (Brisbane), 24 December 1988.
82   Ibid.
83   '$100m Expo Slug Claim Taxpayers Hit Hard: Report', *Sun* (Brisbane), 31 March
     1989.
84   Ibid.
85   Stubbs, '$120m Expo Loss!'; '$100m Expo Slug Claim'; 'Taxpayers Left with the
     Bill: Report', *Sun* (Brisbane), 31 March 1989.
86   'A Financial Hangover from Expo?', *Sun* (Brisbane), 31 March 1989.
87   'Taxpayers Left with the Bill'.
88   Ibid.
89   Peter Carroll and Kerry Donohue, 'Accounting for Expo '88', *Directions in
     Government* 3, 1 (1989), 64.
90   Ibid.
91   Ibid.
92   Ken McElligott (20 April 1989), *Queensland Parliamentary Debates*, 5019–21.
     This was at the second reading of the South Bank Corporation Bill.
93   Carroll, 'Intergovernmental Relations', 457–8.
94   Ahern, interview with the author.
95   Goldston, interview with the author.
96   Shane Rodgers, 'Piece-by-Piece Tender for Expo Commerce Area', *Courier-Mail*
     (Brisbane), 10 May 1989.
97   Ibid.
98   Ahern, interview with the author.
99   Llew Edwards, interview with the author.
100 Donna Lee Brien, 'Celebration or Manufacturing Nostalgia? Constructing
     Histories of World Expo '88', *Queensland Review* 16, 2 (2009), 79; Goldston,

interview with the author. Goldston invited Expo's site-scaping maestro, John Truscott, to advise on the redevelopment, but he grew ill and was unable to continue.

101 Carroll and Donohue, 'Accounting for Expo '88', 62.

102 Jennifer Craik, 'The Expo Experience: The Politics of Expositions', *Australian-Canadian Studies* 7, 1–2 (1989), 102.

103 Hogan, 'Long Queues'.

104 Mark Voisey, '$11m Expo Battle', *Sun* (Brisbane), 30 March 1989. Corruption allegations included the purchase of Abeles' knighthood.

105 Ibid.; John Stubbs, Greg Abbott, and Sally Fitzgerald, 'TNT Fights $11m Expo Debt', *Sunday Sun* (Brisbane), 2 April 1989.

106 Stubbs, Abbott, and Fitzgerald, 'TNT Fights $11m Expo Debt'.

107 Goldston, interview with the author.

108 'Expo Park Management Deny Bad Debts with World Fair Body', *Courier-Mail* (Brisbane), 31 March 1989.

109 Goldston, interview with the author.

110 Jennifer Craik, 'Expo 88: Fashions of Sight and Politics of Site', in eds Tony Bennett, Pat Buckridge, David Carter, and Colin Mercer, *Celebrating the Nation: A Critical Study of Australia's Bicentenary* (St Leonards: Allen & Unwin, 1992), 147.

111 Ibid; Goldston, interview with the author.

112 Goldston, interview with the author.

113 Keith De Lacy (4 October 1989), *Queensland Parliamentary Debates*, 1225.

114 Ibid., 1123–4.

115 Margaret Bridson Cribb, 'The National Party', in eds Rosemary Whip and Colin A. Hughes, *Political Crossroads: The 1989 Queensland Election* (St Lucia: University of Queensland Press, 1991), 121.

116 Wayne Goss (8 June 1989), *Queensland Parliamentary Debates*, 5381.

117 Ibid., 5382.

118 Steve Bishop, *The Most Dangerous Detective: The Outrageous Glen Patrick Hallahan and the Rat Pack*, 2nd edition (Brisbane: Steve Bishop, 2015), 360. Don Lane reportedly claimed his unexplained income was from abuse of ministerial expenses rather than graft, as he felt (wrongly) that he would not be jailed for it. Instead, he triggered an inquiry into ministerial expenses that resulted in the aforementioned jail terms.

119 Rae Wear, *Johannes Bjelke-Petersen: The Lord's Premier* (St Lucia: University of Queensland Press, 2002), 146. Two property developers were later found guilty of bribing Hinze.

120 Ibid., 102–3.

121 Evan Whitton, *The Hillbilly Dictator: Australia's Police State*, rev. ed. (Crows Nest: ABC Books, 1993), 211–13.

122 Ibid., 201. Other developments included Winchester South, a cultural centre on the Gold Coast, and three prisons.

123 Paul Reynolds, *Lock, Stock & Barrel: A Political Biography of Mike Ahern* (St Lucia: University of Queensland Press, 2002), 186–7, 204.

124 Ibid., 183, 204.

125 Peter Coaldrake, 'The Campaign', in Whip and Hughes, *Political Crossroads*, 87–9.
126 Ahern, interview with the author.
127 Jamie Walker, *Goss: A Political Biography* (St Lucia: University of Queensland Press, 1995), 122.
128 Ibid., 125. This included adverts showing Labor being soft on drugs and abortion, and creating an environment that attracted homosexuals from Sydney.
129 Ibid.
130 Anthony Steel, *Painful in Daily Doses: An Anecdotal Memoir* (Kent Town: Wakefield Press, 2009), 314. Steel says Brisbane was the only mainland capital without a major arts festival at this time. He was asked to run the resulting event, the Brisbane Biennial International Music Festival, and Barbara Absolon was appointed general manager.
131 Reynolds, *Lock, Stock & Barrel*, 206.
132 'Goss Says Expense Letter May Have No Legal Standing', *Queensland Times* (Ipswich), 7 December 1989. The 1987 Cabinet decision was itself a reversal of an earlier decision, in which ministers, their partners, and their guests were permitted to attend Expo at no cost – but at an anticipated $33,000 cost to the public. The decision was rescinded after a public outcry.
133 John Stubbs, 'Goss to Expose Expo Secrets', *Sunday Sun* (Brisbane), 17 December 1989.
134 Sallyanne Atkinson, *No Job for a Woman* (St Lucia: University of Queensland Press, 2016), 181–2.
135 Atkinson, interview by Spearritt, Miller, and Talbot. Atkinson says that, many years later, Hutton confided to her that he regretted the preferences decision, to which she laughingly replied, 'Don't tell me that *now!*'
136 Walker, *Goss*, 176.
137 Ibid., 184.
138 Ibid., 153, 159, 160–4.
139 Ibid., 227; Bob Weatherall (executive officer of FAIRA), interview with the author, July 2017. Weatherall says, 'Bloody Wayne Goss was as conservative as buggery – and we had major problems with him and the *Native Title Act* because he had bloody Kevin Rudd as his senior adviser.'
140 John Macarthur, 'On Kodak Beach: Technical Developments in Imaging and Architecture', *Transition* 48 (1995), 21.
141 Ibid., 20.
142 Ibid., 19.
143 Ibid.
144 Donna Lee Brien, 'Brisbane Will Never Be the Same: Tasting Change at World Expo '88', *Queensland Review* 15, 2 (2008), 4.
145 Goldston, interview with the author.
146 Moore, interview with the author.
147 South Bank Corporation, *Annual Report 2012/13*, 2013, 7, accessed 6 October 2014, http://www.southbankcorporation.com.au/corporate-publications/annual-report-2012-2013.
148 Andrew MacDonald and Des Houghton, 'How the ABC's Sweetheart Deal for Riverfront Land at South Bank Will Keep Getting Better', *Courier-Mail*

(Brisbane), 19 July 2012, accessed 6 February 2016, http://www.couriermail.
com.au/realestate/how-the-abcs-sweetheart-deal-for-riverfront-land-at-south-bank
-will-keep-getting-better/story-e6frequ6-1226429445446; Tony Moore, 'Aunty
Heads to South Bank Parklands', *Brisbane Times*, 10 December 2008, accessed
6 February 2016, http://www.brisbanetimes.com.au/news/queensland/aunty
-heads-to-south-bank-parklands/2008/12/10/1228584880788.html.

149   Des Houghton, 'Secret Deal between ABC and Bligh Government for Prime
Land at South Bank', News.Com.Au, 19 July 2012, accessed 6 February
2016, http://www.news.com.au/realestate/news/secret-deal-between-abc-and
-bligh-government-for-prime-riverfront-land-at-south-bank-revealed/story
-fncq3gat-1226428771685.

150   Katherine Feeney, 'Days Numbered for South Bank Corporation', *Brisbane
Times*, 11 December 2012, accessed 6 February 2016, http://www.
brisbanetimes.com.au/queensland/days-numbered-for-south-bank-corporation
-20121211-2b6zc.html.

151   South Bank Corporation, accessed 27 June 2017, http://southbankcorporation.
com.au/about-us/overview.

152   Tony Moore, 'South Bank Parklands Extended for 25th Birthday', *Brisbane
Times*, 20 June 2017, accessed 20 June 2017, http://www.brisbanetimes.com.
au/queensland/south-bank-parklands-extended-for-25th-birthday-20170620
-gwupeu.html.

153   Rosanne Barrett, 'Queen's Wharf Mega-Project to Reign over 20pc of City',
Australian, 2 June 2017, accessed 27 June 2017, http://www.theaustralian.com.
au/business/property/queens-wharf-megaproject-to-reign-over-20pc-of-city/news
-story/4976feade473200812eaece37063baf4.

154   Queensland Government, Department of State Development, 'Queen's Wharf
Brisbane', accessed 6 February 2016, http://www.statedevelopment.qld.gov.
au/major-projects/queens-wharf-brisbane.html. The consortium is composed
of The Star Entertainment Group (formerly Echo Entertainment Group), Far
East Consortium, and Chow Tai Fook Enterprises. Echo was assisted by former
Queensland premier turned lobbyist Rob Borbidge.

155   Cameron Atfield, 'South Bank CEO Says Precinct Will Rise to Queens Wharf
Challenge', *Brisbane Times*, 25 October 2015, accessed 6 February 2016, http://
www.brisbanetimes.com.au/business/south-bank-ceo-says-precinct-will-rise-to
-queens-wharf-challenge-20151024-gkhluj.html.

156   Sarah Vogler, Peter Michael, and Jason Tin, 'Casino Brisbane: New Casino,
Mega Resort by Echo Entertainment at Queens Wharf Precinct', *Courier-Mail*
(Brisbane), 20 July 2015, accessed 6 February 2016, http://www.couriermail.
com.au/news/queensland/casino-brisbane-new-casino-mega-resort-by-echo
-entertainment-at-queens-wharf-precinct/news-story/53850d5629ff9f1d1b53810
359ebd3b9.

157   Queensland Government, 'Queen's Wharf Brisbane'.

158   Tony Moore, 'Will Brisbane Get "Expo-Like" Transformation from New Casino
Complex?', *Brisbane Times*, 25 July 2015, accessed 6 February 2016, http://www.
brisbanetimes.com.au/queensland/will-brisbane-get-expolike-transformation
-from-new-casino-complex-20150724-gik6nt.html.

159 Bureau International des Expositions, 'Our History', accessed 10 February 2015, http://www.bie-paris.org/site/en/bie/our-history; Robert W. Rydell, 'New Directions for Scholarship about World Expos', in eds Kate Darian-Smith, Richard Gillespie, Caroline Jordan, and Elizabeth Willis, *Seize the Day: Exhibitions, Australia and the World* (Clayton: Monash University ePress, 2008), 21.2.

160 Ibid. US secretary of state Colin Powell informed the BIE of the country's withdrawal. Both Canada's and America's withdrawals are believed to have been the result of cost-cutting directives.

161 The White House, Office of the Press Secretary, 'President Donald J. Trump Signs H.R. 534 into Law', 8 May 2017, accessed 27 June 2017, https://www.whitehouse.gov/the-press-office/2017/05/08/president-donald-j-trump-signs-hr-534-law.

162 Jeremy Venook, 'The Olympics Haven't Always Been an Economic Disaster', *Atlantic*, 4 August 2016, accessed 24 August 2016, http://www.theatlantic.com/business/archive/2016/08/the-olympics-havent-always-been-an-economic-disaster/494534/; Robert A. Baade and Victor A. Matheson, 'Going for the Gold: The Economics of the Olympics', *Journal of Economic Perspectives* 30, 2 (Spring 2016), 213–14.

163 Adam Nash (co-writer of the protest song 'Cyclone Hits Expo'), interview with the author, February 2012.

164 Carl Malamud, *A World's Fair for the Global Village* (Cambridge: MIT Press, 1997). The experiment attracted sufficient interest at the time to secure a foreword to Malamud's book by the Dalai Lama and an afterword by Laurie Anderson.

165 Absolon, interview with the author.

166 Ibid.

167 Llew Edwards, interview with the author.

168 Ibid; Queensland, Department of the Premier and Cabinet, *Department of the Premier and Cabinet Annual Report 1997–98* (Brisbane: Department of the Premier and Cabinet, 1998), 6–7; 'Remember When: Confidence of a Gold Coast Win for the 2002 Expo Was High before Vote Lost', *Gold Coast Bulletin*, 8 June 1998, accessed 18 November 2017, http://www.goldcoastbulletin.com.au/lifestyle/gold-coast-130/remember-when-confidence-of-a-gold-coast-win-for-the-2002-expo-was-high-before-vote-lost/news-story/911a82b3ac1914a7be16c6fa6feb6e89. Hayden was by this time a former Governor-General. The bid for a world exposition at Coomera on the Gold Coast was narrowly and controversially defeated by a rival Manila bid (for an exposition that never eventuated). When acknowledging the failed Gold Coast bid in the 1997–8 annual report, outgoing Director General Peter Ellis (who reported to Premier Borbidge prior to his 1998 election loss to Beattie) either tacitly or accidentally acknowledged some of the circumstances complicating the pursuit of a hallmark event in a post-Fitzgerald and Bjelke-Petersen environment: 'Should a similar competitive bid be considered in the future, then special administrative arrangements might be considered to overcome inflexibilities perceived by the Bid Team, with respect to existing State Government tendering and accounting requirements, in view of very short deadlines it commonly faces and a need to make quick decisions in the field.'

169   Goldston, interview with the author.
170   Helen Gregory, 'Brisbane River', *Queensland Historical Atlas*, 2010, accessed
      12 October 2015, http://www.qhatlas.com.au/content/brisbane-river.
171   Pepper, interview with the author.
172   Absolon, interview with the author.
173   Ibid.
174   Ibid. This interview was given in the lead-up to Expo's twenty-fifth anniversary.
175   Rae Wear, 'Robert Edward Borbidge: In the Shadow of Bjelke-Petersen', in
      eds Denis Murphy, Roger Joyce, Margaret Cribb, and Rae Wear, *The Premiers
      of Queensland*, (St Lucia: University of Queensland Press, 2003), 393–8. The
      Westminster convention was violated when Attorney-General Denver Beanland
      was permitted to retain his role after a motion of no confidence was passed against
      him in parliament (in relation to the CJC controversy). Borbidge also threatened
      to defy the Constitution by replacing Mal Colston (a former Labor member
      turned independent) with an independent. Liberal members disallowed it.
176   Noel Preston, 'Peter Douglas Beattie: The Inclusive Populist', in Denis Murphy
      et al., *Premiers of Queensland*, 417–19. The Shepherdson Inquiry led to the
      resignations of the deputy premier, two backbenchers, an Australian Workers'
      Union party member, and a former Goss staffer. Beattie was considered supportive
      of this inquiry and of the investigations relating to Nuttall.
177   Chris Masters, 'Moonlight Reflections', *Griffith Review* 21 (Spring 2008), 68.
178   Jane Edwards, interview with the author.
179   Carol Lloyd (joint creative director for the Expo 88 advertising account),
      interview with the author, December 2012.
180   Peter Spearritt and Marion Stell, 'Queensland Brand', *Queensland Historical Atlas*,
      2010, accessed 20 October 2015, http://www.qhatlas.com.au/queensland-brand.
181   Swan was state secretary and Rudd was director general of the Office of Cabinet.
      Michael Bryce is an architect and graphic and industrial designer.
182   For recent comedic examples, see 'First Dog on the Moon: Clive Palmer – The
      Truth!', *Guardian*, 28 January 2016, accessed 6 February 2016, http://www.
      theguardian.com/commentisfree/picture/2016/jan/28/first-dog-on-the-moons
      -guide-to-solving-clive-palmer-and-fixing-democracy; and Alex McKinnon,
      'Queensland's Having a Surprise Election and It's Going to Be Pretty Weird, Even
      for Queensland', *Junkee*, 6 January 2015, accessed 6 February 2016, http://junkee.
      com/queenslands-having-a-surprise-election-and-its-going-to-be-pretty-weird
      -even-for-queensland/48112. This style of criticism typically emanates from the
      southern press and is directed at controversial public figures based in Queensland.
      Controversial public figures based outside Queensland, such as Tony Abbott, Fred
      Nile, and Cory Bernardi, are more typically assessed independently of the state in
      which they are based.
183   Daniel Hurst, 'Old Ties: Newman Connections Occupy Games Board',
      Brisbane Times, 9 May 2012, accessed 6 February 2016, http://www.
      brisbanetimes.com.au/queensland/old-ties-newman-connections-occupy-games-
      board-20120509-1ycir.html. This article notes that the previous chairman of
      the Gold Coast 2018 Commonwealth Games board was sacked to make way
      for an associate of Newman's. See also Shae McDonald, '"Overcooked" Media

Tart: Gold Coast Mayor Lashes Beattie', *Brisbane Times*, 12 July 2017, accessed 12 July 2017, http://www.brisbanetimes.com.au/sport/commonwealth-games/gold-coast-2018/overcooked-media-tart-gold-coast-mayor-lashes-beattie-20170712-gx9t74.html. This piece echoes the scandal over Expo ministerial expenses under Cooper. Chairman Peter Beattie (the former Labor premier appointed to the position by Labor premier Palaszczuk, who denied it was a job 'for Labor Party mates') castigated the Gold Coast City Council for gifting tickets to councillors.

184 Tony Moore, 'G20 Will Give Brisbane an Expo 88 Boost: Minister', *Age, IT Pro*, 12 November 2014, accessed 6 February 2016, https://www.brisbanetimes.com.au/national/queensland/g20-will-give-brisbane-an-expo-88-boost-minister-20141111-11knje.html.

185 Tony Fitzgerald, 'Submission to the Legal Affairs and Community Safety Committee, Crime and Misconduct and Other Legislation Amendment Bill 2014', 27 March 2014, accessed 15 February 2015, http://www.parliament.qld.gov.au/documents/committees/LACSC/2014/CMOLAB2014/submissions/004.pdf.

186 Stephen Keim, 'Newman's Queensland: Here We Joh Again', *Independent Australia*, 14 April 2014, accessed 6 February 2016, https://independentaustralia.net/politics/politics-display/newmans-queensland-here-we-joh-again,6383.

187 Andrew Stafford, 'Why Queensland Will Never Joh Again', *Friction*, 1 February 2015, accessed 6 February 2016, http://www.andrewstaffordblog.com/why-queensland-will-never-joh-again/.

188 Larissa Waters, 'The Queensland of Old', *New Matilda*, 4 June 2017, accessed 20 June 2017, https://newmatilda.com/2017/06/04/larissa-waters-asked-one-question-too-many-about-labors-new-mega-casino/. Waters echoed concerns about the social downsides of Expo, and the public's right to have some input into the uses to which such prime real estate is put.

189 'Tony Fitzgerald Outlines Principles for Pollies in Federal ICAC Push', media release, The Australia Institute, 12 June 2017, accessed 20 June 2017, http://www.tai.org.au/content/tony-fitzgerald-outlines-principles-pollies-federal-icac-push.

190 Adam Gartrell, 'Majority of Federal MPs Refuse to Sign Up to Tony Fitzgerald's Ethical Standards', *Brisbane Times*, 10 July 2017, accessed 11 July 2017, http://www.brisbanetimes.com.au/federal-politics/political-news/majority-of-federal-mps-refuse-to-sign-up-to-tony-fitzgeralds-ethical-standards-20170710-gx820x.html.

191 Ahern, interview with the author.

192 Ibid.

193 Ibid.

194 Atkinson, interview with the author.

195 Des Power (former chairman of Queensland Events Corporation and executive producer of *Today Tonight*), interview with the author, March 2013.

196 Weatherall, interview with the author; Julie Go-Sam, Garry Cole, and Mark Sherry, 'Assessing the Bicentennial: Interview with Bob Weatherall', *Social Alternatives* 8, 1 (1989), 7.

197 Weatherall, interview with the author.

198 Philip Day, *The Big Party Syndrome: A Study of the Impact of Special Events and Inner Urban Change in Brisbane* (St Lucia: Department of Social Work, UQ, 1988), iv.

199 Drew Hutton (Expo 88 protester and co-founder of the Queensland Greens), interview with the author, May 2007.

200 Ibid.

201 Anne Jones (an editor of *The Cane Toad Times*), interview with the author, December 2012.

Conclusion   Shine on Brisbane

1   Sir Llew Edwards (former Queensland Liberal Party leader, deputy premier, and chairman of Expo 88), interview with the author, October 2012; Lady Jane Edwards (née Brumfield, Communications director for Expo 88), interview with the author, October 2012.

2   Sir Llew Edwards, interview by Roger Scott and Ann Scott, *Queensland Speaks*, Centre for the Government of Queensland, 22 September 2009, accessed 20 October 2013, http://www.queenslandspeaks.com.au/llew-edwards.

3   Peter Goldston (Site Development director for Expo 88, and founding general manager of the South Bank Corporation), interview with the author, November 2012.

4   'Stefan Skyneedle on Fire', YouTube, 2006, accessed 28 August 2014, https://www.youtube.com/watch?v=pgG6kdywRbQ. The tower was swiftly restored.

5   The exhibition was called 'Light Fantastic: Expo 88 Rewired'.

6   This writer edited archival footage of Expo for the South Bank Corporation and produced a short video on Expo Oz for the Queensland Museum.

7   One such event was the 'Expo Revisited' exhibition at Circle Gallery, West End, in May 2008, in which Expo 88 protest ephemera was displayed, and which resulted in a compilation publication, *Expo Revisited*.

8   Donna Lee Brien, 'Celebration or Manufacturing Nostalgia? Constructing Histories of World Expo 88', *Queensland Review* 16, 2 (2009), 84.

9   Andrew Stafford, *Pig City* (St Lucia: University of Queensland Press, 2004), 172–3.

10 Frank Bongiorno, *The Eighties: The Decade that Transformed Australia* (Collingwood: Black Inc., 2015), 35–9.

11 Ibid., 37–8.

12 David Anderson, 'Visitors' Long-Term Memories of World Expositions', *Curator* 46, 4 (October 2003), 401, 407, 408.

13 Ibid., 409.

14 Barbara Absolon (Entertainment deputy director and Walkways producer for Expo 88), interview with the author, December 2012.

15 Jane Cadzow, 'Expo City A-Flutter, but with a Touch of the Butterflies', *Australian*, 28 April 1988.

Index